The
Assertive
Librarian

The Assertive Librarian

by Janette S. Caputo

ORYX PRESS
1984

The rare Arabian Oryx is believed to have inspired the myth of the unicorn. This desert antelope became virtually extinct in the ealry 1960s. At that time several groups of international conservationists arranged to have 9 animals sent to the Phoenix Zoo to be the nucleus of a captive breeding herd. Today the Oryx population is over 400 and herds have been returned to reserves in Israel, Jordan, and Oman.

Library of Congress Cataloging in Publication Data

Caputo, Janette S.
  The assertive librarian.

  Bibliography: p.
  Includes index.
  1. Librarians—Psychology. 2. Library employees—Psychology. 3. Assertiveness (Psychology). 4. Library science—Philosophy. 5. Libraries and readers. I. Title.
  Z682.C26   023′.9   83-43252
  ISBN 0-89774-085-8

This book is dedicated to four people whom I admire immensely and who have had a positive role in my own life as an assertive librarian:

Kenneth J. Bruza, Ph.D.
Thomas J. Cinque, M.D.
Sally Harms
Vern M. Pings, Ph.D.

Table of Contents

Preface

This book is written for all librarians and library employees, working at any level, in any type of library. My belief that the professional role of any librarian can be enhanced through the appropriate application of the principles of assertion training is based on my own discoveries as an assertive librarian, on the library situations that many assertive colleagues have shared with me, and on my experiences as both developer and teacher of library continuing education courses in assertiveness and human relations skills. Thus, the focus of this book on assertiveness is practical, not theoretical, and its scope is professional, not personal.

Assertion training workshops for librarians have been developed by the author. It is hoped that this book can serve as a text for future workshops in which personal development for application in a library setting can be introduced and practiced.

Assertiveness training is based on the theory that behavioral responses are learned rather than instinctual, and that we therefore have control over the responses we wish to learn, unlearn, and select for use. Perhaps the most distinctive characteristic of assertiveness training is its practicality. The models of behavior that are defined as assertive are presented as part of a wide range of alternative behaviors that are available to every individual as a matter of choice, adaptable and adoptable as they fit each person's unique value system, philosophy, and style. Assertive techniques are specific, definable, understandable, and workable. They can be immmediately applied in both our personal and professional lives. They enhance humanistic beliefs and provide alternatives for conflict resolution.

For the professional librarian, assertive skills can be employed in problematic situations to avoid sullen withdrawals, hostile confrontations, misunderstandings, and inappropriate emotional responses (e.g., guilt or anxiety). They can be selectively used to turn win-lose conflicts into win-win transactions. There is little to be won, however, and perhaps much to be lost, from the acquisition of abrasive and obnoxious behaviors in the guise of "assertion training." This book is meant to be eminently practical, presenting assertive techniques as a repertoire of possible alternative behaviors which a librarian can select based on the perceived needs of each individual situation, time, and place, rather than as a standard package of presumably assertive "tricks" that can be used in a manipulative fashion without regard for the long-term interpersonal effects they may produce.

No single style of behavior can be effective for all times, in all places, for all people. Assertiveness, as presented in this text, will be considered a continuum of behaviors of varying strengths and designs. These behaviors will be shown in a variety of library situations.

In this book, library situations appear more frequently in some chapters than in others, and this may tempt readers to read them prematurely; it is strongly recommended that readers read the entire text in sequence, as each new concept builds on those previously presented. The foundations for a thorough understanding of the many nuances in Chapter 9, "The Assertive Library Supervisor," in particular, are found in Chapters 1 through 8; consequently, Chapter 9 cannot be fully understood without the framework of these previous chapters.

To date, only one research study has been undertaken to measure the effects of assertiveness training on librarians. Stead and Scamell (1981) distributed questionnaires to 72 librarians attending a management development seminar sponsored by the Special Libraries Association at a regional conference. Their questionnaire included some demographic data, a recognized scale measuring job satisfaction (Smith, Kendall and Hulin's Job Descriptive Index), and a recognized scale measuring assertiveness (the Rathus Assertiveness Schedule). The questionnaire results, from 68 usable responses, indicated that assertiveness training for low-assertive librarians may increase their job satisfaction, but that, for the subgroup of librarians 41 years of age or older, with 11 or more years of professional work experience, assertiveness training may lead to a decrease of job satisfaction in terms of relating to their co-workers. The authors collected data that showed some statistical significance but carefully point out that "any conclusions drawn from this study must be tempered by the fact that the data were derived from self-reporting measures, and the analysis was correlational in nature" (Stead & Scamell, 1981, p. 388), as well as that the data came from a very small, self-selected sample of single-type (i.e., special) librarians. They suggest a need for further research. I heartily endorse that need; I hope this text may serve as a catalyst to pique the interest of library researchers in addition to providing readers with descriptions of the practical applications of assertiveness to the library environment.

The
Assertive
Librarian

Chapter 1
Introduction

The basic concepts of modern assertion training were first outlined in 1949, when a book called *Conditioned Reflex Therapy,* written by Andrew Salter, was published by Creative Age Press in New York. In this book, Salter described "the inhibitory personality" and defined six rules of "excitatory reflexes," which he believed would strengthen the inhibited patients he treated. These six rules of excitatory reflex concerned (1) feeling talk, or the saying of what we feel; (2) facial talk, or the nonverbal expression of our feelings; (3) frequent use of I-statements—sentences beginning with the pronoun "I"; (4) the ability to accept praise and give compliments; (5) the ability to make contradictory statements when we disagree with another person; and (6) the ability to live for the present and be spontaneous. This classic work has been identified as the foundation for the current practice of assertion training. Salter used his rules of excitatory reflexes to treat patients suffering from shyness, claustrophobia, low self-sufficiency, depression, stuttering, alcohol addiction, and sexual or psychosomatic disorders. Later behavior therapists Joseph Wolpe (1958) and Arnold Lazarus (Wolpe & Lazarus, 1966) treated people with similar problems, but in their work they differentiated between assertive and aggressive behaviors. In the 1970s, assertion training began to enjoy a widespread popularity which Arthur Lange and Patricia Jakubowski (1976), two of the leading assertion trainers/therapists of this decade, explained was the result of two important social changes in the 1960s. First, people began to place a higher value on personal relationships as a source of self-worth and satisfaction with life. Second, as alternative life-styles became more openly declared and more accepted, the range of socially acceptable behaviors was considerably expanded. The next step in this popularization process, noted by Alberti and Emmons (1977), was the acceptance of assertiveness training by minority groups as a successful means of training their members to stand up for their rights in appropriate and meaningful ways.

THE ASSERTIVE CHOICE

Assertive behavior is typified by calm, rational thinking, self-confidence, healthy self-esteem, a regard for others and for self, and a sense of responsibility. It is based on the recognition that every situation includes a variety of alternative potential responses, and that we, as rational beings, can choose from among those alternatives in order to find the responses that (1) best meet our needs, (2) allow us to avoid causing harm to others, (3) allow us to interact with other people in a productive and satisfying manner, and (4) allow us to approach the resolution of conflict in ways that maximize the gains for all parties to the conflict.

The history of humankind shows centuries in which people made behavior choices by habit, custom, or externally imposed limitations, rather than by conscious thought. It is this habitual responding that is the target for change in assertion training. The roles of behavior modification and cognitive-emotive processes in assertion training can be stated very simply: (1) all behaviors are learned; (2) assertive behaviors can therefore be learned; (3) rational thought can assist in the analysis of our learned behaviors and the objective assessment of real situations; (4) rational thought can help us select the learned behaviors we would like to abandon as well as the learned behaviors we would like to adopt and use more often; and finally, (5) a cycle of practice, feedback, assessment, and additional practice can result in the replacement of other, more satisfying, learned behaviors for those learned behaviors which we have found to be unsatisfying in the past (Ellis, 1973; Wolpe, 1982).

What Is Assertiveness?

Since 1949, psychologists have been defining and refining the definition of assertiveness, trying to state it in easily understood terms, yet also trying to instill in the definition an expression of philosophy as well as a description of behaviors. Joseph Wolpe defined assertion as "the proper expression of any emotion other than anxiety toward another person" (1973, p. 81). At roughly the same time, Fensterheim defined assertiveness as "the act of declaring oneself, of stating this is who I am, what I think and feel; it characterizes an active rather than a passive approach to life" (1972, p. 161). Rimm and Masters (1974) said that assertive behavior is the interpersonal behavior involving the relatively direct expression of feeling in a socially appropriate manner, while Spencer Rathus, a psychologist who has been very active in conducting research on assertive behaviors, defined it as "the expression of oneself in a positive, productive manner" (1975, p. 9). In the second edition of *Your Perfect Right,* a book that was written in part for the therapeutic community and in part for the general population, Alberti and Emmons (1974) defined assertiveness as "behavior which enables a person to act in his own best interests, to stand up for himself without undue anxiety, to express his honest feelings comfortably, or to exercise his rights without denying the rights of others" (p. 2). Jakubowski (Jakubowski-Spector, 1973) also formulated a definition that included the concept of standing up for one's rights, defining assertion as "that type of interpersonal behavior in which a person stands up for her legitimate rights without denying the rights of others" (p. 76). These latter definitions, which include the concept of rights, have been repeatedly paraphrased in the literature of assertion training for the therapeutic community (Galassi & Galassi, 1978; Groth, 1977; Hauser, 1979; Hughes, 1981; Lange, Rimm, & Loxley, 1975; Mamarchev, 1977); for the general public (Ashby, 1975; Fensterheim & Baer, 1975; Jakubowski & Lange, 1978); and for the work environment (Becker, 1980; Brockway, 1976; Caputo, 1981; MacNeilage & Adams, 1982; Pardue, 1980; Pugh, 1979).

The definitions that seem to be the most applicable to the work environment are these:

- *Assertion* is standing up for your rights without violating the rights of others.
- *Nonassertion* is not standing up for your rights (remaining passive).
- *Aggression* is standing up for your rights without concern for (or conscious avoidance of) the violation of others' rights.

Assertion. Assertive people are described as those who may insist on what they feel is correct but who will not generate gratuitous hostilities while doing so, who can confess to errors without loss of self-esteem, and who can choose to forego redress for grievances if a rational view of the entire situation warrants it (Rathus, 1975). Stated simply, assertive people attempt to strike a balance between passive and aggressive behaviors that emphasizes their self-responsibility (O'Donnell & Colby, 1979). Assertive people make requests of others, speak clearly, maintain appropriate eye contact, take less time to respond than others do, use "I" more often to describe their feelings, and are direct (Williams & Long, 1979). They also present themselves in a comfortable, confident way, take an active orientation toward work, are able to give and take criticism constructively, and deal with anxiety and fear in ways that allow them to continue to function effectively (Clark, 1979). Assertive people communicate openly, honestly, and directly, with consideration for others, cutting through arbitrary differences in status in order to communicate on an equal level (MacNeilage & Adams, 1982) because they represent a healthy balance between self-orientation (selfishness and aggression) and social orientation (compliance and passivity) (Ames, 1977). Assertive people smile, initiate conversations with strangers, say no without feeling undue feelings of guilt (Pardue, 1980), and are both skilled in empathy and sensitive to the feelings of others (Hauser, 1979). Assertive people give and accept compliments, express love and affection, and voice personal opinions, including disagreements, without defensiveness (Galassi & Galassi, 1978). Finally, assertive people take responsibilities for their behaviors and choices of behaviors (Jakubowski & Lange, 1978).

Assertive behaviors are direct actions that allow a librarian to attempt the resolution of interpersonal conflicts in rational and considerate ways. They are characterized by honesty, objectivity, accuracy, respect for self and others, reasonable tolerance, and self-expression. Librarians who are able to give a personal opinion on a controversial issue while at the same time recognizing the rights of others to hold differing opinions, perhaps based on the same rationale and strength of affective feelings, are engaging in assertive behavior. The assertive librarian can face conflict with an investigative assurance that problems can be solved and decisions can be made through an appropriate analysis that allows respect for human rights. The assertive librarian can take appropriate disciplinary or other negative action without feeling inappropriate guilt and is equally adept at providing positive feedback such as sincere compliments and rewards. One of the most significant payoffs for the assertive librarian is the enhanced self-esteem and improved personal relationships that can result from appropriate assertion.

Nonassertion. Nonassertive people show deference, timidity, and meekness; have difficulty dealing with feelings of anger; make efforts to suppress their feelings; and feel frustrated much of the time (MacNeilage & Adams, 1982). They have a detrimental effect on the work environment as well; their reluctance to express their opinions or feelings denies their colleagues an opportunity to interact, while their frustrations lead them to disgruntlement and a negative effect on morale. The nonassertive supervisors who yield to every request easily produce confusion and inconsistency in their staff members (Hulbert,

1982). Nonassertive people are prone to suffer hurt feelings, resentment, low self-esteem, and psychosomatic illnesses (Groth, 1977). They tend to avoid seeking information, asking for help, and asking questions when they don't understand (Neiger & Fullerton, 1979). Nonassertive people have a tendency to avoid eye contact when talking with others, may sit or stand with head lowered or body drooping, and may exhibit nervous behaviors such as tics or excessive blinking (Williams & Long, 1979).

Alberti and Emmons (1982) make a distinction between generalized and situational nonassertion. Some people are generally nonassertive, acting timid, shy, or reserved in most or nearly all circumstances, while others are normally able to function adequately, in self-enhancing ways, but become unassertive in certain situations that cause them undue anxiety.

Passive behaviors are characterized by nonaction. The passive librarian is characterized by avoidance behaviors, silent acceptance, self-denial, and overtoleration. The nonassertive librarian allows, for example, powers external to the library to dictate policy, procedure, or collection development decisions without providing his or her professional opinion on appropriate service rationale or library administration to those outside powers. Assertive behaviors do not guarantee acceptance of a librarian's input, but nonassertive behavior does guarantee that such input will not be accepted, as it is never offered. Nonassertion provides very little satisfaction to the librarians who choose it; it may bring some short-term satisfaction in avoidance of the dreaded conflict, but it brings a long-term decrease in self-esteem and a feeling of helplessness. Nonassertive librarians may begin building a large store of unverbalized resentment toward the people perceived as having power, and this resentment can severely limit their ability to behave assertively. When it finally becomes clear that they must speak up on an issue, their verbalization too often explodes into inappropriately aggressive complaints and hostility.

Aggression. When we think of aggression, we often think of hostility, rage, violence, and other extreme outward expressions of anger and frustration. We may also think of extraordinarily fierce competition. The usual goal of aggression is domination, or winning, forcing the other person to lose. Winning is ensured by humiliating, degrading, belittling, and overpowering other people until everyone but the aggressor is weakened and less able to express and defend their needs and rights (Lange & Jakubowski, 1976). Aggressive people are stubborn and resistant to change. They are highly defensive of potential damage to their self-esteem because their self-esteem is usually rather low and vulnerable; thus, they make extra efforts to make it appear to be high and invincible. Their requests are made as demands. They are impulsive, reacting instantaneously to the stimulus of real or perceived opposition from others. Aggressive people blame others for the negative things that they experience.

Aggressive people express anger in destructive ways, intensifying interpersonal conflict rather than helping to resolve it; aggression is a behavior that is intended to threaten or injure the security or self-esteem of others (Hoffman, Kirwin & Rouzer, 1979). Aggressive people may inflict harm or violate others' rights by verbal or nonverbal, direct or indirect, immediate or delayed, conscious or unconscious means (Duncan & Hobson, 1977). Aggressive people often exhibit assertive behaviors such as honesty and clarity, but their goal-directed behavior includes manipulation, domination, excessively inappropriate fury (instead of controllable anger), and hostility (Ellis, 1976).

Aggressive behavior in a library may appear as irrational tirades by supervisors over subordinates' errors, or conversely, by irrational rages from subordinates against supervisors. It may be indicated by brusque responses or no response at all to patrons at the reference desk, refusal to listen to reasonable requests for exceptions to rules, refusal to perform certain functions or to assist certain patrons, conscious fiscal irresponsibility, purposeful attacks on staff morale, or vengeance through evaluation forms and memorandums. The aggressive librarian may find some short-term satisfaction in a momentary feeling of superiority but suffers great loss in terms of long-term destructive action on interpersonal relationships.

Passive-Aggression. Aggression is characterized as very direct, but it may also be expressed in indirect ways. MacNeilage and Adams (1982) define passive-aggression as "the unhappy marriage between superficial acquiescence and underlying resentment, bitterness or rage" (p. 6). Typically aggressive people may exhibit bullying and bravado as standard modus operandi; passive-agressive people appear to exhibit nonassertive behavior. The clinical definition of passive-aggression is "a mechanism of defense, a personality trait, or maladaptive pattern of coping behavior" (Perry & Flannery, 1982, p. 164). In Chapter 8, the difference between defense mechanisms and coping mechanisms will be reviewed. It is important to determine, when you must deal with passive-aggressive people, whether their behavior is a result of a defense mechanism or a maladaptive coping mechanism.

Passive-aggressors who are responding to defense mechanisms are unaware of the aggressiveness of their intent. They see themselves as victims, as people for whom things just always go wrong. They are very successful at hiding their true feelings from themselves, often more successful at that than at hiding those true feelings from others. A colleague who truly likes you may hide her/his resentment at your being named the chair of an exciting new committee and sincerely congratulate you, then show up late for every meeting or procrastinate on committee assignments s/he agrees to do for you. When a defense mechanism is responsible for this behavior, a passive-aggressive person will have absolutely valid excuses for each lapse: tardiness is the result of being unable to find their minutes from the last meeting (which were right there a minute ago) or being unable to end a telephone conversation in time; procrastination is caused by illness or over-whelming demands on their time by someone with higher authority than yours. It is important to note that these passive-aggressors *do not consciously know* that they are doing these things purposely.

Passive-aggressors who are using maladaptive coping behaviors are aware of the aggressive intent of their actions, however. They attempt to hide their aggression by expressing it in passive ways or by exhibiting it in nonactions. Their behavior is the result of deliberate conscious thought, a maladaptive coping mechanism that successfully allows them to be aggressive without experiencing the overt social sanctions offered to aggressors. Common work examples of deliberate passive-aggressive behavior are dawdling, procrastination, intentional inefficiency, stubbornness, and forgetfulness. These are the people who harm you by:

1. Agreeing to perform a task for you but not meeting your deadline or forgetting about it completely.
2. Consistently misunderstanding what you want: "*I thought* you said...."
3. Consistently procrastinating and accompanying it with attempts to instill guilt in you: "Don't be so impatient."
4. Frequently, but intermittently, forgetting routine assignments, requiring you to monitor them daily.
5. Chronic tardiness.

Table 1 compares the characteristics, consequences, and payoffs of assertive, nonassertive, and aggressive behavior.

8 The Assertive Librarian

Table 1
Comparison of Behaviors

	Nonassertion	Assertion	Aggression
Characteristics	Tolerance when your rights have been violated; emotional dishonesty; indirect or no communication; self-denying; inhibition; weakness.	Standing up for your rights when they have been violated; emotional honesty; direct communication; self-enhancing; lack of inhibition.	Standing up for your rights by denying or violating the rights of others; emotional honesty with inappropriate extreme expression; self-enhancing at others' expense; lack of inhibition.
How You Feel	Timid; shy; helpless; meek; hurt; anxious; humiliated; "I'm nobody."	Confident; self-respecting, satisfied that you are treated with respect; "We're both somebody."	Righteous; superior; courageous; depreciatory of others; may feel guilty later; "You're nobody."
How Others Feel	Frustrated by your inaction; overvalued by you.	Valued; respected; satisfied; maybe guilty if others have been aggressive with you.	Devalued; unrespected; used; defensive; humiliated; hurt; manipulated.
How Others Feel About You	Irritated; disgusted; pitying; disrespectful.	Respectful, although there can be adverse reactions from nonassertive others.	Angry; vengeful; disrespectful.
Approach to Conflict	Avoiding open conflict; rarely showing anger.	Bringing conflict into open; expressing anger to assist in solving problems.	Seeking conflict; expressing anger to punish and control.
Conflict Outcome	Your needs remain unsatisfied.	Your needs are usually satisfied.	Your needs are usually satisfied at others' expense.

Table 1
Comparison of Behaviors (continued)

Action Pattern	Nonassertion	Assertion	Aggression
	Underreacting.	Acting directly, appropriately.	Overreacting.
At Work, Superiors Tend to	Discount your opinions; ignore you; take advantage of you.	Trust you; invite your participation; negotiate with you.	Challenge you; punish you; retreat from you.
Payoffs	Avoidance of conflict; tension; unpleasantness.	Increase in self-esteem; improvement in interpersonal relations.	Venting of emotions immediately; superior feelings.
Payments	Building up resentment and anger; risk of explosion into aggression at inappropriate time or place.	Possible break-down of relationships with others who will not accept your assertiveness.	May have build-up of guilt; probable loss of interpersonal relationships.
Intent	To please; to gain approval.	To communicate; to solve problems.	To dominate; to control.
T.A. Viewpoint	I'm not OK; You're OK.	I'm OK; You're OK.	I'm OK; You're not OK.
Leadership Style	Fleeing; giving in.	Negotiating; evaluating; acting.	Controlling; dominating; intimidating.
Decision Making	Making decisions that avoid conflict or that allow others to make decisions.	Making own decisions based on information and needs.	Making own decisions; ignoring impact on others; trying to make others' decisions for them.

Table 1
Comparison of Behaviors (continued)

	Nonassertion	Assertion	Aggression
Interpretation of Success	Getting lucky.	Realistic assessment of actual situation.	Beating out others and winning.
Self-Sufficiency	Low.	High.	Looks high—may be high or low.
Communication Process	Giving little input.	Free flow.	Accepting little input.

A Behavioral Continuum

The borders between assertive, nonassertive, and aggressive behaviors may be difficult to discern. The *appropriateness* of a particular behavior for that particular time and place, with that particular person, for each individual's unique personal style, may be the deciding factor in classifying behaviors.

> It is clear that there are no absolutes in this area, and that some criteria may be in conflict. A particular act may be at once assertive in behavior and intent (you wanted to and did express your feelings), aggressive in effect (the other person could not handle your assertion), and non-assertive in the social context (your subculture expects a powerful "put-down" style). It may not be possible to reconcile such mutually exclusive classifications.... In any event, the question "Is it assertive or aggressive?" is not one which may be answered simply. The issues are complex and each situation must be evaluated individually. Indeed, the labels "non-assertive," "assertive," and "aggressive" themselves carry no magic, but within the framework described here may be useful in assessing the *appropriateness* of a particular action. (Alberti, 1977, p. 354)

A useful way to think of these behaviors is to imagine them existing around the edges of a circular continuum, along which we can choose to move freely. (See Figure 1.) Assertive people may sometimes choose to behave more passively, sometimes more aggressively, but will strive to remain somewhere on the portion of the circumference labeled as assertive, sometimes purposefully moving to the nonassertive section, but rarely choosing fully aggressive behaviors and avoiding passive-aggressive actions. In the real world, behaviors may appear at any point along this continuum and may appear to be mixtures of two types of behavior; the appropriateness and analytical intent of the behaviors must be considered in defining and classifying them as primarily one type or another.

Why Be Assertive?

The benefits of assertiveness include higher self-esteem, reduced anxiety, effective resolution of conflict, reduced psychosomatic illnesses, enhanced interpersonal relationships, and increased work effectiveness (Alberti & Emmons, 1982; Fensterheim & Baer, 1975; Jakubowski & Lange, 1978; MacNeilage & Adams, 1982). But assertive behavior is an energetic undertaking. It is unlikely that anyone could be assertive 100 percent of the time even if s/he tried to be. Thus

Figure 1

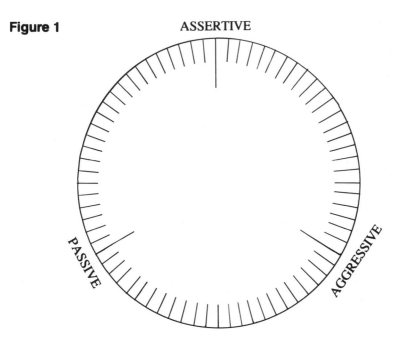

assertive behavior *always* involves a choice of alternatives. While it is often very helpful, effective, and satisfying to behave assertively, there is no obligation to behave assertively in all situations at all times (Lange, Rimm & Loxley, 1975). No single behavior pattern is always right. The repertoire of assertive behaviors is a menu rich in its variety. Assertive librarians are free to choose when and how much they will assert themselves as well as choosing those assertive behaviors that fit their own styles and with which they feel comfortable.

There is a danger in diluting your perspective on the importance of undesirable events or opportunities for assertive behavior. Every undesirable event need not be considered a threat to one's personhood. For example, you can easily maintain your self-esteem without expressing your opinion at every opportunity or taking instant offense at minor, unintentional violations of your rights. Constant assertion over both major and minor events quickly becomes obnoxious assertion and is ultimately self-defeating (Jakubowski & Lange, 1978).

Assertion training often focuses on the techniques that make up the assertive behavior repertoire, but living assertively requires self-knowledge more than it requires techniques of self-defense. Substantial and long-lasting behavior changes are possible only when people add them to a solid base of verbalized beliefs and values. The modification of nonassertive and aggressive habits requires intrapsychic efforts as well as simple behavioral learning (Fischoff, 1977). Groark, who supports assertion as a technique for handling troublesome library patrons, summarizes the assertive choice quite neatly:

> ...assertion is not a personality trait but a series of learned responses to specific situations. Most people who have received assertiveness training agree that these responses are relatively easy to learn. It is up to the individual to decide when and to what extent to apply them (1979, p. 172).

THE LIBRARY STEREOTYPE

The concept of stereotypes as both a consequence and a predictor of behavior has been part of the social sciences literature since 1922. More recently stereotype has been defined as a classification that allows attribution of assumed characteristics of a group of people to single members of that group. The validity of the assumed characteristics is unimportant; people react to the stereotype of the group, not to the individual her/himself (Cauthen, 1971).

Research on the formation and maintenance of occupational stereotypes has shown that the traits of assertiveness, intelligence, and responsibility are highly related to the prestige dimension of the occupation under consideration (Crowther & More, 1972). Although Melvil Dewey declared in 1876 that "the time has at last come when a librarian may, without assumption, speak of his occupation as a profession" (p. 5), the library literature of today, more than a century later, is still filled with articles questioning whether librarianship is truly a profession or simply an occupation (Biggs, 1981). When those of us within it have difficulty defining librarianship, it is a rather safe assumption that the prestige dimension of our profession in comparison with others is relatively low. The historical age of an occupation has been shown to be a determinant in the development of stereotype, so that well-established, familiar occupations (such as that of librarian) are defined much more sharply as stereotypes, with far more resistance to change, than newer, comparatively unfamiliar occupations (such as that of information manager). Stereotypes about the kinds of people apt to be employed in designated occupations have been found to be comparable in strength and magnitude to stereotypes about ethnic groups (Crowther & More, 1972).

McCauley, Stitt and Segal (1980) defined stereotypes as the "generalizations about a class of people that distinguish that class from others," stating that stereotyping "is differential trait attribution or differential prediction based on group membership information" (p. 197). From a research viewpoint, this definition is workable, and the study shows that stereotype prediction is probabilistic in nature. But from a perspective inside the stereotype of librarians, we should perhaps be far more concerned with the Crowther work (Crowther & More, 1972) which indicates that the strength of a stereotype may act on the members of the occupation as well as on those outside it, in that it forces certain attributes on them as societal expectations.

Librarians are service professionals who are skilled in the organization of information, yet the business acumen, marketing skills, financial skills, and management skills that necessarily support the provision of library services are not part of our stereotype. We are represented as meek, timid, and dowdy. The general public responds to the discovery of one's library profession with comments on how nice it must be to work in a quiet place, or with evident surprise that anyone with obvious normality works in a library by choice, or merely with a blank question of "but what is it you actually *do?*"

What other data support the maintenance of this negative image? A 1957 doctoral dissertation on the personality of a librarian (Biggs, 1981) found data showing that the general public consistently stereotypes librarians as orderly, conforming, passive, and unsociable. The findings suggested that this stereotype was not only self-perpetuating, it was based on fact. The librarians studied did exhibit the sterotyped behaviors. More recent research studies by librarians, about librarians, has also shown that, unfortunately, many of the stereotypical attributes of librarians actually do exist in a large number of librarians. Clayton (1970) studied male library science students in 1967, using the College Personality Inventory, comparing their scores to composite scores representing 14 other occupational groups. The library students scored significantly lower than the composite scores on poise, ascendency, self-assurance, socialization, maturity, responsibility, and general orientation toward achievement and intellectual efficiency. The only area in which the library students scored significantly higher than the other occupational groups was femininity. Bailey's 1981 study of library supervisors and middle managers reviewed research literature that indicated librarians had a distaste for and lack of aptitude for supervision.

In a thought-provoking monograph challenging librarians to change, Paul Wasserman wrote,

Certain characteristics of librarianship and of library administration tend to constrain leadership. One is a kind of waiting and hoping born of desires and wishes but not translated into forceful action....Another characteristic of librarianship is the longing to enshrine a leadership figure in whom to impute godlike wisdom and understanding....An even more subtle factor affecting the presence or absence of leadership behavior is related to the perception which those who hold positions of responsibility have of their roles and of the image they reflect to others. A...self-assurance, confidence...sparks the behavior of a leader...[that is] seen by others...it is just such a quality which separates the winners from the losers, differentiating those who will be humbly accepting from those who will fight for more. An administrative class with such a personality, such a style, becomes a leadership class. And almost as a direct consequence of such self-perception and acting out of such behavior, this becomes the view also held in the mind's eye of those who observe them. But this is hardly the self-perception of most librarians. The stereotype of submission and toleration of marginal conditions persists among the library administrative class, and a static condition is inexorably perpetuated. For it makes the alternative, a genuine leadership stance founded upon promise and bold operations, seem unrealistic, daring, or ridiculous (Wasserman, 1976, p. 105).

Cowell (1980) has published one of the most picturesque descriptions of the stereotype and laments that the types of people who are likely to be attracted to the profession based on this public image are far more likely to perpetuate it than to correct it.

In our media-oriented image-conscious society, the librarian may very well seem particularly unfortunate, reflected in the imagination of the general public as a fussy old woman of either sex, myopic and repressed, brandishing or perhaps cowering behind a date-stamp and surrounded by an array of notices which forbid virtually every human activity. The media, for whom the librarian is frustration personified, have reinforced this stereotype, hitherto transmitted solely by superstition and hear say....On the few occasions that authors do stretch their imaginations to envisage librarians at work they are usually occupied with...tasks guaranteed to emphasise aspects of the job both trivial and unglamorous (pp. 167–169).

Asheim calls the library image compliant, inoffensive, and nonassertive and describes it as a self-fulfilling prophecy, for whenever librarians "accept the role that society has defined for them, they do not consider it appropriate to exhibit the sense of commitment, the drive to lead rather than follow, the necessary assertiveness required to prescribe, or to demand professional rights and responsibilities" (1978, p. 237).

Assertiveness cannot eradicate the library stereotype; it has much too firm a hold. Studies show that stereotypes tend to be maintained even when the holders of the stereotype are exposed to information that fails to conform to the expectations generated by the stereotypical image (Hamilton & Gifford, 1976), and that people like and need predictability, so they maintain stereotypical beliefs (Aboud, 1976). But assertive skills can help librarians cope with the problems generated by their nonsatisfaction of the stereotypical expectations of patrons and public. The use of assertive skills can raise the self-esteem of librarians and can also be effective in helping librarians exhibit their sense of commitment and drive to lead. In addition to teaching librarians to make the assertive requests that their needs be met and that appropriate responsibilities be given to them, assertion can help to keep librarians from falling into the seductive trap of Asheim's self-fulfilling prophecy.

THE ASSERTIVE RISK

Somewhere, 'somewhen,' someone said "without risk, there is no gain." This truism applies to assertion. There is no doubt that any behavior change includes some risk, and a change to assertive behavior is not only risky, it is fallible. The assertive librarian may choose totally appropriate assertive language, coupled with totally consistent assertive body language, in a situation that is entirely appropriate for an assertive effort, and still find that the conflict remains unresolved or actually increases. Assertion can be very effective, and it frequently is, but it carries no guarantees.

The decision to engage in assertive behaviors in a given situation should be based on a conscious analysis of the realities of the situation (Hauser, 1979; Heffner, 1981) with a careful analytical weighing of the importance, to the asserting librarian, of each factor in the situation. As each person is unique, this analysis will differ with each librarian, but many of the questions which should be consciously considered are essentially the same:

1. What possible gains are there? Will I increase my self-esteem? Will I change the situation? Could I earn a promotion or other reward? Might I get more responsibility or autonomy? Could it enhance the honesty in my relationship? Would the relationship itself get better? Will I increase communication or understanding?

2. What possible losses are there? Could I suffer a decrease in my self-esteem? Would there be a negative change in the situation? Could I be terminated or given some other sanction? Might I get a decrease in autonomy or responsibility? Would this put more openness and frankness in the relationship than I really want? Could the relationship worsen? Would this increase *mis*understanding?
3. What do the possible losses *really* mean to me? How awful would it be if they happened? Could I handle it?
4. Is this situation a recurring one, or does it occur only rarely?
5. Is the person who has violated my rights unaware of that violation, or was it done with intent to harm?
6. How important is this to me? If I risk getting fired over it, is it worth it? If I stand an equal chance of being promoted or being fired over it, is the possible promotion worth the possible termination?
7. Are there alternative actions that might increase the likelihood of the potential gain and also decrease the likelihood of the possible loss? Could I say something a little differently or choose a different time or place for my assertion?
8. Are there alternative opportunities immediately available that decrease the possible loss if I risk termination? Do I have another job offer? Could I get one? Could I transfer within the organization?
9. Is there a higher authority that can be consulted? Before the assertion? After the assertion? Is there someone who should be present during it?

Millburn and Billings (1976) are two psychologists who have studied the factors of risk and uncertainty in the psychological process of decision making. According to them, risk is perceptual and subjective, not objective, and by definition is actual risk only when the individual involved believes it to be. When all other things are equal, the perception of risk increases whenever the probability of negative consequences ("losing") is greater than the probability of positive consequences ("winning"), and this makes sense to most of us. But this study also showed that our perception of risk also increases when the variance in the probabilities is very wide or whenever the positive and negative consequences are very different from each other, as compared to situations in which the alternatives are relatively neutral or similar. The perceived risk is greater in behavior that may lead to being promoted or being fired than it is in behavior that may lead to winning a 3.5 percent merit increase instead of a suggested 2.5 percent increase.

One of the greatest risks to assertive behavior, and one that is often unrecognized as a risk, is the reactions of people who know you well. When you change the way you behave, they no longer have the comfort of being able to anticipate your responses in a given situation; they must adapt their own actions and may become ill-at-ease. Pugh (1979) notes that this seems to be true even when the old behaviors have been troublesome, and people have been expressing a wish for change. Shelton (1977) warns that sudden behavior changes can produce such enormous stress that, on occasion, they precipitate the termination of interpersonal relationships. In a work situation, Shaw and Rutledge (1976) point out that the nonassertive manager is often viewed as a "nice person," so that her/his initial assertions are perceived as aggression rather than as a calm assertive statement of goal or purpose. Even minor assertions should thus be approached analytically, for they may have great impact if they represent a new type of behavior.

In some situations, the analysis of your considered assertive behavior may lead you to classify it as unadaptive; i.e., it may lead to negative consequences that far outweigh the merits of the assertion (Fiedler & Beach, 1978; Getter & Nowinski, 1981). In these cases, assertive librarians may choose to assert their right to behave nonassertively. This decision to be nonassertive is, in itself, assertive, as it is based on a rational, conscious decision rather than on an unwitting, habitual reaction (Cotler, 1975; Hulbert, 1982).

There are inherent risks in assertion. Both Levinson (1968) and MacNeilage and Adams (1982) note some of these risks. Assertion brings with it a risk of your being misunderstood, the risk of suffering political losses within the organization, the risk of giving people information they have trouble handling (thereby increasing your risk of feeling guilt), the risk of others increasing their expectations of you, a risk of negative responses from people who don't like assertion, a risk of less approval and support from some colleagues, the increased risk of finding things you don't like about yourself as you you engage in more self-scrutiny, the risk of pressure from others to back down when you have chosen to be assertive, and the risk that your analysis failed to discern that the matter of minor importance to you is of great importance to the other person and has much greater negative consequences than you anticipated.

SUMMARY

Assertion is learned behavior that can help you resolve conflicts, is based on a realistic analysis of situations and a variety of alternatives, is a matter of choice in every situation, and is defined as standing up for your rights without violating the rights of other people. Assertive behaviors can be useful to librarians in the daily practice of their profession, in conflicts with colleagues, patrons, governing boards, supervisors, or subordinates. They can help librarians deal with the problems generated by socially imposed stereotypical expectations. Assertion is part of a circular continuum of behaviors that includes nonassertion (passivity), aggression, and passive-aggression. Movement along this continuum is constant; and no single point, no single type of behavior is right for every situation, place, and time. Assertion is probably not possible, and is certainly not appropriate, 100 percent of the time. Assertive behavior carries no guarantees and may in fact be quite risky, but it does have benefits: it increases a librarian's sense of self-esteem for having taken positive, realistic action in an appropriate and considerate manner, and it may bring a wide variety of positive resolutions to conflicts. Assertive behaviors are neither genetic nor natural to certain personality types; they are learned behaviors, and librarians can build a wide range of possible behavior choices by simple practice, assessment, and adaptation.

Chapter 2
Your Assertive Rights

Throughout this book and the many other publications meant to assist self-development in assertiveness, you will find the concept of interpersonal rights presented as an integral part of assertiveness. The basic definitions that are used to discriminate among assertive, nonassertive, and aggressive behaviors include the concept of rights. But why is this concept emphasized so heavily? Just what, exactly, *are* these interpersonal rights? And finally, does everyone have these same rights?

THE IMPORTANCE OF PERSONAL RIGHTS

Jakubowski (Jakubowski-Spector, 1973) explains that people are much more likely to assert themselves once they have accepted the fact that there are basic, interpersonal, assertive rights. They no longer feel guilty about asserting themselves, and they no longer need another person's good wishes to continue to act assertively. Hutchings and Colburn (1979), who conduct assertion training workshops for nurses, agree. They state that one of their major tasks in training is to help participants incorporate assertive rights into their personal belief systems because, unless this internalization occurs, the participants will probably not use any of their learned assertive skills. They will not believe they have the right to act assertively.

Fensterheim and Baer (1975) note that we must recognize our rights and stand up for them, for, if we do not, other people define our roles for us and we lose autonomy and the freedom to be ourselves. Jacobson (1972) wrote that to be assertive we must assume an equal share of consideration and courteous treatment, for it is only through this assumption that we can act in ways that tend to equalize power. Psychotherapists express the view that people not only have certain basic, assertive rights that they are entitled to exercise, but that these rights should be exercised in order to achieve a healthy adjustment in life. When our rights are not exercised, excessive anxiety, inappropriate guilt feelings, psychosomatic disorders, and even pathological changes in predisposed organs may occur (Alberti & Emmons, 1982; Jakubowski & Lange, 1978; Wolpe & Lazarus, 1966). All this gives us an idea of why interpersonal rights are heavily emphasized; now it is time to explore what these rights actually are.

The Personal Rights Everyone Shares

An incredible number of specific individual rights have been identified and detailed in the literature of assertion training, and each writer seems to have her/his own favorite list of which are the most important. Jakubowski and Lange (1978) note that everyone has the right to decide her/his own values and lifestyle as long as they don't violate the rights of others and expand this to mean that you have a right to be yourself and feel good (not guilty) about yourself so long as you don't damage others in the process. Later they expand this belief of a basic right to dignity and self-respect into a list of 10 basic rights that they believe everyone has:

1. The right to be treated with respect.
2. The right to say no without feeling guilty.
3. The right to experience and express feelings.
4. The right to take time to think.
5. The right to change your mind.
6. The right to ask for what you want.
7. The right to do less than you are humanly capable of doing.
8. The right to ask for information.
9. The right to make mistakes.
10. The right to feel good about yourself.

The early self-improvement book by Smith, *When I Say No, I Feel Guilty* (1975) is somewhat extreme in its suggestions for appropriate assertive behavior, but it is useful in adding to the list of everyone's interpersonal rights. It, too, lists 10 rights. One, the right to change your mind, is included in the Jakubowski and Lange list noted above. The other nine, however, are different, and their contribution to our review of rights is significant, for they begin to indicate the notion that self-responsibility is an inherent factor in our basic rights:

1. The right to judge your own behavior, thoughts, and emotions, and to take responsibility for their initiation and consequences upon yourself.

2. The right to offer no reasons or excuses to justify your behavior.
3. The right to judge if you are responsible for finding solutions to others' problems.
4. The right to make mistakes and to be responsible for their consequences.
5. The right to say "I don't know."
6. The right to be independent of the good will of others before coping with them.
7. The right to be illogical in making decisions.
8. The right to say "I don't understand."
9. The right to say "I don't care."

Nussbaumer (1978) lists two rights that can be added to our growing basic list, which are of special importance in the application of assertiveness in any work environment and which continue the concept of responsibility:

1. The right to be listened to and taken seriously.
2. The right to perform skills in a responsible manner.

Alberti and Emmons (1982) also contend that each person has the right to be and express her/himself and to feel good (not guilty) about doing so, as long as s/he does not hurt others in the process; they also emphasize that we each have the obligation to accept responsibility for our actions and feelings. In their "Universal Declaration of Human Rights" (1974, pp. 201–206), which they propose as a standard for "all peoples and all nations," they present an extensive list of universal rights that ranges from rights to "life, liberty, and security of person" through rights to nationality, to marry, to peaceful assembly, to education, and to rest and leisure.

A quick perusal of some of the popular works on assertiveness add 35 more basic rights to our list (Bloom & Coburn, 1975; Bower & Bower, 1976; Butler, 1981; Kelley & Winship, 1979; and Shaw, 1980). Thirty-one of these are of a general nature and are applicable to both personal and professional roles, while the last four (numbers 32 through 35) are specific rights for people who choose to work:

1. The right not to take responsibility for another person's needs.
2. The right not to be used.
3. The right to spend your time with people you choose.
4. The right to get the service you are paying for without having to argue your case.
5. The right to structure your own time without feeling guilty.

6. The right to assess and decide which of your needs are the most important for you to meet.
7. The right to have knowledge about the treatment of your body.
8. The right to be treated with dignity and not be patronized.
9. The right not to be bribed by your parents.
10. The right to have all your questions answered even if the professional serving you is very busy.
11. The right, as an adult, to participate in deciding how much contact with parents is reasonable or desirable.
12. The right to be treated as a competent adult.
13. The right to have different values from your parents.
14. The right to tell someone of your needs.
15. The right not to be railroaded into agreeing with someone else.
16. The right to assume responsibilities.
17. The right to share responsibilities.
18. The right to decide how you will handle your responsibilities.
19. The right to repeat the "mistakes" of others.
20. The right not to be talked down to.
21. The right to meet your needs, to be fulfilled.
22. The right to achieve at a level that you are satisfied and comfortable with.
23. The right to seek reasons for someone's treatment of you.
24. The right not to have to fulfill another person's needs or expectations.
25. The right to have your opinion as valued as anyone else's.
26. The right to say what you want done with your possessions and to be informed in a courteous way about what needs to be done, to or for them, why, and how much it will cost (e.g., in repair situations).
27. The right to accept or reject an offer without being pressured.
28. The right to complain about services rendered.
29. The right to have your feelings respected.
30. The right to defend yourself when unfairly attacked.
31. The right to make choices about your commitments to causes.
32. The right to know what will be expected of you in a job.
33. The right to know what specific conditions will control your salary increments.
34. The right to know what the specific opportunities for advancement are.
35. The right to bargain for possible job duties and salary.

RIGHTS AND RESPONSIBILITIES

In a course in job seeking and job survival skills specifically designed to train unemployed workers, Heffner (1981) includes an "Every Person's Bill of Rights" (p. 24). After selecting and listing his favorite list of rights (all of which are included in the review lists noted above), Heffner states emphatically that "rights involve responsibilities." Everyone does have the same rights (Heimberg, Montgomery, Madsen & Heimberg, 1977), and, as Levinson (1968) notes in a rather tongue-in-cheek comment, every other person "has as much right to his distorted view as you have to yours" (p. 32). Thus if you accept your right to ask questions of others, you have the responsibility to accept that other people have the same right and may ask questions of you. If you claim the right to respect, you have the responsibility to respect others. Whenever you assert your right to have feelings, you must accept others' rights to have feelings, even when those feelings differ from yours. Each one of the 56 rights reviewed so far carries an unwritten companion responsibility to accept that right for others as well as for yourself.

Pugh (1979) believes there is a common misunderstanding that achieving individual rights automatically excludes the rights of others, and she warns that hard-fisted demands for rights may have the effect of building barriers rather than bridges to better working relationships. Similarly, Casriel (Ellis & Casriel, 1971) warns that a mature person mustn't feel so entitled that s/he doesn't take into account her/his role in reality. If a major consequence, such as losing your job, has a high probability of occuring after a blunt claim for one of your rights, such as holding a different opinion on censorship from the president of the library board, a mature person has the responsibility of considering the results of claiming that particular right at that particular time. Understanding your rights and knowing how to be assertive in claiming them do not oblige you to action; they oblige you to be responsible in choosing how and when to act or not act.

RIGHTS IN THE LIBRARY ENVIRONMENT

There are certain human rights that all people share, but in addition to these, there are some situational (or environmental) rights that exist solely because of the social system in which people live and function. Situational rights include general legal rights, such as those shared by all the people of a specific state who are governed by state laws. More specific legal rights, such as the right of certain occupations to handle, prescribe, and distribute controlled drugs, are also situational rights. Specific work environments have situational rights that may be defined by contractual agreement, by written policies, or by stated authority structures. These situational rights do not undermine or eliminate any basic human rights. They may, however, temporarily affect basic human rights for a specifically defined purpose, at a specific time. Your right to ask questions, for example, may be limited to a certain number or a certain format. Your right to say no will always exist, but it may lead to very specific consequences governed by the situational rights in your work environment.

For the purposes of this book, we will assume that all people share five basic rights:

1. The right to have respect.
2. The right to feel.
3. The right to make mistakes.
4. The right to say no.
5. The right to ask questions.

Given these five basic rights, we will also assume each person has these five responsibilities:

1. The responsibility to respect other people.
2. The responsibility to accept the expressions of feelings of others.
3. The responsibility to accept the fact that others make mistakes.
4. The responsibility to accept no as an answer.
5. The responsibility to accept questions from others.

We are now free to explore the more specific rights and responsibilities in the library environment that are not shared universally but that are different for librarians, for library users, and for the governing bodies of libraries.

Librarians' Rights

Librarians have many specific rights in their professional role. Librarians who supervise the work of others have some additional rights. There are concomitant responsibilities for each of these rights. The following paragraphs will describe some of these rights and responsibilities in detail.

The Right to Understand Expectations Governing Work. Although the responsibilities of specific librarians (e.g., reference or technical services librarians) in a variety of libraries may be similar, each individual library interprets these responsibilities uniquely. Librarians have the right to understand, thoroughly, what expectations are held for them by the governing body of the library, by the library director, and by their supervisor, if any. These expectations will be the measure against which the competencies and value of librarians will be judged. Some expectations may be in writing as part of a job description, others may be unspecified. When expectations are not specified, librarians have the responsibility of asking what they are. When they are specified, either orally or in writing, librarians have the right to ask about them and to expect accurate, complete replies.

The Right to Be an Equal Member of the Library Staff. Regardless of status in a particular library, all librarians have the same basic human rights as others. They have the right to state their opinions, to change their minds, to speak for themselves, to be listened to, and to be respected. They also have the responsibility to accept that others have these same rights.

The Right to Recommend Changes. Librarians have the right to challenge directives, policies, or procedures with which they disagree, but they have the responsibility of working within those directives, policies, and procedures as long as they choose to work in that library, or until they can negotiate the changes they desire.

The Right to Have a Reasonable Work Load. Often librarians feel overwhelmed by the many demands on their time, yet they may feel at the same time that there are additional library responsibilities not assigned to them that they could or would like to accept. Librarians have the right to spell out what they believe a reasonable work load to be and what combination of library responsibilities they feel would suit them best. They have the right to request additional support staff or changes in work assignments. When administrative decisions are made in response to their requests, librarians have the responsibility of choosing to accept them or seeking an alternate route to meet their needs (e.g., getting another job or revising their request).

The Right to Make Decisions Regarding Information Needs of Patrons. Librarians are experts in the organization and retrieval of information. When a patron requests information, librarians have the right to decide what sources are most appropriate to answer the request and how much information they should give the patron. They have the responsibility, however, of revising these decisions based on the evaluation of the patron as to whether or not her/his needs have been met.

The Right to Dislike a Patron. Librarians are no more human and no less human than any other occupational group. Librarians are service professionals, but they are not under any obligation to like everyone to whom they provide service. As a librarian, you have a right to dislike a library user, even if that dislike has no "reasonable" foundation. You have a *responsibility,* however, not to allow that dislike to interfere with the provision of library services. Kroll and Moren (1977) conducted an experiment that provides data to suggest that librarians clearly accept this responsibility. Based on other studies with both general groups and other occupational groups, which suggested that 'clean-cut' versus 'hippy' or unkempt appearances of college students significantly affected responses to their requests for help, political support, acceptance of rights, directions, and pleas for petition signatures, the two investigators set up a study of reference service in eight public libraries. They measured speed of service, amount of help provided (measured by whether the librarian took the patron to the shelves or catalog versus just pointing to them), diversity of the information sources provided, and friendliness. Contrary to their expectations, they found no significant differences on any of the measures and concluded that "a deviant-appearing person was just as likely to receive prompt, helpful, and friendly service as a conventionally dressed person" (p. 130).

The Right to Limit Areas of Expertise. Libraries of the 1980s and those of the future are and will continue to be highly complex institutions. Library educators manipulate library school courses and curriculums in increasingly sophisticated ways to prepare their graduates for a variety of library roles and careers. However, just as individual libraries can no longer be self-sufficient in providing all the resources their users need, individual librarians cannot be self-sufficient in all aspects of librarianship. Even in one-person special and school libraries, librarians have the right to set limits on how many aspects of librarianship they will attempt to maintain at a high level of expertise. The standards of the library profession will be maintained if, along with claiming this right, librarians maintain their concomitant responsibility to form networks and establish relationships which allow them to supplement and complement their own skills with the skills of others.

The Right to Deny Out-of-Scope Requests. Many libraries, particularly special libraries, have policies prohibiting their use by the general public, or have collections that are limited by subject area, by format, or by educational level. Librarians have the right to refuse to answer requests for information that are out of scope for the library or to refuse access to the library according to the policies of the institution. Assertiveness training sessions usually emphasize that people have the right to say no and to express opinions without justifying themselves or giving reasons. With this specific library right, however, librarians have the responsibility to provide more information than a simple negative in saying no. A statement as simple as "This is not a public library; we are not open to the public" is enough to provide the library seeker with minimal information on seeking alternate sources. Users, like librarians, have the basic right to make a mistake. Unless librarians accept some responsibility for providing at least minimal information with which the user can correct her/his mistake, the library will continue to be sought inappropriately.

The Right to Seek Information and Set Priorities. In order to meet all the information needs of the library's users, librarians have the right to seek information about the nature, scope, and urgency of a user's request and to use this information in setting priorities for the provision of information. Their responsibility extends to making valid decisions for those priorities and to revise them in the light of additional information.

The Right to Fail. The librarian who satisfies every user's request without delay, with totally accurate information, and with as much easy-to- read-and-decipher information as the user wants is a fantasy of first semester library school students. You have a right not to be able to do everything the users want, and you have the right to state your inability to meet their needs without making excuses. You do have a responsibility, however, to ensure that the alternatives you can provide are clearly stated and made available.

The Right to Respect for Library Property. You have a right to expect that library property will not be abused or mutilated and that library materials will not be lost. You have a responsibility to express your concern and to take appropriate action when damages to library property or losses of library materials occur.

Collection Development Right. You, the librarian, have the right to build, balance, and maintain an appropriate library collection to support the library uses defined by your parent government, organization, institution, company, or community. You have the responsibility to consider recommendations from library users, library staff members, and advisory bodies such as library committees in your collection development work. You have the right to defend the library's collection development policies from external efforts aimed at censorship of materials, but you have the responsibility to be able to validate the choice of controversial materials with appropriate documentation.

The Supervisory Right to Evaluate. Library directors and supervisor librarians have the right to judge the work and evaluate the performance of those who work under their supervision. When these evaluations are negative, they have the right to investigate reasons for performance deficiencies. With this right, they have the responsibility to be objective, open, and fair in their evaluations. They have the responsibility to indicate positive and negative evaluations to staff members and to answer questions about how their conclusions were drawn.

The Supervisory Right to Reassign. Directors and supervisors who assign tasks and responsibilities to library staff members have the right to reassign those tasks and responsibilities as necessary. They have the responsibility to explore other possible alternatives and the effect such reassignments may have on staff members before making such changes.

Right to Be Assertive. All librarians have both the right and the responsibility to be assertive in their interactions with colleagues, library users, members of library support staffs, and all others with whom they communicate as professional librarians.

Library Users' Rights

Library users have the same basic rights that librarians and all other people share. They also have some very specific rights that pertain to their use of libraries.

Right to Be Treated Equally. Library users have the right to be treated equally, without regard to age, occupation, dress, race, sex, community standing, or any other characteristic upon which discriminatory practices could be based. They have the responsibility not to expect preferential treatment for any similar characteristic.

Right of Free Access. Groark (1979), who supports the acquisition of assertive skills by librarians to assist them in dealing with troublesome library patrons, notes that troublesome patrons often exhibit behaviors that violate other patrons' rights to use the library without their being disturbed by annoying, antisocial, or illegal behavior. Patrons do have the right not to be disturbed by other patrons who are behaving in a disruptive manner; in order to stand up for this right, they have the responsibility to voice complaints to members of the library staff so that necessary assertive action may be taken on their behalf.

Right to Request Priority Service and Exceptions. Patrons may have special needs for information that cannot be handled through routine services but could possibly be satisfied by exception. Patrons have the right to express these special needs and to request that exceptions be made for them or that a high priority be given to their request. They have the responsibility to accept the response, positive or negative, that is given to their request, or, when the response is negative, to carry their request to a higher authority, without harrassment or disparagement of the librarian making the initial response.

Right to Dislike Libraries. Many library users find a lot of pleasure in their trips to the library, but there are many other people who go to the library as a last resort. Some are nonassertive people who are simply hesitant to ask for help and feel unsure and anxious in the library environment. There are other people, however, who for any number of reasons find themselves uncomfortable in libraries or have negative images of people who work in libraries and who consequently dislike libraries and librarians and are not the least bit nonassertive, particularly in actively exhibiting their dislike. These users have a right to dislike you and your environment. They have a responsibility, however, not to allow this dislike to interfere in the information process. You, as an assertive librarian, may find that the users who wholly and enthusiastically claim their right to dislike the library and you are not willing to accept the responsibility of separating their feelings from their overt behaviors toward you. Your assertiveness will allow you to resist getting defensive or reciprocating their animosity.

Right to Evaluate. Library users have the right to evaluate the library, the collection, the staff, and the library services according to their own unique interpretation of what a library should be, whether or not this is a valid assessment of your abilities to satisfy their information needs. They have the responsibility to communicate this to you. You have a responsibility to accept their input and a right to select how much weight you will give to these opinions. Users have the right to accept or reject the actions (or nonactions) you take based on their evaluations and make complaints to library committees, library boards, or managers over the library department. They have the responsibility to accept final decisions as final until they have new information to provide.

Governing Board Rights

The rights of committees, councils, boards, and other library governing bodies to approve or recommend library action are usually defined by the by-laws, charter, constitution, or laws of the organization, corporation, city, institution, or other parent body. Members of these groups and individual nonlibrarian administrators who supervise library directors have two special pairs of rights and responsibilities that need to be defined here, however.

Right Not to Understand Libraries. Nonlibrarians have a right not to make special efforts to obtain a professional understanding of library systems and information services and not to apologize for a lack of knowledge in these areas. They do have the responsibility to listen attentively to presentations about library service and to carefully read materials about the library that are sent to them due to their role in or relationship to the library.

Right to Request Justifications. Members of governing bodies have the right to request justifications for library actions, whether these be staffing patterns, collection development, or budgetary concerns. They have the responsibility to ensure that they consider these justifications objectively and fully and if they do not completely understand them, to ask questions until they have a full understanding.

The preceding paragraphs and pages are not meant to be an inclusive list of all the rights that exist in the library environment; such a list is infinite according to the nature of each unique library, librarian, and total library staff. It is meant to describe the relation of basic human rights to the library as a work environment and to provide groundwork for the remainder of the book.

SUMMARY

The definitions of assertion, nonassertion, and aggression are all concerned with interpersonal rights. These are basic human rights shared by all people. A review of the many rights listed in a variety of publications on assertiveness show that they range from very general, as a right to feel good about oneself, to very specific, as a right to know what conditions control salary increments. Five basic human rights given special emphasis in this book are (1) the right to have respect, (2) the right to feel and express feelings, (3) the right to make mistakes, (4) the right to say no, and (5) the right to ask questions. Every right also includes a responsibility. These responsibilities are (1) to respect others, (2) to accept the expression of others' feelings, (3) to accept the fact that others make mistakes, (4) to accept no as an answer, and (5) to accept that others will ask questions of you.

Basic human rights always exist in both personal and work environments. The work environment, however, may have some situational/environmental rights that are specific to the work environment and its authority structure. The library environment includes some specific situational rights of librarians (and library directors or supervising librarians), library users, and the governing bodies over libraries. Each has a concomitant responsibility.

Chapter 3
Setting Assertive Goals

Before you can begin to set goals for achieving your new assertive behaviors, you must do two things. First, you must identify how assertive you are now and which kind of situations you habitually handle assertively (Bower & Bower, 1976). Second, you must identify those areas in which you feel uncomfortable behaving assertively and the kind of situations in which you habitually behave nonassertively or aggressively (Alberti & Emmons, 1975; Butler, 1981). This chapter includes two inventories, the Librarian's Assertiveness Inventory and the Librarian's Discomfort Inventory, which have been developed to help you set goals for assertive behaviors and plan personal strategies for achieving assertive behavior in the library.

HOW ASSERTIVE ARE YOU NOW?

The psychological research literature includes a variety of assertiveness inventories that have been published, tested by complex statistical procedures for reliability and validity, and that are in regular use as measures of how assertive people are before and after they undertake assertiveness training. The Rathus Assertiveness Schedule (Rathus, 1973) is widely used as a measure of general assertiveness. Other scales that have been developed through research to measure assertive skills include the Gambrill and Richey Assertion Inventory (1975), the Adult Self-Expression Scale (Gay, Hollandsworth & Galassi, 1975), and the College Self-Expression Scale (Galassi, Delo, Galassi, & Bastien, 1974). Many of the measures tested in the past two decades were developed from the work of Wolpe and Lazarus, whose Wolpe-Lazarus Assertiveness Scale appeared in their 1966 book, *Behavior Therapy Techniques.* There are also a wide variety of assertion measures that have been developed from experiential and literature bases without extensive research testing. Nearly every book on assertiveness includes a self-measurement tool, and there are a number of specific measurement devices for varied occupational groups. The Sundel Assertiveness Scale I (Sundel & Sundel, 1980) is excellent as a measure of professional assertiveness for human service workers, and MacNeilage and Adams include a scale for measuring assertiveness in the work environment in their 1982 book *Assertiveness at Work.*

The Librarian's Assertiveness Inventory which is presented here includes some material adapted from the Rathus Assertiveness Scale and the MacNeilage/Adams Checklist for Work Stress. In addition to these two excellent sources, data from three years of teaching assertiveness workshops for the Medical Library Association and the Special Libraries Association have been used to design this scale. Librarians from a wide variety of types and sizes of libraries helped test the scale by responding to the 60 unique statements designed for it while responding at the same time to both the complete Rathus Assertiveness Schedule and the MacNeilage/Adams Checklist for Work Stress. The scores on all three measures were then correlated to determine the approximate reliability of the Librarian's Assertiveness Inventory. When indicated revisions were completed, an additional correlative test was conducted. The original list of 60 library related statements was reduced to 45 to eliminate inappropriate statements and redundancy, and some wording changes were made.

It is extremely important to determine 'where you are'or a point of reference before undertaking any course of change, desirable or otherwise. This assessment is useful in setting goals for change and also in measuring change after a learning experience or over time. You are thus encouraged to take time at this point to respond to the Librarian's Assertiveness Inventory before reading further.

Librarian's Assertiveness Inventory

Instructions: Indicate how characteristic each of the following state-ments is of you, using the following scale of 1 to 5:

    1 = Never or almost never true of me, totally uncharacteristic.
    2 = Rarely true of me, quite uncharacteristic.
    3 = Sometimes true of me, depends on the circumstances.
    4 = Usually true of me, quite characteristic.
    5 = Always or almost always true of me, totally characteristic.

_____ 1. I am able to give constructive criticism to another librarian without jeopardizing our relationship.
_____ 2. I find it difficult to criticize or discipline a subordinate.
_____ 3. When I interview people, I put them at their ease.

_____ 4. People seem to take advantage of my good nature and willingness to help.

_____ 5. I serve on more committees than I would like to.

_____ 6. I tell people exactly what I think even when I suspect it will hurt their feelings.

_____ 7. If someone argues with me, I give in to avoid bad feelings.

_____ 8. I ask for the autonomy I believe I can handle.

_____ 9. I do not make exceptions to library rules.

_____ 10. I speak freely in staff meetings, voicing my opinion even when I know it is a minority view.

_____ 11. When I get a job evaluation I disagree with, I state my disagreement either verbally or in writing.

_____ 12. I find it easy to give suggestions to my boss.

_____ 13. I don't bother to correct people who accept the librarian stereotype.

_____ 14. I have difficulty accepting criticism.

_____ 15. When someone teases me too far, I blow up.

_____ 16. When someone teases me too far, I cry.

_____ 17. I feel more comfortable with other librarians of my own sex than with librarians of the opposite sex.

_____ 18. When a co-worker asks me personal questions, I answer because I don't know how to get out of answering without offending her/him.

_____ 19. When a co-worker asks me personal questions, I never answer no matter how offended s/he is. I just ignore her/him.

_____ 20. I am a risk-taker.

_____ 21. I can say "I don't know" easily.

_____ 22. Every time I disagree with someone, s/he gets mad at me.

_____ 23. When a colleague has really done a good job on something, I tell her/him.

_____ 24. I secretly tell annoying people off while I am driving home from work.

_____ 25. I brood over the things I say to people when I think I should have said them differently.

_____ 26. I am not afraid to take a controversial stand with the library board/committee.

_____ 27. When I have a bad day at work, I usually wind up in an argument at home or out socially.

_____ 28. I won't ask a colleague to change work days with me, even though there have been times the schedule has wrecked my personal plans.

_____ 29. When a patron gets visibly upset about something, I remain calm.

_____ 30. When I think I am handling more than my share of the workload, I complain loudly.

_____ 31. When I am getting overcommitted, I say "no" to new requests for my time.

_____ 32. If I feel incapable of doing a task assigned to me, I am afraid to admit it.

_____ 33. I find it difficult to relate to my boss as an equal.

_____ 34. Even when I agree with other people, I don't speak up in meetings.

_____ 35. I compliment myself when I've done something good, even where other people can hear me.

_____ 36. When someone has been unfair to me, I let her/him know I think s/he has been unfair.

_____ 37. If I am late to a meeting and the only seats left are in the front row, I stand in the back of the room.

_____ 38. I look forward to expressing my opinion at staff meetings.

_____ 39. I am often at a loss for words.

_____ 40. I don't know where to look or put my hands when I'm talking with someone.

_____ 41. I try not to hurt someone else's feelings.

_____ 42. When patrons are clearly disruptive, it is easy for me to calmly ask them to leave.

_____ 43. I try to swallow my anger when I'm at work.

_____ 44. I reciprocate when people try to 'put me down.'

_____ 45. I am willing to call other librarians for advice when I'm stumped.

The Appendix provides a response key for the Librarian's Assertiveness Inventory. In it, the numerical responses to each statement are identified as aggressive, nonassertive, or assertive. There is no numerical total against which you can judge your total assertiveness, as a single compiled score has little meaning for use in setting individual goals. The inventory is designed to show behavior patterns rather than an overall single assessment. As you compare your responses to those shown in the Appendix, you should search for two patterns. Both patterns are important to consider in setting goals for yourself.

First, do your responses show an overwhelming preponderance of one type of behavior? If you show a disproportionate number of nonassertive responses, for example, you may wish to set goals involving confidence building as well as learning some appropriate assertive skills. If you have a disproportionate number of aggressive responses, you may wish to concentrate on learning to discriminate between assertion and aggression more carefully so that you can replace aggressive reactions with assertive responses.

Second, do your nonassertive and aggressive responses seem to be elicited by similar types of situations? If you find five statements relating to similar types of situations, and four of your responses are rated as high assertive while the fifth is rated as nonassertive, you can reasonably assume your nonassertive response was selected assertively, that is, you assumed elements in the situation that led you to choose nonassertion in that instance. Your choice was not habitual but reasoned. If, however, you responded nonassertively to four of five similar type situations, you may wish to consider whether your nonassertive responses were based on reason or habit.

When you have completed an evaluation of your responses, you will have gained some important information about the types of situations you might consider as goals for new assertive behaviors. Now you need to determine when, how, and how much you want to practice assertion.

HOW COMFORTABLE ARE YOU?

Assertive behavior, like other types of learning, is transferable. The same techniques can be employed in varying situations, with different people, at different times. But many people find that techniques that work well for them in certain situations, and with which they are very comfortable, simply do not work for them in other situations, or do not feel *right* to them in other situations. How you respond depends very much on the specific circumstances of the situation (Hughes & Mullins, 1981), and circumstances change: your feelings about different people may be different, your mood may change, or your needs may change. Your level of comfort is vital to your ability to act assertively, and your level of assertive living can affect your feeling of comfort.

The Librarian's Discomfort Inventory is designed to help you determine your level of discomfort in a variety of potential library circumstances. In 1976, Bower and Bower published a general book on assertiveness in which readers were asked to remember past experiences in which they had felt inadequate. A worksheet (Worksheet #2, pp. 14–16) was provided to assist readers in this identification task.

This worksheet served as a stimulus for the Librarian's Discomfort Inventory, which evolved into the form presented below. Other publications provided ideas for the discomfort possibilities included in the inventory list. These included works by Baer (1976), Caputo (1981), Donald (1980), Kelly (1982), and Lange and Jakubowski (1976). Again, you are strongly encouraged to take time to respond to the Librarian's Discomfort Inventory before reading any further.

Librarian's Discomfort Inventory

Instructions: (1) Place a mark (a check, an ''x,'' or whatever you prefer) by each of the lines below that you feel are true for you. You need not be concerned with the level of their importance, simply check off *all* that apply. (2) Go back through the list a second time, and *circle* those marks that indicate areas you want very much to change. Circle only those things that are *really* important to you, those things that give you the most anxiety or are the biggest obstacles to your professional development. (3) *Do not* try to do both things at the same time. It does take longer to go through the entire list twice, but your results will be much more accurate if you take an extra few minutes to do it this way.

What nonassertive or aggressive *behaviors* describe you?

_____ blushing
_____ stammering, stuttering
_____ mumbling
_____ low speaking voice
_____ no eye contact
_____ mixing words up
_____ few or no gestures
_____ sitting on edge of seat
_____ making excuses
_____ forgetting what you are saying and how to say it
_____ crying
_____ tensing of jaw muscles
_____ clipping words for emphasis
_____ growling, grumbling
_____ shouting, or loud voice
_____ glaring, staring
_____ purposeful repetition
_____ exaggerated gestures

_____ slouching, sprawling
_____ rationalizing
_____ being determined to get your message across regardless of response
_____ cursing

Who are the people with whom you have difficulty being assertive?

_____ professionals from other disciplines
_____ librarians from other types of libraries
_____ co-workers in your library
_____ co-workers from other libraries within your organization
_____ supervisees/employees
_____ supervisor/employer
_____ library committee/board/governing body members
_____ the general public
_____ students
_____ faculty
_____ your regular library patrons
_____ patrons who are not part of your usual patron population
_____ people who have personal characteristics you dislike (e.g., loud voices, unkempt appearance, etc.)
_____ people who ask questions that violate your personal value system (e.g., who want information on gay rights when you are totally opposed to the concept)
_____ authority figures (e.g., clergy, physicians)
_____ administrative authorities over your library setting (e.g., city council)
_____ service representatives
_____ vendors of library services
_____ vendors of library equipment and supplies
_____ officers of professional library organizations
_____ former library school faculty/former mentors

When do you find you have difficulty being assertive?

_____ when you are giving instructions to a subordinate
_____ when you are accepting instructions from a supervisor
_____ when you are giving constructive criticism
_____ when you are accepting criticism, constructive or otherwise
_____ when you are angry
_____ when you are upset over nonlibrary concerns
_____ when you are speaking up in a group
_____ when you wish to give an unsolicited suggestion

_____ when your suggestions are solicited and you have none
_____ when your suggestions are solicited and you have one you think will be poorly received or controversial
_____ when you feel someone has treated you unfairly
_____ when you need help
_____ when you don't want to do something you have been asked to do
_____ when you must speak in front of a group
_____ when you must chair a meeting
_____ when you disagree with someone
_____ when you don't know something
_____ when you are being interviewed
_____ when you are interviewing someone else
_____ when you are being given a performance appraisal
_____ when you are giving a performance appraisal
_____ when someone you dislike wants to work closely with you
_____ when someone you like has offended you

What topics do you find unpleasant to discuss?

_____ your successes
_____ your errors
_____ others' successes
_____ others' errors
_____ your supervisor's good points
_____ your supervisor's faults
_____ your subordinate's good points
_____ your subordinate's faults
_____ librarianship (with nonlibrarians)
_____ professional issues
_____ budgetary concerns
_____ budget requests (for increased dollars)
_____ library politics
_____ library policies
_____ library procedures
_____ library networks/cooperatives
_____ differences of opinion with other librarians from the same type of libraries
_____ differences of opinion with other librarians from different types of libraries
_____ objections you have to rules and regulations of networks your library belongs to

There are no right or wrong answers to this discomfort assessment tool, nor is there a response key. Its entire use is to assist you in setting your own assertive goals, and its use in this regard is very simple: *Do not use circled marks as your first assertive goals.* For your first goals, try for behavior changes in the areas that are *not* important to you. This significantly decreases your potential anxiety over the outcome of your target situation. If it doesn't work out exactly as you hoped it would, your losses will not be great, and your concern should be similarly small. When you have practiced your new assertive skills often, when they have become replacements for formerly habitual behavior, when you can control your emotional responses in high anxiety situations, then, and only then, should you consider tackling one of your circled goals.

THE GOAL PROCESS

You are ready to begin selecting personal assertive goals when you have completed an objective assessment of your strengths and limitations. Goal selection has been called the most critical part of the goal process, and many writers warn how easily your desires can remain unsatisfied due to the inappropriate selection of goals (Pardue, 1980; Williams & Long, 1979). But how do you actually select your first goal?

A useful way to begin is to subdivide a long-term goal into multiple short-term goals. For example, if your long-term goal is to handle excessive anger which you habitually exhibit in aggressive behaviors at work, such as sarcasm or belittling statements when you talk with colleagues, a first subgoal might be to learn to investigate your anger each times it arises, analyzing it to determine why you are angry. Your second subgoal might be to learn a relaxation technique which will allow you to decrease your physiological response to the affective state of anger without denying your right to feel angry. A third subgoal might be to learn assertive ways to verbalize feelings without violating others' rights. Your fourth subgoal could be to practice these new skills in nonwork situations of minor importance to you: at the grocery store when you encounter a needless delay, at home with a persistent telephone salesperson who has called for the third time, or at the hotel desk when your room has not been made up all day. Finally, when you have been successful with all of your subgoals, you will be ready to approach your real goal of using new behaviors to express your anger in work situations. This step-by-step process is very important. As Neiger and Fullerton (1979) note, it is relatively easy to get rid of a pesky telephone salesperson once you have learned assertive behaviors, and it may be a little harder to be assertive with someone who cuts in front of you in a line, but these situations "pale in significance and become quite trivial when you compare them to ongoing working relationships" (p. 31), as working relationships are long-term relationships that you will be likely to want to cultivate, build, and deepen. Pugh (1979) adds that realistic subgoals minimize the risks of assertion and increase chances of success in attaining the desired changes.

According to Williams and Long (1979), there are certain characteristics of goals that you should also keep in mind. First, a goal must be measurable if it is to be easily evaluated. In the example above, where your long-term goal is to control your anger in work situations, your first two subgoals could be measured by noting the length of time it takes you to determine the underlying cause for your anger each time it occurs and by noting both how long and how much you can control your physiological responses. Second, the level of the goal you set should start at a minimum, and more readily attainable, level that can be increased as you are successful in attaining that level. If your long-term goal is to speak up in large meetings, and your current behavior is to make no comments at all, an attainable, minimum level goal would be to speak up once, at a single meeting, by agreeing with a statement already made, e.g., "I agree with that." After this success, repeated over several meetings (and probably varied somewhat, e.g., "I think Val is right"), the goal level could be increased to two comments per meeting or to one comment of agreement with a supporting reason. Moving from no comments to group orator is much too great a leap to take in a single step.

A third characteristic to consider is the connotation of a goal, positive or negative. Although the elimination of a negative behavior can be seen as a positive goal, it has a more positive connotation if a positive behavior replaces the negative behavior. It is also far easier to eliminate negative behaviors when they are carefully paired with incompatible positive behaviors that can be substituted for them. For example, if you have a habit of assessing everything as "OK," and you have noticed that this habit has a negative effect on your colleagues, you would be more likely to achieve your goal of providing more positive reinforcement by substituting phrases like "That's great" or "I like that," than by simply reminding yourself not to say "OK" at each opportunity that arose.

Although goal setting in this way may seem to be very self-centered, it is vital that this orientation take place before you can begin to live assertively. Donald (1980) believes that the goal setting process is an integral part of confidence building, which is the base upon which assertive living must rest. She lists five basic questions to be asked during the goal setting process, pointing out that each answer should be scrutinized for how realistic it is. Her first question is, Is this goal consistent with my personal characteristics and abilities? If the answer to this question is no, you should consider whether the attainment of those characteristics and abilities should be set as first-step goals leading to the long-term goal. Donald's second question is, How long do I need to reach this goal? This can be difficult to assess, and setting specific deadlines for the first step and other subgoals can be helpful in estimating how long it will take to effect a behavior change. Habits that have developed over years are quite likely to be highly resistent to change. Donald's remaining three questions all relate to time and reality: What can I do today? What can I have realistically accomplished by one week from today? What specifically can I do within a month to implement or reach my goals? Long-term goals may seem to be impossible unless their attainability is reinforced by small step successes as subgoals are reached.

BLOCKS TO ASSERTION

After you have defined your goals and begun to learn varied assertive techniques and skills, you may still encounter blocks that inhibit your use of assertive behaviors to attain your goals. Although the variety of blocks to any type of goal attainment is as infinite as the human mind is creative, they tend to fall into five specific categories (Lyon, 1980):

1. Lack of knowledge or skills necessary to attain the goal.
2. Lack of resources needed to attain the goal.
3. Internal constraints (e.g., fear of consequences).
4. External constraints (e.g., policy/authority).
5. Lack of time necessary to achieve the goal.

In relation to assertion, some of these categories are less inhibiting than others. When a lack of knowledge or skills necessary to attain the goal is discovered, it may be possible to overcome these deficiencies by setting them as first-step goals. Similarly, a lack of resources may be overcome by increasing resources before attempting the desired goal.

A lack of time may be overcome by reducing the goals sought to a realistic expectation for the length of time available or by seeking to expand your time frame through extension of deadlines. In assertion training research, it has been shown that most blocks to assertive behavior fall in the category of internal constraints (Alberti & Emmons, 1982; Cotler, 1975; Flowers, 1975), and overcoming these constraints is a major focus of most assertion training. External constraints may also inhibit assertive behaviors significantly, and in this regard, assertion trainers emphasize the process of reasonable, logical, rational, cognitive choices as assertive behavior (Lange & Jakubowski, 1976).

As internal constraints have such major importance in blocking the acquisition and use of assertive behaviors, they will be the major focus of this section. Internal constraints can be divided into three major kinds: (1) fear of consequences, (2) a belief that others should know what we want and need without our telling them, and (3) anticipation of a "perfect" environment in which to behave assertively (Caputo, 1981).

Fear of Consequences

A fear of negative consequences is a very common block to assertion (Montgomery & Heimberg, 1978). It is felt by most people, and it is hard to overcome even though it is self-imposed. The fears people harbor range from minor to major fears and include both affective and situational consequences. A minor affective fear is "they'll think I'm pushy," while a major affective fear is "s/he won't love me any more." A minor situational fear is "they'll take twice as long to do it for me now," while a major situational fear is "I'll lose my job if I do that." Fears that librarians have expressed in assertion courses presented by the Medical Library Association are representative of this wide range, and they are presented in Table 2.

Table 2
Reasons Librarians Give for Not Being Assertive

Reason Given	What Is Often Meant	Resultant Behavior
It's not important enough to bother with.	I'm not important enough to say it. No one would listen to me anyway.	Nonassertive
I don't have time to think about that.	I'm too afraid to do anything about that, so I'll keep too busy to find time for it.	Nonassertive
I'm right!	I'm smarter and better than everyone else.	Aggressive
I had to be honest about it....	I violated her/his rights, but I was justified because honesty is a virtue.	Aggressive
I might lose my job.	I don't dare rock the boat.	Nonassertive
S/he made me do it.	I violated her/his rights, but I'm justified because s/he deserved it anyway; s/he asked for it; I'm guiltless.	Aggressive
I wouldn't give her/him the satisfaction!	I'm afraid if I stand up to him/her, s/he'll attack me (and win), and that will give her/him pleasure	Nonassertive
It wouldn't make any difference anyway.	I'm powerless/helpless.	Nonassertive
It wouldn't be nice.	At all costs, people have to approve of me and think I'm nice.	Nonassertive
I might make her/him feel bad.	Her/his feelings are more important than mine.	Nonassertive

Table 2
Reasons Librarians Give for Not Being Assertive (continued)

Reason Given	What Is Often Meant	Resultant Behavior
Anybody else would have felt exactly the same way I feel.	I probably violated someone else's rights, but I've been treated badly, so I'm justified.	Aggressive
It'll just make matters worse.	I can't possibly do anything to make matters better, I'm too helpless, too dumb, etc.	Nonassertive
I never liked her/him anyway.	I violated her/his rights, but I'm justified, because s/he never earned my approval or respect.	Aggressive
They never did anything for me.	I violated their rights, but I've earned better treatment than they have given me.	Aggressive
S/he will think I'm mean.	At all costs, I must have approval. I cannot stand it if someone thinks I'm mean.	Nonassertive
I should have gotten that; it should have been mine.	No one else will give me what I've earned even if I ask for it, so I won't bother to ask, I'll just take it.	Aggressive
This will just pay her/him back!	I think someone else violated my rights. S/he wouldn't listen if I complained, so my only recourse is to seek revenge.	Aggressive and Passive-aggressive

Many of our minor affective fears are a result of early socialization. We are taught to be polite, to be unselfish, to be modest, and, above all, to be "nice." Alberti and Emmons (1974) noted that quiet behavior in American children is rewarded to such an extent that natural spontaneity and assertive behavior is conditioned out of them no later than the fourth or fifth grade. American women fall into what Phelps and Austin (1975) call the "Compassion Trap" when they learn society's role expectations that women should provide tenderness and compassion at all times, and that they will be rewarded with love or affection when they place others' needs and feelings before their own, even to the exclusion of any consideration for their own feelings.

Jakubowski and Lange (1978) also have shown a concern for the way society's expectations affect our assertive behavior. We are taught not to be selfish, and the sharing we learn to exhibit as children is quickly translated into the thought that, unless we think of others first and give until it hurts, we are being selfish. But being selfish is more than not thinking of others first: being selfish is concern with one's own welfare, in disregard of others, excessively or exclusively. Our early socialization leads us to generalize that saying no to someone or setting limits on how much of yourself you will give to them is selfish behavior. However, a healthy, reasonable person realizes that (1) it is not healthy to hurt yourself; (2) caring for others does not prohibit you from also caring about yourself; (3) you do not have limitless energy to give either to others or yourself; and (4) you have a responsibility to yourself to value your own needs as highly as you value the needs of others. Similarly, our childhood lessons about politeness lead us to nonassertive behavior in order to avoid the "rudeness" of telling someone we are offended by her/his behavior. Early lessons on modesty teach us that complimenting ourselves is "bragging," a behavior that cannot win friendships. In *Creative Aggression; The Art of Assertive Living,* Bach and Goldberg (1974) describe our cultural expectations of "niceness" in a variety of roles, occupational as well as familial. They also specify the high price this "nice" behavior demands of individuals as well as the rewards it may offer. The "nice" teacher is defined in this way:

> Little or no homework, lots of rapping in class about "feelings," no required attendance, and easy exams are the hallmarks of the "nice" teacher. He or she tries to be everybody's friend, and runs a "hang loose" class.
> "Nice" teachers can be easily manipulated by a tale of woe. They promise everything to everybody. "Nice" teachers will align themselves with student causes, and may even let students decide themselves on what grade they want.

THE REWARD "Nice" teachers can see themselves as special heroes, and martyrs to the establishment. Students "dig" them, and they get lots of compliments and flattery.

THE PRICE ..."Nice" teachers provide students with an unreal model...[as] they don't set meaningful standards and are equally "nice" to all students, the "nice" teacher's grades and letters of recommendation eventually become worthless...their students are less prepared...they often disappoint students (p. 13).

Bach and Goldberg go on to define the "nice" boss in this way:

A "nice" boss...keeps a large calendar on his wall on which he circles the birthdays of every employee...he gives two major parties a year to which everybody is invited...he keeps his office door open at all times, smiles, and says "How're things going?" as people walk by. He is eager to be the "nice" guy and help others out. For example, late one afternoon he sat around helping to stuff and seal envelopes that needed to go out that day while his own work sat waiting on his desk.

In general, he hesitates to ask an employee to do anything out of the ordinary, such as to work late or carry an extra assignment. He secretly shudders at the thought of giving orders. He never gets openly angry and studiously avoids criticizing anybody. To the contrary, he always looks for the positives and goes out of his way to find something nice to say about everyone's work. Nobody ever gets fired once they've been with the office more than three months. He himself is the very model of a hard worker, frequently at his desk well past 7:00 p.m., and often coming in to work on Saturdays. But if anybody in his office looks overtired, he is quick to tell the person to take the rest of the day off. Clearly, nobody would call this "gentle soul" who never yells, criticizes, or makes demands on anybody, anything but "nice."

THE REWARD The "nice" boss does manage, by and large, to avoid being involved in the conflicts, or disharmony around him. Employees smile when they're around him, rarely raise their voices, nor make anything but positive, happy-type conversation with him.

Those who quit their jobs to go elsewhere never tell him the truth about their real sources of discontent or frustration. He is therefore never made to feel that personnel dissatisfaction has anything to do with him. The behavior of others around him allows him to see himself as a person who creates an atmosphere of peace, love, and harmony around him. This self-image is very satisfying to him.

THE PRICE The heaviest price the "nice" boss pays at work is that he loses his best employees. This happens for several reasons. Since he is loath to criticize or be disliked by anybody, he does not really discriminate between an excellent performance and a lesser one. The genuinely talented, productive employees begin to feel it's not worth extending themselves. They begin to feel stagnant and unchallenged. Eventually, they become so bored and frustrated that they quit. Over the years, as the best people leave, the "nice" boss finds himself increasingly surrounded by the clingers, the lesser competent, and the syncophants, who can't really produce well but who feel safe and protected because they can survive by smiling and playing the game of being "nice." The more manipulative employees begin to see that they can get away with anything and so they take more and more liberties: long coffee breaks, coming to work late, and leaving early. Consequently the quality of work steadily declines.

Inside himself, the "nice" boss is chronically tense, worried, and prone to psychosomatic problems like ulcers and hypertension. Because he carries so much unnecessary responsibility on his shoulders, it also has a particularly disastrous effect on his home life. He arrives there in the evening totally exhausted....Eventually everything in his life begins to feel meaningless and empty. He doesn't understand why, with all of his good intentions, he feels so lonely, friendless, and neglected (pp. 9–11).

These descriptions are extreme, but they do make a point. We are socialized to believe that "nice" means nonassertive. A similar description of a "good" librarian based on our common experiences regardless of the type of librarianship we practice, and on the unspoken messages included in some library science curriculums, is easy to describe in similar nonassertive terms:

The "good" librarian responds to every patron demand as fully as possible, as quickly as possible. Questions never remain unanswered, and patrons are not expected to do any portion of the work themselves. Books and journals are ordered on demand in response to each patron request, regardless of budgetary limitations. Other parts of the budget, like librarian travel, simply have to be sacrificed when necessary. The librarian always runs a neat, organized library, where nothing is ever missing or mutilated, and where, to be absolutely sure everything is in the right place, s/he often shelves materials her/himself.

The "good" librarian is always patient, particularly when explaining library policies and collection decisions to anyone who questions them and never shows her/himself to be harried, harrassed, ruffled, annoyed, irritated, or upset any more than s/he would exhibit overt signs of happiness or amusement in the library. Flexibility is a staple characteristic of the "good" librarian, who is willing to change policies, hours, or collections on demand of influential patrons, the library committee or board, or members of the library staff. This same flexibility is seen when the "good" librarian eagerly acquiesces to a command to develop a new subject area collection with one week's notice about a curriculm change, new department, or new city plan for industrial expansion.

The "good" librarian is able to differentiate between the "important" and "unimportant" patrons, and, although being very careful to see that the "unimportant" patrons get all the same services as the "important" people, makes sure that the "important" patrons know their importance is recognized. This may be exhibited in a slight display of deference or affective expression, or it may take the form of special exemptions to otherwise rigid library policies.

The "good" librarian never troubles the users with involved reference interviews, s/he just takes whatever minimal information is offered and goes straight to the best source of information to instantaneously find an answer at no cost to the user. The really "good" librarian is never absent or ill, knows how to work (and repair) every machine in the library, and never speaks above a whisper.

THE REWARD "Good" librarians need no more reward than the satisfaction of providing people with the information they need. Compliments from patrons, which come in readily (especially from "important" patrons), and the "peace" of a "well-run" library (avoidance of conflict is an important goal for them) are icing on the cake. Accepting orders for collection development or policy decisions allows them to share responsibility (and therefore any potential blame) for library services with the staff, library committee, library board, or even their patrons.

THE PRICE Employers are eager to recognize the reward of satisfaction "good" librarians seek and give them fewer material rewards than other employees: they are paid less than others with equivalent or less professional education and experience, they get less employee benefits than others in their organizations (e.g., sabbatical time for professional development), and less recognition (e.g., department head status in a corporate structure). Their self-esteem is undermined by this differential reward system, which then inhibits their abilities to negotiate for the more material rewards.

Compliance responses to all the varying patron, staff and committee/board demands result in unbalanced or inappropriate collections, budgetary mismanagement, staff unrest and inconsistent policies. They also help perpetuate the library stereotype.

This myth of the "good" librarian can lead us into a whole range of behaviors governed by the rules of good and bad behavior. If we define "good" behaviors as those that fit society's expectations of librarians and define all other behaviors as "bad," we can hardly help damaging our self-images as it is impossible not to engage in this socially defined "bad" behavior at times.

Fear of consequences may be exhibited as a reluctance to hurt someone's feelings, which Neiger and Fullerton (1979) call a thinly disguised fear of disapproval, or as shyness, which "can serve as a convenient excuse for avoiding challenges, unpredictable situations or people, and the possibility of rejection" (Zimbardo, Pilkonis, & Norwood, 1975).

Diminishing your fears. An excellent way to control your fear of consequences is to face them realistically. Assertive behavior *is* risky. You may hurt someone's feelings, or be disapproved of, or be rejected. So, given that reality, what, exactly, will happen to you if any of these things occur? Try saying, "*So what, if...*" for each of your fears:

- *So what,* if I make a mistake?
- *So what,* if my opinion is challenged?
- *So what,* if s/he doesn't like me any more?
- *So what,* if I lose my job?

Then, immediately, answer yourself as realistically as possible:

- *So what,* if I make a mistake? Some people may think I was stupid to make that mistake. I may have to do this over. I may have to ask someone else to help me. I may lose a little time. But, I may learn a lot.
- *So what,* if my opinion is challenged? I may learn something I didn't know before. I may be asked to justify my opinion. I may change my mind. My feelings may be hurt. But, I may enjoy the resulting discussion.
- *So what,* if s/he doesn't like me any more? I may be unhappy at losing this friend. I may have to look for new friends. I may be inconvenienced. But, I may feel free to do new things my friend and I never did.
- *So what,* if I lose my job? I may have trouble finding another one right away. I may have to give up my apartment or cut back on spending money. Things will probably be pretty rough financially for a while, and it will probably be tough to explain how/why I lost this job. But, I may decide to start my own business at last.

Finally, realistically assess how many of those consequences you want to risk, and choose the type of behavior which logically follows for you:

- *Making a mistake* might work out just fine. The boss knows I have never worked on this kind of a project before and has already indicated the deadline can be flexible. I'll get a lot more satisfaction trying my ideas out, even if I make a mistake that costs me time, than if I just follow someone else's orders. And, since everyone makes mistakes, it's no big deal if I make one. If someone thinks I'm stupid for making mistakes, I will disagree.

- *Having my opinion challenged* has always been tough for me, but I have learned a lot about myself recently, and I know better than to let my whole ego ride on a single experience. I have thought about the subject a lot, so I can justify my opinion if I choose to answer the challenge. If my feelings are hurt, I can cope with it; I know that everyone has as much right to disagree with my opinion as I have to hold it. I may be wrong, but I may have a good point, I'll never know what the others think of my idea unless I take the plunge.
- *Losing this friend* over this issue is more than I want to risk. We have had disagreements in the past, and I may be able to state my concern in a more acceptable way to decrease the chance of losing this friendship, but if I can't, I would rather not state my concern. There may be a future issue that's more important to me, and I may have to risk this friendship then, but for now I'm going to choose to be nonassertive over this issue.
- *Risking my job* is the toughest decision I have ever had to make. I am really worried that I won't find another job right away, and I certainly can't afford to start my own business just now. Yet every day I am finding myself more upset and incapable of handling the constant conflicts between the job requirements and my personal values. I know I'd be happier somewhere else, but it would really be hard to explain why I left, especially if I get fired for refusing to do this assignment. I think my best alternative is to update my resume and start serious job hunting. I can tolerate this situation and be cooperative for another 6–12 months, as long as I know it will eventually end. It would be foolish to jeopardize my chances of getting another job by getting fired tomorrow.

These examples show how an assertive, rational, assessment of the many consequences we fear can assist us in choosing our behaviors. Whether we choose to take the risk of realizing the consequences we fear, to avoid the feared consequences, or to delay action until we can take steps which will eliminate or alleviate the undesirable consequences, should depend on our cognitive analysis of what we want, what realistic consequences could occur, and how much those potential consequences mean to us. Few of us really wish to take continuous risks, yet few of us wish to live the bland life that never taking a risk entails. Our responsibility is not simply to take risks, but to select those risks that we analytically deem worth taking.

We no longer need to be bound by habitual reactions or irrational fears.

You Should Have Known...

Another common block to assertive behavior exists when someone interacts with us regularly and knows us well, because we are then tempted to believe that person should intuitively know when s/he has hurt our feelings or given us cause for anger. We expect certain people to be sensitive to our needs without our having to state what those needs are. When we interact with strangers, we are very aware that our wants, needs, and feelings will be unknown unless we make an effort to state them clearly. We tend to expect our closest friends and relations, however, to know all about our wants, needs, and feelings wihout our telling them. The result is that we often act far less assertively with those who are close to us than with total strangers (Liberman, King, DeRisi & McCann, 1975).

We not only see the need for assertion with strangers more clearly, we find it easier to exhibit new behaviors with them. Our habitual behaviors toward strangers are generalized to a class of people, all the people we don't know well. Our habitual behaviors toward those we know well, however, are specific for each individual we are close to, and changing these is a greater task. We are socialized to believe that good friendship includes a continuous sensitivity to our needs, and that the closer the relationship, the greater that sensitivity. But when we act as if our friends or relations are continuous monitors of our feelings and needs, we essentially deny them the right to have feelings or needs of their own which may temporarily mask their sensitivity to us.

We engage our close friends and relations in what Alberti and Emmons (1982) call "hidden bargains," which account for many of our habitual behaviors. A librarian who silently accepts unreasonable deadlines, works overtime whenever asked, and puts up with a supervisor's inappropriate temper tantrums may believe "If I put up with all the bad things about this job and never complain, you will give me regular raises without my having to ask for them, and you will never fire me." The librarian essentially has made an unspoken bargain with the supervisor: the librarian will exhibit certain behaviors (acceptance, compliance, noncomplaining), and the supervisor will respond with specific rewards (raises, continued employment). The problem with this agreement is that the supervisor has not only not agreed to it, but the supervisor does not, in fact, even know it exists.

When the librarian does not receive a raise, or if employment is terminated for any reason, this librarian will feel betrayed and bitter. A bargain or contractual agreement with an employer or employee can be very useful, but the hidden bargain demands sacrifices of the person who has formed it without guaranteeing any response at all from the other person with whom the "bargain" has (not) been "made."

The Perfect Environment

The final common block to assertion is an unrealistic, irrational definition of a perfect environment in which to be assertive. When we use these excuses, *I'll be assertive* depends on:

- *If so-and-so is in a good mood.*
- *If someone else doesn't say it first.*
- *Waiting till tomorrow if they don't do it today.*
- *If the time is right.*
- *If I'm sure I'm right.*

We may be rationally assessing the situation and choosing to be nonassertive at this time, or we may simply be postponing assertive behavior as a way of avoiding it. Timing is vital to making an assertive statement, as we will see in Chapter 5, but waiting for the "perfectly right" time can be dangerous. The longer assertive behavior is postponed waiting for the right time, the more rigid our requirements for the right time become, until very few situations can measure up to our requirements. Then we need only be assertive on rare occasions, if at all (Butler, 1976).

Blocking by Choice

Assertion is always a matter of choice. Alberti and Emmons (1982) assure us that, as long as we are certain that we *can* be assertive in varied instances, we are free to choose not to exercise our skills in given instances. Neiger and Fullerton (1979) add, "If you know how to and *can* act assertively when you choose to, your *decision* not to assert yourself is vastly different from your *inability* to assert yourself" (p. 33). Here are some of the instances cited in the book by Alberti and Emmons and in the article by Neiger and Fullerton in which a rational decision to behave nonassertively may be made:

Dealing with the Overly Sensitive. When you know that the person you are dealing with is an overly sensitive person who cannot accept even the slightest criticism or the most minor assertions on your part, you may choose to maintain the relationship without agitation. This may be your best choice for short-term relationships or relationships requiring infrequent contact. A long-term relationship that is one-sided may not be in your best interests, however. If you have an overly sensitive boss you may eventually choose to seek another job, while if you have an overly sensitive employee you may eventually have to choose between her/his agitation and ending her/his employment.

Triviality. When the circumstances are trivial, you may decide they are simply not worth the effort it would take to be assertive. If someone walks into your closed door office without knocking, and you're neither talking with someone else nor attacking a project with special concentration, you may not care that they forgot to knock. Unless this person habitually shows you personal inconsideration, or you want to practice your new assertive skills on less important goals, there's not much payoff in being assertive about the incident.

Redundancy. Sometimes people notice that they've violated your rights and apologize or seek to remedy the situation in some other way. It is unnecessary to add your assertive request for a remedy to what they have already done.

Understanding and Kindness. Now and then you may have information about extenuating circumstances that are affecting another person's normal behavior. You may choose to overlook some infringements on your rights at that time. It is easy, however, to turn kindness into habitual nonassertion, so if the unusual circumstances persist, you may wish to point out that your nonassertive behavior stems from kindness and you will be less tolerant on other occasions: "I know this month has been exceptionally difficult for you with the new computer system being installed four months early and three people on vacation, so I have decided not to be concerned over your temporary short temper. I am confident you'll be more relaxed soon."

No Gain. When you no longer have anything to gain by being assertive, you may decide not to bother. If the issue involves others, and it is settled before you make your assertive statement, you may choose to pass up the opportunity. If you missed an opportunity to be assertive, it may be illogical or inappropriate to try to insert your assertion now.

No Choice. Whenever it is clearly beyond your power to change an event, it may not be in your best interests to assert yourself. When, in spite of everything you could do to justify it, your budget increase request is not approved, and you are suddenly forced to take a budget cut midway through the fiscal year, an assertive statement that you have the right to more advance warning might be true but will probably do you no good.

In Error. If you have incorrectly interpreted a situation, or are not sure that you have the complete facts, you may choose not to assert yourself until you have them all. If you assert yourself in error, you have a responsibility to apologize or otherwise make amends.

Conflicting Rights. Your rights may conflict with another person's rights, especially in the library environment where the rights inherent in the authority hierarchy are added to the human rights we all share. You have a right to choose to smoke, but the library director has the right to set policies concerning where in the library you may smoke. Even if you strongly disagree with the policy, you may not exercise your right to smoke in the areas designated by policy as nonsmoking.

Physical Harm. When you feel you are in danger of physical harm if you are assertive, it is wise to choose nonassertive behaviors until the danger has been alleviated or eliminated. If a potentially dangerous and disruptive patron enters the library, it is wiser to retreat and perhaps contact security than to request that the patron leave you alone.

SUMMARY

Before you can set assertive goals for yourself, you must determine how assertive you are now by identifying the situations in which you usually behave assertively and the situations in which you usually behave nonassertively or aggressively. You must also review and identify the people and instances in which you are not comfortable using assertive skills, targeting some as major goals and others as minor goals. You should then plan to practice your new skills only on the minor goals until you have had sufficient success and have become sufficiently skilled to tackle major goals. Most blocks to assertive behavior come from a fear of negative consequences, and these fears may be affective or situational or both. The way to overcome these fears is to learn to assess which parts of them actually exist in reality and to objectively assess exactly what it will mean to you if these real consequences do occur. Other blocks to feedback include a belief that others should know you well enough to preclude any need to behave assertively with them and a belief that there is a perfect environment in which to be assertive, and you must wait for it to occur before using your skills. These blocks affect your ability to be assertive.

The use of assertive skills is always a matter of choice, and there are some instances in which you may choose to behave nonassertively. These blocks to assertion differ from the fears and beliefs previously considered in that they are based on rational assessments of reality and occur, by choice, when you are capable of assertion but choose not to use it.

Chapter 4
Self-Esteem and Self-Confidence

Self-esteem should be SELF-esteem. What you think of yourself is much more important than what others think of you. Ugly duckling or swan? You are the only person who can answer. Somewhere along the road to assertiveness lies self-acceptance (Chenevert, 1978, p. 36).

People with low self-esteem devalue their achievements, are excessively dismayed by perceptions of personal shortcomings, feel inadequate, and give over-emphasis to personal faults, real or imagined (Levy, 1982). In this state of mind, assertive behavior requires more effort than an individual can give. Unfortunately, Shaw and Rutledge (1976) note that the price people pay for nonassertive and aggressive behaviors is a decrease in both self-worth and self-confidence. As low self-esteem and lack of confidence are obstacles to assertive behavior and lead to nonassertive or aggressive behavior, which in turn leads to even lower self-esteem, the unwary are trapped into a continuing cycle of nonassertion or aggression and the misery of self-dislike. Once behavior is directed toward assertiveness, however, this vicious cycle can be broken (Brockner, 1979). In the experience of Hutchings and Colburn (1979), the newly assertive person often gains enhanced feelings toward her/himself, and this increase in feelings of self-worth leads to further assertion, creating a new constructive cycle to replace the former destructive one.

SELF-ESTEEM, SELF-CONFIDENCE, AND ASSERTIVENESS

According to Hulbert (1982), self-esteem influences your hopes, ambitions, moods, and behavior. It directly affects whether or not you are able to act assertively. Your assertiveness can be seriously inhibited by low self-esteem, for when you continue to compare yourself unfavorably with the ideal you think you should strive for, you will eventually be convinced that you are hopelessly inadequate, unable to affect any interpersonal situation regardless of your behavior. So before you can use assertive skills, you must strengthen your self-image. Once you have assimilated the concept of assertiveness, however, and have found success in using assertive communication, you will develop greater self-confidence in handling interpersonal situations (Pugh, 1979). With this growing mastery of various interpersonal situations comes greater self-respect (Cotler, 1975).

It is not unusual for people to avoid activities in which they believe they will show up poorly, through fear of humiliation, disapproval, or loss of others' respect. Most people, for example, will avoid showing anger at work if they think others will clasify their behavior as out of control or bitchy. In the library, this may be exhibited as avoidance of conflict with staff or patrons for fear that they will think of us as unapproachable, unhelpful, or unwilling to listen (Cotler & Guerra, 1976), all of which are out of place in our picture of a good librarian. As the dissonance between our behavior and our idealization of what that behavior should be increases, our sense of self-worth decreases.

The Psychological Concept of Self-Esteem

Self-esteem can also be called self-regard, self-image, self-concept, and self-structure, but regardless of the term used, the definition remains the same: one's perception of one's self (Harper, 1981). This perception cannot be assessed, however, unless one has something against which to measure it. Argyle (1972) gives us a measureable definition of self-esteem when he defines it as the extent to which a person approves of and accepts her/himself, in comparison with an absolute or in comparison with others. The dimensions of self-esteem must then include both a perceptual, current view of what we think we are like and an idealized, timeless view of what we think we ought to be like, in order to make a comparison which indicates positive or negative worth (Caputo, 1981).

Ego-Ideal. Freud's classical theory of psychoanalysis defined the ''ego-ideal'' as the kind of ideal person we would most like to be, and Freud theorized that when we behave in accordance with this ego-ideal, we feel proud of ourselves (Nordby & Hall, 1974). This ego-ideal includes the values we learn as children and all the values we choose (consciously and unconsciously) to add as adults. Although the ego-ideal is not static and unchanging, it is more resistant to the elimination of old values than to the addition of new values. Freud believed that the ego-ideal was quite rigid, formed in childhood and highly resistent to any change. Later theorists provide more latitude for alteration and development of the ego-ideal after childhood (Hall & Lindsay, 1978). The ego-ideal is gradually shaped by parents, teachers, and significant role models as we learn rules of conduct (Hulbert, 1982). For our view of self-esteem in relation to assertiveness, it is important to note that we can, and do, select the components of the ego-ideal which we consciously wish to maintain, add, or eliminate. As adults, we do not need to be bound to the values our parents instilled during our formative years. The ego-ideal is unresponsive to the passage of time unless we consciously instill new values in it or unconsciously absorb the changing mores of society over its development. Ellis (1966) believes that, when powerful social propaganda supports the kinds of ideation we become addicted to as children, we tend to remain fixed on childish, nonsensical, overgeneralized ideals that, if we used our intelligence and capabilities, we would weed out of our ego-ideals.

Ego-Identity. For purposes of comparison, we will call the current perception of what we are our ego-identity (Caputo, 1981). Although the ego-identity is a current picture of what we believe ourselves to be, it may or may not be a valid one, as our self-perception may or may not be highly skewed. The validity of ego-identity is another variable over which we can, and do, have some conscious control. If we try to be objective and factual in our observations, rather than inferential, this control is facilitated. The mental picture we maintain of our strengths, weaknesses, and personality traits can be changed by what others tell us about their observations of us as well as by our own observations of ourselves (Hulbert, 1982).

Self-Esteem. Figure 2 represents how self-esteem is related to the concepts of ego-ideal and ego-identity. We compare the behaviors of our ego-identity, the current picture of what we believe ourselves to be, with the idealized behaviors of our ego-ideal, the picture of what we believe we ought to be. When the comparison shows little discrepancy, when our ego-identity appears to be similar to our ego-ideal, we experience positive self-regard, or high self-esteem. When the comparison shows a lot of discrepancy, when our ego-identity appears to be very dissimilar to our ego-ideal, we experience negative self-regard, or low self-esteem.

Imagine that the mercury in the thermometer pictured in Figure 2 is your self-esteem. It rises to the level at which your ego-ideal and ego-identity match. As they each move along their slanted lines, they approach each other but never quite meet. The farther they each move along their respective lines, the more they match each other, and the higher your self-esteem (the level of mercury in the thermometer) rises.

Even when we have a positive self-concept and behave assertively, we may still experience guilt feelings based on dissonance with the picture of our ego-ideal. Alberti & Emmons (1974) explain that the institutions of society have so carefully taught us the inhibition of even our most reasonable rights in the guise of courtesy, that we may still feel bad even though we have stood up for ourselves appropriately. Many of our basic societal systems have an anti-assertive influence in the limits that they place on our self-fulfilling actions. In order to behave assertively, we must learn to discriminate between appropriate feelings of guilt when we have really violated our own moral code and inappropriate feelings of guilt when we have only violated a standard-

Figure 2

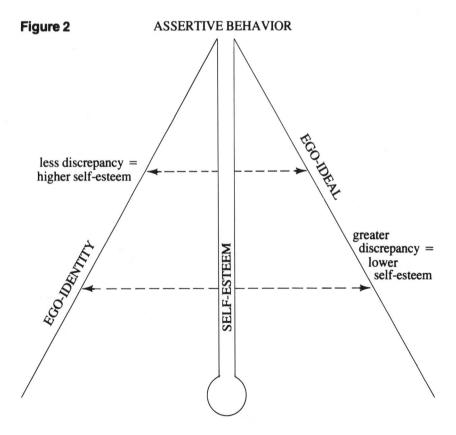

ized, generalized, attitude about behavior (e.g., "you shouldn't be selfish").

Wessler (1975) points out that when we violate other's rights our bad feeling about the violation need not be as strong as guilt. Guilt is more than a simple feeling of regret or sorrow over actions; it includes a concept of right and wrong and comes from the erroneous evaluation or rating of one's worth as a person based on the correct evaluation of one's erroneous acts. This is not the same as rationalization, which is a purposeful mis-evaluation of one's acts. Regret or sorrow, which do not include the self-condemnation of guilt, can help one correct behaviors one prefers to change. Guilt seldom leads to behavior correction. It leads, instead, to excessive condemnation, which leads to low self-esteem, which inhibits correction of the faults.

Self-Esteem in Transactional Analysis. Transactional analysis (TA) defines both our self-esteem and our regard for others by the kind of interchanges we have with other people. In the popular book *I'm OK, You're OK* (Harris, 1967), four life positions are presented. These are commonly depicted by a quadrant figure; Figure 3 is a modification of the commonly seen quadrant diagram. In this drawing, the positions are identified as nonassertive, assertive, aggressive, and passive-aggressive.

Nonassertive behaviors exist in quadrant 1, which is the home of defensive, inhibited people who lack self-confidence and put themselves down through excessive use of negative self-labels. They acquiesce to the wishes of other people by agreeing, assisting, obliging, and cooperating even when they (secretly) disagree. They attribute successes to getting lucky for a change and tend to harbor strong feelings of loneliness, isolation, and depression. They attempt to resolve conflict situations by withdrawal and other avoidance behaviors, quitting jobs, shirking responsibility, and allowing others to take over projects or give them orders. They behave as if they truly believe that they are *not OK* and that all others are better.

Aggressive behavior patterns are found in quadrant 3, which is the home of critical, snobbish people who boost their self-esteem by using negative labels for others as a means of putting other people down. They dominate other people by critical analysis, disapproval, harsh judgments, and manipulation. They attribute their successes to beating other people out and being natural winners. They approach conflict resolution with an "offense is the best defense" attitude, attacking and blaming others instead of seeking mutual solutions. They behave as if they believe that everyone else is *not OK* and they, alone, are best.

Figure 3

NON-ASSERTIVE POSITION	ASSERTIVE POSITION
I'M NOT OK	I'M OK
YOU'RE OK	YOU'RE OK
1	2
4	3
PASSIVE-AGGRESSIVE POSITION	AGGRESSIVE POSITION
I'M NOT OK	I'M OK
YOU'RE NOT OK	YOU'RE NOT OK

Passive-aggressive behaviors are found in quadrant 4, which is the home of the people who classify themselves as victims and losers. They use negative labels for everyone, themselves included. They are unhappy people who evade, concede, retreat, relinquish, and withdraw. They do not recognize that they have any successes and envy the successes of others. They approach conflict resolution with the belief that they are victims who can only hope to win through cheating. They behave as if the world is a chronically problematic reality, and no one, especially themselves, could possibly be classified as OK.

Assertive behaviors appear in quadrant 2, which is the ideal life position according to Harris and other proponents of TA. This is the home of optimistic survivors who busy themselves with getting on with life, striving to be the best they can be. They use positive labels for everyone, themselves included. They are happy people who combine dominance traits of control with affiliation traits of warmth and caring in order to achieve by coordinating, initiating, leading, and advising. They attribute successes to fair competition and are able to classify losses in the same way. They approach conflict resolution with problem-solving techniques and hope to achieve a win-win result. They believe they control their own destinies and behave as if everyone, themselves and others, are all OK.

MEASURING SELF-ESTEEM

Haldane, Alexander, and Walker (1982) note that insight and self-awareness are not qualities with which most people are heavily endowed. How, then, do we objectively measure our self-esteem? There are formal self-acceptance scales and self-image checklists that have been developed by psychologists for use as assessment tools, and these can usually be interpreted to reflect either a mostly negative or mostly positive view of oneself. It is more difficult to interpret a normal or average level of self-acceptance or self-image because both vary with the varied life roles people play each day (Berger, 1981; Weiner, 1981). However, a review of the self-labels that we habitually use, and of feeling statements related to the library work environment, might be useful in providing a sense of high or low self-esteem for librarians.

Lists of positive and negative self-labels adapted from Butler (1976) and Gazda, Childers and Walters (1982) appear in the exercises on the following pages. *Note that there are three words on each list that are starred.* These words are classified as positive or negative according to their common usage as *self*-labels. When we use the word "young" to describe ourselves, we commonly mean that we are energetic, a positive attribute; when we use the word "old," we commonly mean to describe ourselves as tired or wearing down. Similarly, the word "human" when applied to ourselves usually means we have erred, but the fault is justified because we are naturally imperfect, while when we use the word "perfect" to describe ourselves, we are usually using it sarcastically or facetiously. We use the word "controlled" to describe the positive aspects of keeping emotion at acceptable social levels and the word "emotional" when we mean too emotional for society's conventional behavior.

In order to get an idea of how you use self-labels, go through both exercises, checking off the labels that you believe describe the way you are now, those that describe the way you would like to be, and those that you would not like to apply to yourself. Although it takes more time, it is more effective to go through each list twice, checking off only one column at a time.

POSITIVE SELF-LABELS EXERCISE

I THINK I AM:		I WOULD LIKE TO BE:
_____	enthusiastic	_____
_____	confident	_____
_____	responsible	_____
_____	assertive	_____
_____	talented	_____
_____	capable	_____
_____	bright	_____
_____	good-natured	_____
_____	fair	_____
_____	warm	_____
_____	honorable	_____
_____	optimistic	_____
_____	young*	_____
_____	self-reliant	_____
_____	stable	_____
_____	interesting	_____
_____	reasonable	_____
_____	witty	_____
_____	knowledgable	_____
_____	considerate	_____
_____	dynamic	_____
_____	secure	_____
_____	daring	_____
_____	tolerant	_____
_____	polite	_____
_____	strong	_____
_____	dedicated	_____
_____	obliging	_____
_____	sensitive	_____
_____	contented	_____
_____	sure	_____

I THINK I AM: **I WOULD LIKE TO BE:**

_____   creative   _____
_____   competent   _____
_____   liked   _____
_____   generous   _____
_____   thoughtful   _____
_____   graceful   _____
_____   satisfied   _____
_____   flexible   _____
_____   human*   _____
_____   bold   _____
_____   grateful   _____
_____   even-tempered   _____
_____   receptive   _____
_____   outgoing   _____
_____   serene   _____
_____   controlled*   _____
_____   accepted   _____
_____   friendly   _____
_____   conscientious   _____
_____   easy-going   _____
_____   direct   _____

NEGATIVE SELF-LABELS EXERCISE

I THINK I AM: **I DON'T WANT TO BE:**

_____   unenthusiastic   _____
_____   anxious   _____
_____   irresponsible   _____
_____   nonassertive   _____
_____   untalented   _____
_____   incapable   _____
_____   not particularly
                 bright   _____
_____   ill-natured   _____
_____   unfair   _____
_____   cold   _____
_____   dishonorable   _____
_____   pessimistic   _____
_____   old*   _____

I THINK I AM:		I DON'T WANT TO BE:
_____	helpless	_____
_____	unstable	_____
_____	dull	_____
_____	unreasonable	_____
_____	biting	_____
_____	ignorant	_____
_____	inconsiderate	_____
_____	anemic	_____
_____	insecure	_____
_____	cautious	_____
_____	intolerant	_____
_____	rude	_____
_____	weak	_____
_____	bad tempered	_____
_____	disobliging	_____
_____	insensitive	_____
_____	discontented	_____
_____	uncertain	_____
_____	unimaginative	_____
_____	incompetent	_____
_____	disliked	_____
_____	miserly	_____
_____	thoughtless	_____
_____	awkward	_____
_____	dissatisfied	_____
_____	obstinate	_____
_____	perfect*	_____
_____	timid	_____
_____	ungrateful	_____
_____	moody	_____
_____	blunt	_____
_____	shy	_____
_____	out-of-sorts	_____
_____	emotional*	_____
_____	rejected	_____
_____	unfriendly	_____
_____	unconscientious	_____
_____	hard-to-get-along-with	_____
_____	indirect	_____

Now count up the number of positive and negative labels that are matches. A match occurs each time you checked off the same word in both columns on that list. If most of your matches appear on the positive list, you have a reasonably positive self-image. If most of your matches appear on the negative list, you may want to try some of the suggestions at the end of this chapter on how to boost your self-esteem.

Take a closer look at both lists. They are the same length and contain opposite pairs of the same concepts. First, look at the words you checked to describe yourself now, the left-hand column of both lists. Do your unchecked positive words seem to pair up with your negative labels (e.g., you did not check happy and did check unhappy)? Are there positive or negative labels here that you regularly use when you think about yourself? Which negative labels could you replace with positive labels? Now, look at the two right-hand columns, the lists of what you wish you were like. Do these pairs seem to match (e.g., you want to be happy and don't want to be unhappy)? When you look at the totality of what you have checked off for your ideal self, are your expectations realistic?

Let's take a look now at how your self-esteem is affected when you consider your role as a librarian. For this exercise, check off the statements that are true of you:

Librarian's Positive Self-Statement Exercise

_____ I am aware of my positive qualities when I am at work.

_____ I remind myself of successes I have had in the past when something goes wrong in the present.

_____ I congratulate myself when I do something especially well.

_____ I am self-confident about the quality of my work.

_____ When someone in the library is rude to me, I don't let it spoil my whole day; I think it over and forget it if I feel I have nothing to correct in my behavior.

_____ I set realistic goals for each day's work and usually achieve them.

_____ Most of my colleagues like me most of the time.

_____ I can handle interruptions that come my way.

_____ I say positive things to myself more frequently than negative things.

_____ When a crisis occurs, I usually make good decisions on dealing with it.

_____ When a library user gets to me, I remember that they're not all like that.

_____ I remember past compliments when I'm feeling low about my work.

_____ I believe I deserve the praise I get for my work.

_____ I work efficiently and effectively.

All of these statements are evidences of high self-esteem in your work. You should look at them as an indication of your library self-esteem and compare them with your level of self-esteem from the labeling exercise. If you have more self-esteem at work than in general, you may wish to apply some of your assertive library skills to other parts of your life. If you have less self-esteem at work than in general, or if you have low self-esteem both in and out of work, you may want to try some of the suggestions on boosting your self-esteem which follow.

BOOSTING YOUR SELF-ESTEEM

Psychological research indicates that people can increase their self-esteem by mentally cataloging their achievements, visualizing favorable images of themselves and their successes and by mentally reciting positive self-statements (Brockway, 1976; Bruch, 1981; Hulbert, 1982). Similarly, negative self-statements and self-labeling inhibit social effectiveness and decrease self-esteem (Brockway, 1976; Bruch, 1981; Montgomery & Heimberg, 1978). The way you talk to yourself (and we all talk to ourselves whether we admit it or not) is crucial in the development of self-esteem.

Donald (1980) uses this illustration to describe the illogic of negative semantic traps:

> All things that swim in the water are fish.
> I sometimes swim in the water.
> THEREFORE, I am a fish (p. 20).

In spite of seeing this as obviously silly and illogical, we use the same illogic on ourselves:

> People who are usually quiet in large crowds, don't often speak up...[and] have trouble making some decisions...are not confident people.
> I sometimes act that way.
> THEREFORE, I am not a confident person (Donald, 1980, p. 20).

We jump from describing behaviors to putting labels on our total selves and therein lies our problem. For we believe we are whatever we say we are.

Recommendations to Increase Your Self-Esteem

1. Talk to yourself, replacing negative labels and self-statements with positive ones whenever you do something you wish you hadn't. Ask yourselsf *how, when, where* and *to what extent* you behaved inappropriately. Then, instead of labeling yourself by saying "I am not a confident person," limit your concern to the actual behavior that occurred, saying instead, "Yesterday I wanted to speak up in the staff meeting and didn't." Then add a positive self-statement that will encourage you: "When I spoke up two weeks ago, people seemed to listen and I felt good about myself. Next time I will say what is on my mind." Then, forget about the incident (Fischoff, 1977).

2. Agree with the compliments people give you. Instead of derogating yourself by saying "Oh, it was nothing," or "Anyone could have done as well," say instead "Thank you, I think I did a good job on that, too," or "I am really proud of that, it was one of my best efforts." If you find this exceptionally difficult, as many people do, think of your current effect on the people who have complimented you. When you belittle the praise, are you saying they have little taste or discrimination? If you agree in an unbragging way, you are actually complimenting their discerning eye in recognizing your good feature. Some people find they can agree with compliments more comfortably by limiting their responses to a simple "Thank you"; "Thank you, that's good to hear"; or "I appreciate your saying that." We are so conditioned toward modesty, however, that even these simple responses feel stilted to some people. If this is true, try accepting a compliment by giving a compliment in return: "What a nice thing to say!" or "It's very kind of you to say that" (Rathus, 1975).

3. Consciously store really terrific compliments away in your memory to bring out when you need a boost. When a library user says, "This library just keeps going downhill, year after year," remember the library committee meeting last month when, out of the blue, one of the more reserved members told you "This used to be a good library, but now it's a great one, and the difference is you." This is not to say you should ignore criticisms, but after analyzing them for relevance and taking any necessary corrective action, you shouldn't bring them to memory any more often than you bring compliments to mind.

4. Reinforce your positive self-statements. Make a contract with yourself that every time you want a cup of coffee (or tea, cocoa, etc.) at your desk, the price is a positive self-statement. Then keep faith by mentally following your urge for a cup of something with a quick mental flip-flop: "Time for some soda. I did a terrific job finding all six of those problem books on OCLC this morning" (Donald, 1980).

5. Make up a special card set cataloging your virtues. On a set of blank catalog cards, list the positive self-labels that describe your good characteristics and place the card set in a conspicuous place, where you can see it easily. Every day, place a new card on top, and read it to yourself several times during the day. You can use your responses to the Positive Self-Labels Exercise given earlier in this chapter to start off your card set. Studies have shown that this technique results in increased frequency of the positive behaviors noted on the cards (Girdano & Everly, 1979).

6. Get in the habit of making two public positive self-statements a day. State them as an expression of how good you feel and they won't sound like bragging: "I really feel good about the annual report, it's coming along so quickly." "I read through all the background material last night, and now I feel good about the meeting this afternoon."

7. Decrease the frequency and effect of negative self-statements by turning them into positive ones. Instead of thinking that you make a lot of mistakes, think to yourself: "I can really learn a lot from the frequent opportunities I get to assess various alternatives."

8. Follow these turnaround statements with simple reinforcement: "Now *that's* the way to deal with making mistakes!"

9. Get into the habit of deliberately greeting other people, using their names, and giving compliments, accompanied with smiling. Positive responses from other people will increase tremendously, and you will have additional reinforcement of your positive characteristics.

10. Give yourself mental reinforcement as you go through anxiety provoking situations. During an interview for performance appraisal, for example, agree with a compliment out loud and then think to yourself "I did that really well."

11. For extremely resistent habits, try thought-stopping. When you 'hear' yourself thinking a negative self-statement, mentally shout "STOP IT!," which will help jolt you into really thinking a positive statement instead of half-heartedly thinking a positive statement while another part of yourself wisecracks sarcastically.

12. Use visual imagery as a reinforcement. When you achieve something you can be proud of, visualize a hand patting you on the back or someone you respect giving you a big grin and a "Well done."

SUMMARY

Self-esteem is crucial to assertive behavior. Low self-esteem inhibits assertions and continued nonassertion or aggression decreases self-esteem, setting up a vicious, negative cycle. The acquisition of assertive skills is not enough for people with low self-esteem; they must also make efforts to increase their confidence and self-regard in order to use their new assertive skills effectively. We define self-esteem as a comparison between our perceptions of what we are with the ideal self we would like to be: the more similar these images become, the higher our self-esteem. There are constructive measures we can utilize to consciously boost our self-esteem and to maintain it at reasonably high levels even when undesirable incidents have occurred.

Chapter 5
Verbal Assertion

Verbal assertions are statements that we make to initiate or continue three kinds of social interactions: requests, refusals, and expressions of feeling. Assertive statements are not characterized by a continuous confrontation or by verbal assault on another person. They are positive, productive, effective ways to relate to other people. Verbal assertions may indicate necessity or dream, firmness or flexibility, anger or joy, yet they are always open and courteous. Assertive statements are the antithesis of inhibition and covert hostility (Bloom & Coburn, 1975; Butler, 1976; Galassi & Galassi, 1977; Herman, 1978; Shaw, 1980).

This chapter will discuss the three key elements that form the core of assertive statements. Seven types of assertive statements will be described with examples of each type of statement. The special techniques involved in saying no and setting limits will also be outlined. The technique of active listening will be described, and its importance in relation to assertiveness will be explored. Finally, a wide variety of assertive techniques and tricks will be described, with examples of their appropriate use and cautions against inappropriate uses.

KEY ELEMENTS

There are three key elements in the making of verbal assertive statements. The first is ownership, and this is evidenced in I-statements, or sentences that use the pronoun "I" more frequently than the pronoun "you." The second element is honesty or sincerity, which is one of the foundations of assertive living. The final key element is spontaneity, which in this text will be widely defined as appropriate timing.

I-Statements

In the earliest work leading to the current practice of assertiveness, Salter (1949) recommended the frequent use of statements with the word "I" in them. Later writers have reemphasized this point (Alberti & Emmons, 1982; Butler, 1981; Caputo, 1981; Jakubowski & Lange, 1978). Perhaps the most explicit modern work that covers the use of I-statements is *Parent Effectiveness Training* by Thomas Gordon (1970), in which the author recommends a four-part formula to use in making I-statements.

In spite of early prohibitions against excessive use of the pronoun I (remember childhood warnings against sounding self-centered?), I-statements are especially important in the expression of feelings. Some sample I-statements that express feelings are:

- I don't like it when you "borrow" things from my desk without asking.
- I feel confident I can handle that responsibility.
- I am annoyed that you want me to make an exception for you.
- I appreciate your concern. This was a difficult decision for me.
- I am angry that the system is down almost 30 percent of the time.

In all these sentences, the subject is "I" and the predicate is very descriptive of what is felt and what specific reality has generated that feeling. The repeated use of "I" to start a sentence may appear to be unimaginative (especially when multiple examples are listed together), but it is an important facet of assertive statements. This ownership of feeling indicates your intention to take responsibility for what you are saying, and allows you to avoid an accusatory use of the pronoun "you." Compare the following you-statements that could have come from the same person-to-person interactions as the five I-statements above:

- You're always taking things from my desk without asking.
- Don't you think I can handle difficult decisions?
- You always want me to make an exception for you.
- Don't tell me what to do.
- Your lousy system doesn't work 30 percent of the time.

The you-statements are much more likely to produce a defensive stance, guilt feelings, or hostility on the part of the other person than the nonaccusatory I-statements are. In addition, the I-statements equalize the power each person has in the situation by creating an atomosphere in which each person can freely state her/his feelings.

Gordon's 1970 formula for I-statements has four component parts, which he recommends, although he notes that after people become comfortable with the formula they might choose to intermix the parts so that the final statement more readily matches their own style of speaking. The four parts of the formula are:

1. When...(with an objective description of the situation).
2. The effects are...(a description of actual consequences).
3. I feel...(a description of the speaker's feelings).
4. I'd prefer...(the speaker requests what s/he wants).

A sample statement using this formula in a library situation might be:

> When you take materials out of the circulating collection to put them in the special reserve section, you often make mistakes on the paperwork. The effects of this are that our library users look in vain for a book that is neither on the shelf nor checked out. I feel angry when people come to me for assistance and I find your error. I'd prefer it if you were more accurate in processing special reserve materials.

This fits Gordon's design, but it is both stilted and likely to sound accusatory to the person who processes special reserves. Lange and Jakubowski (1976) suggest that the entire Gordon formula may not be appropriate for a work situation. A collection of simpler I-statements could be used for the same situation with better effect:

> Today I helped a patron find two books that weren't on the shelf or in the circulation record; it turned out they were both on special reserve. It's a real problem for me when the special reserve paperwork isn't accurate, and I'm sure it disrupts your workflow when these books have to be partially reprocessed. I'd be happy to listen to any suggestions you have for increasing the accuracy level in processing special reserves.

In this example, the specific situation and its effects are accurately described without appearing accusatory, and the feeling and preferential statements are presented as part of a problem-solving approach. Hewes (1975) notes that the communication of strong emotions, such as anger, can be classed as "effective sending" when I-messages are used, and must be classed as "ineffective sending" when you-messages are used, as you-messages are synonomous with verbal attacks.

Honesty and Sincerity

Another crucial element in verbal assertion is honesty. I-statements express feelings that we sincerely feel, not the feelings we think we ought to have, wish we had, or that we believe society would expect us to have. Inappropriate uses of the phrase "I'm sorry" are one of the most common dishonest I-statements. We use "I'm sorry" for a wide variety of situations in which we have no real regrets:

1. I'm sorry, but you had it coming.
2. I'm *sorry!* Excuse me for living!
3. I'm sorry, there are no exceptions to that rule.
4. I'm sorry, we're closing. I have to ask you to leave now.
5. Well, I'm sorry, but I just won't do it!

Osborn and Harris (1975) point out that the only relevant feelings are the ones we honestly feel. When we dishonestly profess to feelings that we think our role dictates, we undermine our credibility in that role. The five examples above can be restated, deleting the insincere apologies:

1. I think you deserved what happened to you.
2. I feel hurt when you talk to me that way. I believe my behavior is appropriate.
3. I cannot make an exception to that rule for you.
4. It's closing time. Please leave by the front exit.
5. I am not willing to do that.

A simple statement of fact or an observation can be substituted when your honest feelings may violate another's right to respect. When a problem employee resigns before a library manager has to take disciplinary action, the library manager is often intensely relieved. Consideration for the problem employee's right to respect will keep the assertive manager from greeting the resignation with "I couldn't be happier than to see you leave," but the honesty inherent in assertion will keep the same assertive library manager from saying "I'm sorry to see you go" when that statement is patently untrue. The library manager could sincerely say "It's important for you to talk with the personnel department about your termination benefits"; "Your twelve years here have given you some good experiences"; or "You seem very happy about your new job." Other, valued, employees who could not have failed to be aware of the problems with this employee will neither think the manager has been too brutally honest nor hypocritical when factual or observational statements are used in place of insensitive frankness or inappropriate and dishonest regret.

Honesty and sincerity are a major component of verbal assertions, but, just as we are taught in our early socializations, it is always important to consider the impact of our communication on the person receiving it (Heisler & Shipley, 1977). In assertion, this consideration leads to substitutions of factual or observational statements for feeling statements rather than leading to insincere or "softened" feeling statements. In an article on assertion training for managers, Shaw and Rutledge (1976) say:

> Participants practice "what's right." Participants define alternatives, clarify consequences, and are provided with some "right" answers. The right answers are broad. They leave a great deal of room for choice and in large measure they are a confirmation of what participants have learned from experience...the fact is that most managers want to increase their capacity to be assertive in pursuing their goals without alienating or diminishing others.
>
> Managers have a right to express their feelings and should encourage others to express theirs. This doesn't mean that people can simply let go. Feelings need to be focused and utilized responsibly. Assertiveness requires that managers recognize their own feelings and utilize them responsively within the framework of the real world in which they are functioning (p. 12).

Honesty, though categorically a virtue, is not always palatable to others. Rathus (1975) warns that expressions that are both honest and appropriate may still lead to social sanctions. It is unrealistic to expect that all honest expressions will be universally accepted. Discretion is sometimes in order, expecially with negative feelings; honest expressions of feelings should undergo constant cognitive filtration so that the exhortation to be honest does not result in emotional harm to others.

Spontaneity

The third important characteristic of verbal or spoken assertions is their immediacy, or spontaneity. This is often the most difficult element to achieve, as our immediate responses to unusual situations are intensely habitual and consequently often nonassertive or aggressive instead of assertive. Alberti and Emmons (1982) highly recommend spontaneity and suggest that hesitating when you are uncertain of just what to say too often lets the opportunity to say anything at all slip by. They have found that the practice of saying something to express feelings at the time they occur is a valuable step toward greater spontaneous assertiveness.

In a work situation, however, it may be more important to define spontaneity as appropriate timing. Lost opportunities can often be recaptured within the formal time frame of the work day, and a pause to frame the wording you wish to use may be invaluable to you as you begin to practice your assertive skills in the library. Interactions with patrons may become lost opportunities if they slip by, but interactions with colleagues, supervisors, and subordinates are easily recaptured with the anticipatory pauses of assertive disengagement, such as "I'm not sure just what to say about that; I'd like to think it over and discuss it with you tomorrow" or through assertive requests to review past actions, such as "That took me by surprise yesterday and I'm not sure my response was appropriate; I've thought about what happened and I'd like to review my thoughts with you." Paris and Casey (1976) say that, as you practice assertion, the recognition and expression of feelings becomes easier until spontaneity follows with relatively little effort. Assertion as a way of life is something you may wish to adopt as a permanent and continuous philosophy, remembering that assertive behaviors are exhibited by rational choice. It is very rational to allow some opportunities to express feelings to slip by until you are comfortable with your ability to be spontaneous without violating the rights of others. Rathus (1975) states emphatically that it can be "highly counterproductive to encourage all clients to express all feelings at all times" (p. 14).

TYPES OF ASSERTIVE STATEMENTS

There are seven major types of assertive statements. It is not important for you to be able to define each of these or to be able to discrimate among them. It is far more important that you understand how they fit the philosophy of assertive living and how you can use them in the library, if you choose to do so.

Simple Assertion

Simple assertions are straightforward statements of need. For example, "Please hand me that book." Assertion and routine courtesy can coexist, so there is no reason to avoid words like "please" in stating a need. The reason you have the need may be stated or unstated, according to your choice: "Please shut the door" is no more or less assertive than "Please shut the door because I want some privacy."

Simple assertions are especially valuable in work situations; try to imagine how you could use the multiple examples which appear below:

1. I need your advice.
2. I need your support on this issue.
3. I have a problem I'd like to discuss with you.
4. Will you help me with this project?
5. I'm confident I can do a good job on that; will you give me the opportunity to try?
6. I'd like to get to know you better. I think we can both accomplish our goals if our departments work together.
7. Our company (university, community, school district) appears to be moving into a new direction. I'd like to be involved. What can I do?
8. What is the fee for this service/equipment?
9. I want more information about this program (procedure, policy).
10. Do you have a complaint? I'd like to help you.
11. I want to tell you how I feel about this. Would you be willing to listen?
12. I did an excellent job on these two special assignments. I deserve a raise. I would like a merit increase of two percent of my salary above the annual salary increase.

Empathetic Assertion

Empathetic assertions acknowledge the feelings of the other person as you make your request, refusal, or express your own feelings. Verbal recognition of the other person's feelings lets them know you realize this may not be the "best" time for your request, so you wouldn't be coming to them unless you had thought it through and belived you had a special need that could not wait for a better time. For example:

> I know you had a rough time with that angry patron just now, but I've run into a problem in the media section. I need your help.

This type of statement is especially useful with, and especially appreciated by, people who are strongly morning or night people. Consider how Nighttime Nell or Evening Ed would react to an 8:00

a.m. problem if you said "I know you hate to hear about problems first thing in the morning, but we are expecting an angry patron at 8:15 and I want to tell you about it" instead of "Ms./Mr. Angry Patron will be here at 8:15 to see you. Good luck."

Soft Assertion

Soft assertions are direct expressions of caring or affection. "I love you" and "I respect you" are both soft assertions. You might feel the former is out of place in the library setting, but certainly the latter is very appropriate. Soft assertions are a way to express your emotions toward others and are often easier for those others to accept than an elaborate compliment might be. An employee who has difficulty accepting praise for her/his work, no matter how well deserved, can literally glow on receipt of soft assertive statements like:

- I'm glad you work here.
- I really enjoy your company.
- You always help brighten my day.

Soft assertions, however, can take on sexist overtones if you use them thoughtlessly. Avoid or be very careful with statements that describe your feelings in terms of another person's physical attributes, such as:

- It's so nice to have a really good-looking person at the desk.
- I love to be in the company of such a handsome fellow.
- You always brighten my day, you look so pretty.

Used thoughtfully, soft assertions can be very valuable in building good interpersonal relationships with colleagues, mentors, supervisors, subordinates, and others you see through your work as a librarian. Some examples of soft assertions that are very useful in the work environment appear below:

1. I really like the way you did that.
2. I want you to know how much I enjoyed your presentation (report, etc.).
3. Thank you for being concerned about me.
4. I really admire the way you handled that problem.
5. I've learned a lot from you.
6. Thank you for your support.
7. I have really enjoyed working on this project with you.
8. You have been very helpful.

9. Thank you for the good advice.
10. Your work deserves a raise (promotion, etc.), and I have recommended you for it.
11. I want you to keep doing that.
12. I'm glad I met you.

Angry Assertion

Angry assertions are the expression of anger as an emotion without aggression or accusation. They are neither hostile nor delivered with aggressive nonverbal messages. They are forthright and objective and are delivered calmly. An example of a calmly expressed angry assertion is: "I am angry that the library opened late this morning. In the future I want you to try to call me when you are going to be delayed so that I can make other arrangements to get the library open on time."

Angry assertions are a "formula" type of assertive statement. First, you need to specify that your feeling is anger, although you may indicate the level of anger you feel by use of terms such as "annoyed" for mild anger and "furious" for great anger. Second, you also need to specify the reason for your anger, and this can be more difficult than it appears. In the above example, you might be tempted to say your anger was due to the fact that this employee didn't call you, but in fact, if the employee had not had the task of opening the library, or if the employee had arranged for someone else to get the library open, you might have been satisfied without a call. If your anger is due to the consequences of the another person's action or nonaction, then it is important to identify those consequences, not the person's action or nonaction, as the cause of your anger. Finally, the third integral part of an angry assertion is a statement of how the situation can be rectified. This may be through a specific course of action, as in the example cited above, or it may be through your statement that you are willing to give up the emotion: "I get irritated when you occasionally demand services in a blunt way, but I realize you only do that when you are very pressed for time and you don't mean to be rude, you're just feeling harried. So I overlook it on the rare occasions that it happens."

In the library, you will find that angry assertions can be used for a wide variety of situations. This more extensive list of sample angry assertions is realistic. Which of these could you comfortably use?

1. I resent your being late this morning. In the future I want you to be here on time.
2. I disagree with you and cannot accept that reason. A bus strike is not an "act of God"; if there is a strike, you must find another way to come in to work or use time from your vacation or sick bank for that day.
3. I feel put down by comments like that. Please stop making them to me.
4. The work you did for me is not what I hoped it would be. You must do it over again.
5. I am annoyed by your flippant responses to patrons who ask for directions to the rest room. I want you to be more polite to them.
6. I am irritated that you want me to make an exception for you. Even though most of your schedule changes can be accommodated, it is irritating to redo the schedule so often; you regularly request last-minute changes. In the future, I will not accept any requests less than two weeks in advance.
7. I am dissatisfied with the condition of the materials you sent. I want you to correct the order without charge.
8. I am furious that you did not keep your promise. I will not be able to recommend your services to anyone else.
9. I am angry that you are smoking here; this is the nonsmoking section. Please put your cigarette out or move to the smoking area.

Confrontation Assertion

Confrontation assertions are used to solve a problem about which a previous, mutual, agreement had been made. They, too are a "formula" type of statement. First, the original agreement is restated. This allows both parties to inspect it for misunderstandings as to what they actually had agreed. Second, the discrepancies between reality and the former agreement are stated, in nonjudgmental terms. Instead of saying "You are unfair," the facts are stated without implications of any judgment of personal characteristics. Finally, a request is made to renegotiate or reaffirm the agreement.

Here is an example of confrontation assertion:

I thought we had agreed that we would share the requests for computer searches equally, since we have both had the same amount of training and experience. For the last two weeks, you have done all the searches before I came in to work. I know the requesters want them done as quickly as possible, but I would like to find a way that we share this work equally. It's important for both of us to maintain our searching skills through constant use.

Negative Assertion

Statements in which you admit to and take responsibility for error are called negative assertions. The important part of a negative assertion is that admitting an error need not be accompanied by defensiveness or guilt. A statement of intention to stick to the original agreement or a request to renegotiate an agreement you have found is not to your satisfaction are equally appropriate. For example, either of the following two negative assertions could be used in response to the confrontation assertion illustrated above. You could say:

> You're right. I did agree that we would share the searches equally, and I haven't kept that agreement. I should have held the nonurgent search requests for you to do in the afternoon. I will do better in the future.

Or, you might say:

> You're right. I did agree that we would share the searches equally, and I haven't kept that agreement. I find it very difficult to tell some patrons that their search requests will be held until the afternoon when I tell others that I will do theirs immediately. There are a lot of search requests first thing in the morning, and I would like to share them with you right then. Can we arrange the schedule so that we are both on duty in the morning? That way we will both get a lot of practice, and we can work on the tough searches together.

Assertive Disengagement

Assertive disengagements are a way to request postponing a discussion until a potentially more fruitful time. This type of statement allows you to set the time that is best for you to respond to another person, and you may choose to postpone your response for as little as 10 minutes or as much as a week or more. The following examples show how you might use assertive disengagement:

1. I'm too upset to discuss that just now. Can we talk about it in the morning?
2. (Looking at watch): I don't have enough time right now to give you the attention you deserve. Let me get my calendar out and we'll set a time that is good for both of us.

3. I haven't had an opportunity to read this as thoroughly as I would like. Could we discuss it an hour from now after I've gone over it one more time?
4. Please come in and sit down. I will be back in a few minutes to discuss this with you.
5. (While on telephone): I see that the person I have an appointment with has arrived. I will call you back later today.

Sometimes your request is denied. But as example number four indicates, sometimes a momentary disengagement is all you need. A statement such as "Let me think about that for a moment" or the nonword "H-m-m-m" will usually elicit 60 or more seconds of quiet in which your mind can consider alternatives and select those most appropriate for the situation. A minute may sound like a very short period of time, but thought processes are four to five times faster than the usual speed of speech (Emery, 1975), and most people speak faster than they think they do. As an experiment, try thinking of what you might be able to tell someone about yourself in 30 seconds, then record what you think you have time to say and play it back while you time it. Most people find they can speak 150–200 words per minute. A single minute thus gives you time to think 600–1000 words. That can be plenty of time (and words) for an assertive disengagement in which to prepare a response.

TAGS, HEDGES, AND COMPOUND VERBS

A research study of speech style found that some styles of speech are more often characterized as assertive than others (Newcombe & Arnkoff, 1979). The use of tag questions at the end of a declarative sentence, such as "It's cold in here, isn't it?" are seen as less assertive, less confident, than the same sentence without the tag question: "It's cold in here." This is evident when we look at the confrontation assertion, which would be diluted if you were to say "We agreed to share searches equally, didn't we?" instead of "I thought we agreed to share the searches equally." Examples of tag questions are:

- Don't you?
- Couldn't we?
- Wouldn't it?
- Isn't it?
- OK?
- Do you mind?

Similarly, hedges dilute the force of your assertive statement. If you offered the soft assertion "I enjoy your company, let's have lunch together more often" by saying "I enjoy your company, maybe we should have lunch together more often," your colleague might wonder whether you really meant either part of the statement. We frequently use hedges to indicate our flexibility, but when they are attached to what was meant to be an assertive statement, they indicate indecision rather than flexibility. Some common hedges are:

- Maybe.
- I guess.
- I suppose so.

The last speech pattern that Newcombe and Arnkoff found which effectively softened the effect of an assertive statement was the use of compound verbs in simple assertions. These, too, tend to decrease the perceived power held by the person making the request. Examples are:

- "Won't you close the door?" *instead of* "Please close the door."
- "Would you tell me what the price of this is?" *instead of* "What is the price of this?"
- "Could you give me an idea of what you think?" *instead of* "I need your advice."

SAYING NO AND SETTING LIMITS

One of the most frequent reasons librarians give for participation in an assertion workshop is the need to learn how to say no without feeling guilty. As service professionals, librarians are socialized into trying to accede to every request and into going to great lengths to satisfy the needs of other people. Most of the time, this is appropriate work behavior for librarians. Unreasonable requests, however, occasionally come to every library from patrons, and there are also times when colleagues make unreasonably heavy demands on one's talents or time. In these situations, it is extremely disadvantageous to say yes when you really want to say no or when it is in your best interests or the interests of the library to say no.

Whenever you say yes when you really want to say no, you run these risks:

First, other people may exploit you. When your inability to say no becomes recognized by colleagues, you can be overwhelmed by committee responsibilities and special projects that take a very heavy toll on your time. If library patrons make unreasonable requests and you satisfy them uncomplainingly, they will have no basis for determining what reasonable requests might be and will continue to bring unreasonable requests to you.

Another risk you take by inappropriately saying yes is that your credibility may decline. If by saying yes you make promises that you cannot deliver, you run a major risk of eroding your credibility with the person to whom the promise was made, regardless of the reason for your failure to comply. People assume, correctly, that, if there were limitations on your ability to comply, those limitations should have been clarified at the time you said yes to their request. Loss of credibility then degrades your ability to engage in honest communications with that person.

You also risk loss of self-esteem when you say yes to activities you believe are wrong for you. You can easily lose respect for yourself by being unable to refuse to comply with these requests. In addition, your hidden resentments may soar. By saying yes to a person when you want to refuse, you pave the way for resentment to build up against the person who made the request. When a library patron asks you to do something that is unreasonable and you fail to say no or to explain that it is an unreasonable request, you may find yourself disliking that patron. It is reasonable to dislike the task, and you may even decide you dislike your too compliant behavior, but it is unreasonable to dislike the patron for making the request you should have denied but didn't.

Frequently, things you prefer to do have to be sacrificed when you say yes to others. When you continuously accede to the requests of others, the calls on your time become greater and greater. Eventually, you will no longer have time to do the things you enjoy doing or that are your primary library responsibilities.

Finally, you risk reverting to passive-aggressive behaviors. This is a very real risk for people who are unable to refuse the requests of others. They may say yes to a task but perform it inadequately, incompletely, or complete it in an untimely fashion as a means of covert refusal.

A special way of saying no is to set limits. This may be easier for you than to begin saying a definite no if, in the past, you have been especially compliant. You have the right to set limits on how you wish to spend your time, how much privacy you desire, and how you want people to treat you. A limit is defined as the boundary you define for others in order to let them know how far you are willing to go. Limits are totally individual, they are determined by your beliefs and feelings, and you have the right to change your mind about them if you choose to do so.

The two exercises that follow list examples of ways to say no and set limits. Read them aloud to yourself, and put a check mark by the ones you would feel comfortable using. If these examples don't fit your personal style or the library environment you work in, pencil in any changes you need to make until you have statements that you could practice and use comfortably.

Exercise in Saying No

_____ No, I can't do it. I have already scheduled something else for that time.

_____ No, I can't do that for you. Our policy is that only students who are enrolled here may have circulating privileges.

_____ No, I have already done my share.

_____ No, I feel I have already done more than my share.

_____ No, I have decided not to accept any more outside commitments at this time.

_____ No, that's your responsibility. I would feel dishonest doing it for you.

_____ No, I'm busy.

_____ No, I just finished serving on a committee and would prefer to give someone else a chance.

_____ I appreciate the compliment, but I am not willing to chair that committee again this time.

_____ I would like to be able to help you, but I don't have time.

_____ No, thank you, I'm not interested.

Exercise in Setting Limits

_____ I would rather not hear about your problems at home.

_____ I really want to talk with you, but I have work to do right now. Can I call you tonight after dinner?

_____ I appreciate your stopping by, but I have cannot fit visits from book vendors in unless you call ahead to make an appointment.

_____ I can't do the whole thing because I don't have time, but I will do the first section to help you get started and you can finish it.

_____ Please stop lecturing me. I have a right to base my behavior on my own assessment of the situation.

_____ I think it is important that we discuss this, but I don't want to continue this conversation until you stop the name-calling.

_____ Please don't smoke in my office.

_____ I will help you out this time, but I won't be able to help you after this.

_____ I will help you write the report if you include my name on it as a co-author.

_____ I can give you emergency help on the reference desk any afternoon, but my mornings are too busy to help you out.

When you have adapted these practice statements to fit your unique individual needs, begin using them in your work environment whenever you feel pressured to agree with unreasonable or inappropriate requests.

ACTIVE LISTENING

Half of verbal assertion is being able to say things assertively; the other half is being able to listen assertively. Unless we actively participate in both halves of the communication process, speaking and hearing, we are likely to misinterpret what people say, jump to wrong conclusions, interrupt inappropriately, anticipate points incorrectly, or make decisions based on incomplete information. Hearing is a physical process, while listening is both a physical and an emotional process. When we listen, we integrate the physical process with the emotional and intellectual processes in order to gather meaning and effectively understand another person (Goldhaber, 1979).

A therapeutic technique called "active listening" was developed in the early 1960s by Carl Rogers, father of "client-centered counseling." The technique consists of "listening for feelings" and reflecting back your guesses about those feelings in simple factual statements, so that the speaker can affirm, deny, or revise what you have restated until communication is specific and complete. More than that, active listening brings the listener into total involvement with the speaker, empathizing with her/his feelings and trying to understand what s/he says. Your understanding is enhanced externally by what you hear and internally by what you empathize.

Active listening encourages interpersonal relationships in five ways:

1. It allows and encourages the speaker to express feelings very openly because s/he can see and hear your interest in her/his message.
2. It helps the speaker to enunciate negative feelings because you create a nonjudgmental atmosphere in which negative emotions can be freely admitted.
3. It promotes warmth in the relationship because the experience of being heard and understood is very satisfying.
4. It facilitates problem solving because people investigate more alternative solutions to a problem when they talk it out.
5. It influences the other person to listen to you as well as you listen to her/him.

Your success with active listening also increases your self-confidence, which enhances your self-esteem (Donald, 1980).

Broadwell (1977) and Donald (1980) both espouse the technique of active listening as a very effective tool for the workplace. Ames (1977) describes it as essential to fact-finding in personnel work. In the library, a library manager might use active listening to solve staff disputes. Here is how a sample scene might read:

Director: (seated at desk, looks up as staff reference librarian storms in): Hi, what's up?

Librarian (pacing nervously): I'm ready to quit! Every 10 minutes the reference schedule gets changed. I can't take much more.

Director: (starting active listening technique): You're clearly upset. I know you wouldn't be upset without a good reason. Tell me about it, I'm listening.

Librarian: I try to be accommodating, but my schedule is always being changed, and it's just been changed again for the fourth time this week. I know we're a little short of people but nobody ever gives a damn about *my* needs!

Director: You try to help out, but right now your needs aren't being met.

Librarian: That's an understatement. I have a class on Tuesdays and Fridays from 6 to 10, and I've just been scheduled to go on the desk at 6:30 this Friday.

Director: You need to be in class at 6:00, so you can't work the desk at 6:30.

Librarian: Right!

Director: Well, that's a need I think I can help you meet. Ask Val to join us, and we'll try to get it set right now.

Smith and Fitt (1982) strongly suggest that active listening is an important skill for library reference work and use the following example to describe its use in this way:

Patron: Excuse me, can you please tell me where the psychology books are?

Librarian: Certainly, they are kept in the west wing of the library. It's right there on the floor map. What do you need?

Patron: Well, I just want to browse through them.

Librarian: There are a lot of books over there; did you want information on a particular aspect of psychology?

Patron: Well, I need something on behavior.

Librarian: You are interested in behavior. (This is the librarian's first active listening statement, and she continues to use them until she is satisfied she understands the patron's request.)

Patron: Yes. I know nothing about psychology, but I want to know the reasons people behave the way they do.

Librarian: You want to know all the psychological theories on human behavior.

Patron: I don't want to know about *all* of them.

Librarian: You don't think all of the theories will help you.

Patron: Right, I guess. The real problem is that I don't know what makes my daughter behave the way she does, and I want to understand her.

Librarian: I see; you would like a book on human behavior that will give you insight into the way young people tend to behave.

Patron: That's exactly right (p. 248).

How is this different from a reference interview where the librarian would have asked a string of questions instead of making a string of statements? One major difference is that many library patrons are reluctant to answer straightforward questions about what they want, so a string of questions appears intrusive. A string of statements indicates a desire to understand without putting any onus on the patron: the patron can *correct* a statement, where s/he must *answer* a question.

Active listening requires undivided attention, a genuine concern for the communication process between you and the speaker, an effort to listen empathetically, and the ability to keep in touch with your own feelings so you will not respond defensively. You can use active listening skills in making a communication as well as in receiving a communication. Table 3 lists some useful active listening skills for encouraging others to listen to you. In each example, Gerry's script illustrates the active listening technique.

Table 3
Active Listening Skills

Technique	Examples
Silent, noninterruptive listening; attending behaviors.	Face to face position, eye contact, nods of the head, quiet brief phrases like "I see" or "Go on."
Open ended questions that cannot be answered yes or no but help the other person explore her/his feelings.	*Gerry:* I'd like to go to the meeting tonight. How do you feel about that?
Parroting—repeating back the same words, occasionally with a change of emphasis (do not over-use; it can be distracting).	*Terry:* I don't mind if you go to the meeting tonight. *Gerry:* You *don't* mind if I go to the meeting tonight?
Paraphrasing or summarizing and asking for confirmation of your interpretation of the message.	*Terry:* I don't mind if you go to the meeting tonight. *Gerry:* Are you saying you don't mind if I go to the meeting tonight even though it means you will have to work alone?
Reflection of feelings, or "reading between the lines"; a response to the feelings of the speaker rather than her/his words.	*Terry* (with sarcastic emphasis): I don't mind if you go to the meeting tonight. *Gerry:* You seem angry with me.

Responses

Oral, verbal responses are important to active listening. Studies show that we assume our message has been heard if people are quiet while we speak, and we also assume that others feel the same way we do if they do not respond to our feelings in any way (Numerof, 1980). The active listening responses allow the speaker to check the message that is being heard and reinforces that the hearer identifies the feelings as the speaker's feelings, which are not necessarily similar to the hearer's feelings. According to Calabrese (1979), good listening skills are directly related to empathizing. We must listen to the underlying feelings of a message as well as to its content.

The International Communication Association has identified 12 basic categories of listening responses that are found in live communication. Five are defined as confirming responses, and seven are defined as disconfirming responses. The confirming responses are those which assist the communication process, while the disconfirming responses are inhibitory in their effect on communication (Dance & Larson, 1982). As you read through these responses, consider how you might feel if you were the speaker in each instance, facing this response.

Confirming Responses

1. Direct Acknowledgement: The hearer reacts to the speaker directly and verbally.
2. Agreement on Content: The hearer reinforces or supports information and opinions expressed by the speaker.
3. Supportive Response: The hearer expresses understanding, reassurance, or emotional support.
4. Clarifying Response: The hearer tries to clarify the content of the speaker's message by asking questions to elicit more information, encouraging the speaker to say more or repeating what has been understood in an enquiring way.
5. Expression of Positive Feeling: The hearer describes positive feelings related to the speaker's message, such as "OK, now I understand what you're saying."

Disconfirming Responses

1. Impervious Response: The hearer fails to acknowledge the speaker's message, even minimally.
2. Interrupting Response: The hearer cuts the speaker short by beginning to respond before the speaker has completed the message.
3. Irrelevant Response: The hearer responds in a way that is unrelated to what the speaker has said or introduces a new topic (or returns to an earlier one) without warning or acknowledgement of the previous topic.
4. Tangential Response: The hearer acknowledges the speaker's message but immediately takes the conversation into a new direction.

5. Impersonal Response: The hearer responds with a monologue characterized by intellectualized, impersonal statements loaded with euphemisms or cliches.

6. Incoherent Response: The hearer responds with incomplete sentences, rambling statements, and interjections such as "You know" or "I mean."

7. Incongruous Response: The hearer responds with nonvocal behaviors that are inconsistent with her/his vocal response, such as "I really care about you" said in tones of boredom with no eye contact.

Blocks to Communication

Eisenberg (1979) notes that average adults spend 7 percent of their time writing, 10 percent reading, 35 percent speaking, and 48 percent listening. Our ability to listen effectively is clearly vital to our overall ability to interact with other people. Our responses as we listen to others are so important to the communication process that they can block it as effectively as the active listening technique can aid it. The table below lists eight kinds of responses that effectively block communication.

Table 4
Communication Blocks

Blocking Response	Example	Message Heard in Block
Evaluation/Judgment	You should have.... It's your duty to....	I know better than you.
Advice Giving	Why don't you.... It would be best....	You aren't bright enough to figure this out without help.
Topping	You think *that's* bad!	Anything you can do I can do better.
Diagnosing	What you need is....	I consider myself an expert in this area.
Prying	Who? What? When? Where? How much?	I must know everything; I am nosy; your business is my business.

Table 4
Communication Blocks (continued)

Blocking Response	Example	Message Heard in Block
Warning/Admonishing/Commanding	You must (will, had better).... If you don't....	I see a terrible future ahead of you.
Logical Lecturing	I've given this a lot of thought... (followed by long monologue).	I want to show you how brilliant I am.
Devaluation	You'll get over it. Life isn't fair. It's no big deal.	Your concerns are not important.

TECHNIQUES AND "TRICKS"

No book on assertiveness would be complete without some mention of the many verbal maneuvers popularized in the "How to Get Your Own Way" type of books. Many of the techniques that are presented here can be useful in the library, but many of them can easily be overused or used inappropriately. Some may seem to fit your own unique style better than others, and some may not appear to be your style at all. The important thing to remember is that assertive behavior is *always* a matter of rational choice, and these techniques should not become unthinking habits any more than aggressive or nonassertive behaviors should be indulged in unthinkingly. Assertiveness is not a game. It is not a win-lose contest. It is not abrasive or abusive. Assertiveness is the rational choice of standing up for your human rights and situational rights by selecting appropriate behaviors and statements which, although they protect and maintain your rights, do not infringe on the rights of others.

An assortment of 22 assertive behaviors will be presented below. Their definitions, examples and comments derive from multiple sources (Ames, 1977; Ashby, 1975; Bower & Bower, 1976; Caputo, 1981; Cotler, 1975; Flowers & Booraem, 1975; Hart, 1977; Hulbert, 1982; Hutchings & Colburn, 1979; Liberman, King, DeRisi, & McCann, 1975; Piercy & Ohanesian, 1976; Rathus, 1975) and are supplemented by personal experiences from workshops presented and attended by the author.

Adult Hookers

These are straight or moderately passive questions added to the end of an assertive statement. They serve to invite the person to whom you have made your assertive statement to become involved in the issue and its resolution. They create a greater sense of freedom for the other person to explore her/his rights and negotiate options along with the asserter. They are used to suggest that the relationship between the asserter and the hearer is equal and that it should be mutually satisfying. Examples of adult hookers are:

- Are you willing to do that?
- Is that OK with you?
- Does that seem fair to you?

Although these mild questions may seem much like the tag endings discussed earlier, there is a difference. Tags are brief questioning phrases tacked on to a declarative sentence, diluting its strength, while adult hookers are separate questioning sentences that assertively request cooperation. For example, a conflict over sharing a workload, which could be approached nonassertively using a tag ending—"We were going to share the filing work, weren't we?"— could be approached more assertively, yet with positive results, using an adult hooker—"I understood that we agreed to share the filing work equally. Are you willing to do that?"

This is a recommended technique, particularly for conflict resolution. It is used for making requests and stating refusals. It is not used for expressions of feelings.

Anger Starvation

This technique is also known as "disarming anger." It is an attempt to calm down an angry attacker so that a problem can be solved rationally. It is used when someone is very angry, appears to be out of control, or appears to have irrationally overreacted to a situation that is a just cause for milder anger. Anger starvation has three separate components. The first is a clear, empathetic recognition of the attacker's emotion and its strength, followed immediately by the second component, a succinct statement of your willingness and intent to help solve the problem. The third component is a removal from the source of anger. If possible, this should be a complete physical removal to another, neutral, location. If not, some steps should be taken to change the current environment so that the source of anger is diluted. Some examples of anger starvation are:

1. I can see that you are very angry about this, and I want to help you as much as I can can. Come into my office, and we'll get a cup of coffee and talk the whole thing over.
2. You are clearly upset over this, and I certainly want to investigate it thoroughly. I would like you to tell me all about it, starting from the beginning. Perhaps if we sit over here by the window, we can "let the sun shine in" and get to a solution that will work for us.
3. I see how angry you both are about this, and I want to work out the best solution for all of us. The conference room is empty just now, so let's move in there. That will keep us from being interrupted, and we can relax and talk over all the details. I'll ask that some refreshments be brought in.

This is a very useful technique, and it is highly recommended. The optimal environment to discuss causes for anger occurs when the anger itself has dissipated. When the anger lingers or reappears, repetitions of empathetic statements and your willingness to listen and help are usually effective. Note also that the cause of the anger is not classified as appropriate or inappropriate, and that defining the situation as an incident or problem is avoided.

Artful Procrastination

This is a technique that uses passivity or nonassertion. Essentially, it is a quiet, deliberate tabling of an issue until it is no longer an issue or has solved itself. It is a way to force the other person to solve the problem for you. Examples of artful procrastination are:

1. I won't be able to consider that problem until next week; if you find a solution in the meantime, please let me know.
2. I will step in to help you solve the problem only if you find you cannot solve it yourself. Work on it for a month, and then get back to me.
3. Oh, just let it sit for a while. It'll keep.

This is not a recommended technique. It is manipulative. It offers a convenient way to shirk appropriate responsibilities or to justify your own inability to be assertive. It is not a rational choice of nonassertive behavior, it is avoidance behavior. An appropriate assertive response to problems you think will be solved by time or should be solved by someone else are to state that you are not taking action at present because you have cause to believe the problem will disappear or to request that someone else solve the problem.

Asking Why

This is a device that can help you if you are habitually nonassertive and have a history of responding to inordinate or inappropriate demands. It can lead to an assertive refusal but not always. It gives you more information upon which to base a rational decision, after which you can choose to deny a request or choose to agree to it. Librarians may feel that asking why they should undertake a task or accept a responsibility is questioning authority, but, as the following examples show, there are many ways to ask why without high risk:

1. That sounds like a very interesting project, but I am unclear as to where I fit in. Would you expand a little on your goals for it and on the responsibilties I would have if I agree to accept it?
2. I know that in the past I have said yes to every new task you have assigned me, but I have often felt overcommitted, so I'm reluctant to continue accepting new tasks without exploring how they will fit into my overall workload. If I agree to do this, how will it affect my regular tasks and priorities?
3. I was taught that it is disrespectful to ask why, so I have never asked you that before. But I have found that I work better when I understand why I need to do something, especially if it has to be done in a certain way. For example, I don't understand why, for some things, speed is most important, and for others, accuracy is most important. I would like to understand, though, because I really enjoy my work here. I won't try to ask you everything today, but perhaps we can start with this new project. Why are we changing the journal check-in system?

This technique is highly recommended for librarians who think they may be too compliant. You may find that you are right, and you have agreed to far more than was appropriate for you, or you may find that you have not agreed to anything that was inappropriate. Asking why is a way to limit compliance that is the result of habit, early socialization, or fear of punishment. This technique can be over-used, however, and becomes old quickly if you are consistently and regularly asking the same person why whenever they make a request of you. It should be used when you really need additional information to make a decision.

Broken Record

This technique is the calm repetition of your statement, usually in the exact same words, which makes you sound something like a stuck record, and which is where the technique gets its name. It is used in two different instances. First, it is used when you are making an assertive statement and the other person tries to sidetrack you or bring up other points, which may or may not be relevant. An example of the broken record technique as it is used to keep the discussion on the point you want to make follows:

> But the point is... [this is a particularly useful phrase] this book is severely damaged and you are responsible for its replacement cost....It doesn't matter who I think I am, we're discussing the fact that you are responsible for the safe return of library materials....That's not the point. We're discussing your responsibility for the library materials you borrow...I'll be glad to discuss that with you when we have settled this issue. We're discussing your responsibility for this damaged material.

This is a very useful way to maintain emotional control in the face of inappropriate or intentionally provocative comments, and it is a recommended technique for library conflicts. It can be especially helpful in conflict resolution with aggressive people. Broken record is occasionally called "back to the main issue" when used in this way.

The broken record technique is also used when you have given an assertive refusal which is not accepted, and you are being pressured into reversing it. This use often includes the repetition of short, exact word phrases, such as "No, I can't do that" in the sample below. When used this way, the technique may be called "parroting" as it can make you sound rather like a parrot that has learned only one phrase. The following example of this technique shows its use as a way to resist pressure to reverse a refusal, without the primary goal of resolving the conflict:

> *Librarian:* If it isn't on the shelf, it may be checked out. Let me look...ah, yes, here is the circulation record. It's not due back for three more days, but I can make a note that you want it when it's returned, and we'll call you then.
>
> *Patron:* Just tell me who has it, and I'll get it myself. It has to be someone I know.
>
> *Librarian:* No, I can't do that.

Patron: But you know who has it, right? It's no big deal, just tell me.

Librarian: No, I can't do that.

Patron: You mean you know who has this book, and you just aren't going to tell me?!

Librarian: No, I can't do that. Our policy is based on the Freedom of Information Act, which protects our right to privacy as well as giving us the right to seek information about ourselves. I couldn't tell anyone else if you had checked this book out either.

Patron: I wouldn't care if you did! I don't have anything to hide, and it's just not that big a deal. It's not a subversive book, you know! I just know I can get it faster by going direct, so please tell me who has it.

Librarian: No, I can't do that.

Patron: This has got to be one of the stupidest policies I ever heard of! I demand that you tell me who has this book!

Librarian: No, I can't do that.

This use of the broken record technique is very frustrating for the other person and does not help resolve conflict. For these reasons, it is not recommended except in situations where an immediate conflict resolution (including negotiation) is not sought or where a long-term close personal relationship is not desired.

Clipping

Clipping is the term given to short answers consisting of simple affirmatives or negatives that give little or no information. It is used when you are under attack and you are unsure why. It can also be used when the verbal content you hear is ambivalent or vague, but the nonverbal signals you pick up are offensive. When you are not certain you are being challenged but think you might be under attack, simple yes and no answers are used until you can identify the issue and respond to it. The following example of clipping is from a hospital library:

Patron (loudly, abruptly): Doesn't this library serve doctors?

Librarian: Yes.

Patron: Well, then, give me a little service! Don't you get JAMA here? The Journal of the American Medical Association?

Librarian: Yes, we do.

Patron: Well, I can't find it. I suppose it's another one of the things you let nurses or anybody take out whenever they feel like it. Nurses and everybody else in this hospital can take books out of here, can't they? I can *never* find what I want in here, and it's always because some damn nurse has it. Your circulation policies need some changing.

Librarian (moving from clipping to anger starvation): I can see that you're very angry about our circulation policies. I was just about to have a cup of coffee, would you like to join me? Then you can tell me which issues of JAMA you need, and we can also talk about the circulation policy. Journals don't circulate to anyone, so I'm sure I can quickly find the issues you need.

A more general example of clipping might be:

Critic: The coffee isn't made this morning!

You (you usually make it, but it's not assigned as your task, you just usually get in first): That's right.

Critic: Something wrong with you?

You: No.

Critic: Well, I can't start work until I have at least one cup of coffee.

You (moving from clipping to an assertive request): Me, neither. I'm moving a little slow this morning, so I would really appreciate it if you would put the pot on. Maybe in the future we can take turns coming in early to get it ready.

Clipping is highly recommended as a means to avoid inappropriate conflict. It keeps you from reacting to the overt components of an attack and allows you to focus instead on investigating the reason underlying the attack.

Contracting

Contracting is a means to negotiate for desired changes by stipulating the specific actions each party in the contract will perform, specifying the consequences for meeting the agreement, and the consequences for failing to meet the agreement. Contracts may be written or oral, sophisticated or simplistic, formal or informal. They may range from agreement on the way a discussion will be held (no name calling, limited time period, equal opportunities to speak, etc.), to acceptance of performance goals included in an annual performance appraisal. They may be sealed by signature, handshake, or a smiling nod. Contracting can work in short-term situations. No name calling, for example, is a contract you might insist upon when confronting a patron at the circulation desk: "I will only discuss this problem with you when you discontinue your name calling." Contracting is highly recommended for long-term behavior change goals. The ten rules for assertive negotiation of a contract, which are presented below, show how the specificity and progressive nature of contracting work. These two factors result in a high probability of success for behavior changes negotiated in this way.

Contracting Rule One. To start with, ask for small changes only. Until you have established a relationship in which contracting is a routine way of resolving conflict, start small. Ask an employee to limit personal calls to no more than two per day, and when that has been accomplished, go on to setting goals for more productive use of work time. These small change mini-contracts are worth the extra time they add to the large change goals you may have.

Contracting Rule Two. Include immediate reinforcements as rewards. Rewards may be tangible and measurable, such as a raise or promotion for improved performance, or they may be rather intangible and difficult to measure, like a promise to be more flexible toward requests for schedule changes when the employee has accomplished the requested changes. The major rewards, however, should also be reducible to smaller, immediate rewards that can be observed or felt. Let's assume, for example, that you specify that you want someone to be less interruptive and to allow you to finish your comments before beginning to speak. The consequences of this contract are (a) if the behavior does not change, you will walk away at each interruption and not resume the discussion until the next day; and (b) if the behavior does change, you will continue the discussion until the other person is ready to terminate it. As the behavior of a habitual interrupter begins to change, you will observe signs of aborted interruptions in facial expressions and choked off words. You may have several discussions that show some behavior change but eventually terminate by your walking away. In order to keep the behavior changes coming until a complete discussion can be held, mini-rewards could be a quiet "Thank you. I could see you were ready to say something before I finished; I'm glad you waited. I'll be glad to listen to what you wanted to say now" inserted in the discussion when you have observed an attempt to perform the desired behavior change.

Contracting Rule Three. Begin with frequent reinforcement, tapering off as the desired behavior increases in frequency. In the example above, the reinforcement of your verbal gratitude would lose its effectiveness if it continued each time you observed overt behavior change signs. You might, if the behavior change was increasing, note that "our discussions are getting longer and more enjoyable" and limit other reinforcing phrases to the rare instances when you observed that major control was exhibited.

Contracting Rule Four. Be consistent, stick to the terms of the contract. If you contract, for example, to allow the interrupter to talk with you (as long as s/he refrains from interruptive behavior, until s/he chooses to terminate discussion), you must not allow other controllable factors to intervene. This means you may have to delay initiation of a discussion that could become lengthy until your schedule has some flexibility, although it does not mean you must allow emergency situations to go unattended.

Contracting Rule Five. Ask for and reward only actual accomplishments, not good intentions. If your interrupting friend says, halfway through your sentence, "But...oops, sorry!," it is an interruption and under your contract terms you should walk away. You might give some reinforcement by saying "We're almost there, tomorrow we'll try again," but you should be saying it as you walk away.

Contracting Rule Six. Require high-quality performance. Don't accept half-baked efforts. A strategically cleared throat may not fit the contract definition of interruption, but if it is clearly interruptive rather than physically necessary, you should walk away.

Contracting Rule Seven. Contract only for active behaviors, not passive behaviors. The individual situation may affect your definition of active versus passive behavior. Nonaction, such as noninterruption, could be classed as a "passive" behavior and certainly would be defined that way in a nonassertive person. In an aggressive person, however, the nonaction of not interrupting could only occur through an active attempt to control habitual behavior. For example, while an interruptive person might not interrupt you in a conversation, s/he may remain passive and sullen, which is substituting passive behavior for the desired active behavior. Similarly, the environment can affect your definition. Interruptive people are often equally disruptive in groups as in one-to-one discussions. But it is easier to "drop out" in a group by simply not attending to the discussion. Noninterruptive behavior in a group situation could thus be accomplished by passive inattention rather than by active attention to the problem.

Contracting Rule Eight. Be sure the terms of the contract are clear. The desired behavior changes and the consequences for achieving it or failing to achieve it must be spelled out in detail, or both parties may feel cheated by fulfilling what they believe is their part of the agreement and finding the other party remains unsatisfied.

Contracting Rule Nine. Be fair and honest in fulfilling the terms of the contract. If you contract to perform specific actions, don't try to rationalize that other actions have the same effect and can therefore be substituted. If you agree to share a distasteful responsibility equally with another person, don't shirk your fair share.

Contracting Rule Ten. Strive for shifting control of the contract to the other person. After you have specified what the consequences will be if the other person upholds or fails to uphold their part of the agreement, be so consistent in holding up your own share of the agreement that responsibility for the consequences are solely related to the other person's actions or failure to act.

Contracting is a highly recommended technique.

Disagreement

Active disagreement can be counterproductive if the asserting person is not prepared to face potentially punitive behaviors on the part of others. In addition, many of us have been socialized that active disagreement is impolite. The technique of simple disagreement is an alternative to active, contradictory disagreement which may be difficult for the asserter to maintain. It is primarily characterized by very simple, passive behaviors. Refraining from smiling or nodding as the other person speaks is a socially acceptable way to indicate nonagreement. Waiting for the speaker to conclude while paying polite attention can be an encouragement for unwanted verbalizations, so letting your attention wander is also a way to indicate disagreement. Another way to indicate disagreement is to find a reason to leave the company of the person who is speaking. In a library, this might be dictated by actual public service schedules, or it might be created by an expressed need to reach another person by telephone or in person, and a prediction that this is the best time to accomplish that. Finally, changing the subject is one way to indicate disagreement.

These forms of simple disagreement are accomplished with less stress than active, contradictory disagreement, and for that reason they may become avoidance behaviors. They are recommended for use in situations where no gain would be forthcoming by active disagreement, where your self-esteem does not require a statement of your own opinion, and where no change would occur in the speaker, others, or the situation as a result of your active disagreement. You are cautioned against overuse of these behaviors, however, as their inappropriate use may serve to decrease your self-respect.

Flipping

Flipping is making a counterproposal in response to a proposal. It is used when you are uncertain of whether you should accept or reject the proposal, or when you are uncertain of whether you want to accept a proposal because the proposer's intentions or motives in making the proposal are unclear. Examples of flipping are:

- *Proposal:* This project is really going to be important to both of us. How about coming over to my place for dinner tonight so we can start talking about it?
- *Response:* I have already made plans for this evening; how about coming to my office at 9:00 tomorrow morning and we'll talk it over until lunchtime?
- *Proposal:* I know exactly what we should do to get the annual book sale off to a fabulous start this year. I'll get started right away, and when you have time to meet with me, we can talk about where to go from there.
- *Response:* I'd love to hear your ideas, and as co-coordinator I think I ought to help out right from the beginning. I'll make time to meet with you as soon as you are free. What time today is good for you?

The way to determine what to offer as a counterproposal is easy to define: it is anything that you would rather do in preference to what has been proposed. This is not as easy to do as it is to say, however. Flipping is a cognitive process which requires practice. Whenever you find yourself reluctant to say yes to a request, but equally reluctant to say no, ask yourself "How can I alter this request so I am comfortable saying yes to it?" Your answer becomes the basis for your counterproposal. This is a highly recommended technique. It is normally needed infrequently, so if you always seem to be making counterproposals you might wish to investigate your relationships or your feelings to determine why you feel uncomfortable accepting proposals that are made to you, or whether you are using counterproposals as a way to manipulate or dominate others. If necessary, you may choose to seek new acquaintances or seek to increase other assertive behaviors.

Fogging

Fogging is a technique that attempts, quite literally, to cloud the issue. It is used to deal with manipulative criticism that implies that you have a need to change your behavior. A lesser known form of fogging is used to cloak refusals in more acceptable terms. Fogging acknowledges some truth in what has been said while allowing the fogger to retain sole responsibility to judge her/his own actions. A standard phrase used when you are fogging in the face of manipulative criticism is "Yes, sometimes I am...." Examples of fogging used to face up to manipulative criticism are:

1. *Critic:* You are always so busy with committees and organizations, you never have any time for the everyday work.

Fogger: You're certainly right about my schedule, it keeps me hopping all the time. I guess sometimes it seems like I am shirking the everyday work.

2. *Critic:* You're too slow to work the reference desk. People are always lined up waiting when you're out there.

Fogger: Yes, sometimes I am slow when I work out there. I like to be absolutely sure I am giving the patrons what they need.

When fogging is used to mask refusals, the technique is to repeat back the request being made, followed by "...but I'm sorry I can't." An example of fogging to mask a refusal is:

Requestor: I have a dentist's appointment tomorrow morning, and I'm scheduled on the terminal for the first two hours of the day. I'd like to switch with you for the first two hours after lunch, when you're scheduled to be on, because I just have to get to the dentist about this tooth.

Fogger: I know how much that tooth has been bothering you, and I'm sure you're anxious to get it taken care of, but my schedule has already been made around the terminal schedule, and I can't trade times with you.

Fogging can be useful, but it is a very manipulative technique. It is certainly equal in manipulative intent to any manipulative criticism that is offered, and its use in masking a refusal can become avoidance behavior. It is therefore recommended for use only by skillful asserters who consistently use rational analysis to select their assertive behaviors, and who will be cautious in using it, aware that it is prone to misuse.

Free Information and Disclosure

These are conversational gambits that are used to initiate and maintain conversations. Free information is the label placed on the clues people give to indicate their interests, opinions, and backgrounds. When you are giving others free information about yourself, it is called disclosure.

Use of free information and disclosure relies on the ability to use open questions instead of closed questions in initiating conversations. Closed questions can be answered yes or no and can unintentionally encourage clipping, while open questions encourage responses with more information than the simple affirmatives or negatives of the clipping technique. "Do you work here?" is a closed question, while "What do you do here?" is an open question. Questions beginning with "how," "what," and "why" are usually open questions. Instances of open and closed questions, with free information, disclosure, and clipping responses are noted in the following two conversations, which could be taking place between two different pairs of librarians at the same meeting, held in a local public library.

PAIR 1, KERRY AND TERRY		PAIR 2, VAL AND SAL	
KERRY:	Do you work here? [closed question]	*VAL:*	What do you do here? [open question]
TERRY:	Yes. [clipping, possibly unintentional]	*SAL:*	I'm the children's librarian. [disclosure]
KERRY:	That's nice. [no free information clues, no disclosure]	*VAL:*	Children can be so satisfying to work with. [free information clue to interest in children]
TERRY:	Yes. [clipping, possibly unintentional]	*SAL:*	It sounds like you work with children too.... [open question]
KERRY:	Well, see you later. [termination of dull conversation]	*VAL:*	I'm a school librarian and.... [beginning of interesting conversation]

These examples show the importance of open questions to the exchange of free information. Closed questions can stimulate free information, but they are frequently answered with simple clipping responses, which inhibit conversation. The other person may not intentionally use clipping; s/he simply may not have good conversational skills and may be uncertain how to add free information in response to a closed question. A good way to practice using open questions is to identify the questions used in TV interviews, listening especially for closed questions which you can try to restate as open questions. Often the interviewer will restate her/his own closed question to make it an open question, giving you some help. The next practice step is to identify the pieces of free information which are elicited by open questions, and you may choose to move from television presentations to overheard conversations in public places for practice examples. Free information is usually of great interest to the person disclosing it, or s/he wouldn't have bothered to do so. When you are adept at picking up the clues people drop, you can begin practicing conversations that follow up on those clues.

The use of open questions to elicit free information and disclosure can be especially effective in the reference interview. A good start is to get in the habit of asking patrons "How may I help you?," which encourages them to make a reference request instead of simply "Can I help you?," which allows them to say no and struggle on without assistance. From there, it is easy to begin using open questions to draw out their real information needs.

Free information and disclosure are highly recommended skills for the assertive librarian. When you are adept at them, professional/ social occasions are very enjoyable. You may also find them useful in giving nonlibrarians a great many clues about what librarianship means to you, helping to decrease their potential acceptance of the library stereotype.

Gaslighting

Gaslighting is not an assertive technique. It is presented here because (1) it is a trap many people fall into, and (2) it can be avoided through the use of assertive skills. Gaslighting is an attempt to make you believe something about yourself that leads you to act in ways defined by the expectations of that other person rather than by your own cognitive analysis of the situation and your own knowledge about yourself. In the following example, an unwary library director falls into the gaslighting trap:

Reference Head: Good morning. The head of circulation hasn't come in yet and hasn't called in sick.

Director: Gee, that's odd. Val is usually here early.

Reference Head: You're worried that Val won't be here by the time we open, especially since that happened once last year. That was a huge problem, with student assistants wondering what to do and not sure where the front door keys were kept and all.

Director (beginning to fall into the trap): Well, Val has been on time ever since, but that sure was a *big* mess that time. I certainly don't want that to happen today.

Reference Head: You probably have a good reason to worry, but whenever you get worried like this, you always get so mad. You'll have to be careful that your temper doesn't get out of control.

Director (falling deeper): Well, let's face it, I have responsibility for this whole place, not just the circulation desk. When Val screws up I have every reason to be mad. But don't worry, I can control my temper!

Reference Head: That's what you said last time, too, but you and Val had quite an argument over it. Your temper is just too big to control.

Director (now firmly entrapped): Well Val will just have to accept the consequences for being late!

When Val walks in, even if there are still some minutes to go before opening time, s/he will assuredly get an irate earful from this manipulated director. Here is how the same example could be handled with a library director who knows how to assertively deny the beliefs the gaslighter attempts to instill:

Reference Head: Good morning. The head of circulation hasn't come in yet and hasn't called in sick.

Director: Gee, that's odd. Val is usually here early.

Reference Head: You're worried that Val won't be here by the time we open, especially since that happened once last year. That was a huge problem, with student assistants wondering what to do and not sure where the front door keys were kept and all.

Director: Well, Val has been on time ever since, so I'm not too worried. Besides, we took special care after that happened to make sure that the students knew whom to go to and what to do.

Reference Head: Well, I'd be worried. I'm sure you're more worried than you're letting on. You're probably just trying to keep your temper under control. You know how mad you get when someone worries you.

Director: No, I'm just not very worried. Val is a very responsible person, and if an emergency has happened, I can handle it.

Reference Head: It's not your handling an emergency that's the problem. It's handling your temper. Last year you two had a big argument over this same thing.

Director: I am confident that if Val does not arrive I can handle the situation. I have been very successful at learning how to identify when my anger is just and how to show it appropriately when I do have just cause to be angry. The problem temper you remember is now a thing of the past.

As the second example shows, the way to fight attempts at gaslighting is to make positive self-statements that emphasize your ability to behave in an appropriate and assertive fashion rather than in the fashion being prescribed for you by the gaslighter. Gaslighting others is definitely *not* recommended for the assertive librarian.

Good Little Victim Trap

This is a device similar to gaslighting, which attempts to make you admit to being in error by highlighting past behaviors and experiences. The person setting the good little victim trap blissfully ignores any present behaviors that deny the role s/he wants you to play. You are tacitly asked to similarly ignore any behavior changes you have learned and accept your characterization as a bad guy by being a quiet, good little victim. Here are some of the favorite phrases used by the people who set good little victim traps:

- You always used to....
- Old dogs can't learn new tricks!
- You said it before....
- It's too late to change now.
- I *know* you.
- If only you could. But....

The way to avoid the good little victim trap is to focus on the present and future instead of the past. Answer with:

- I used to do it that way, but I have changed.
- Fortunately, I'm not an old dog, so I have learned quite a number of "new tricks."
- I may have said that in the past, but now I say....
- It's never too late to change. I keep getting better and better.

- I'm a different person now. The one you knew is gone.
- I'm confident I can.

Like gaslighting, the good little victim trap is definitely *not* a part of the behavior repertoire of the assertive librarian.

Greeting Talk

The focus of assertive behavior is interaction with other people. It is important to observe what are commonly called "social conventions" in order to build and maintain satisfying relationships. This means that you should say good morning to your colleagues when you get to work, whether or not the dog threw up in your shoe, your bus was 45 minutes late, your umbrella blew inside out and you got soaked, or you dropped the only copy of a vital report in the mud. Even if you feel some social conventions are phony or unimportant, observe them, for they do serve an important function. The following stock phrases should be part of your social repertoire:

- Hi, how are you?
- Good morning (afternoon, evening).
- What have you been doing lately?
- My name is...what's yours?
- How are things going?
- How are you doing?
- It's good to see you.

The first two minutes of every interaction are the crucial ones upon which the remainder of the interaction rests. If you use the first two minutes to observe the social conventions, the remainder of the interaction has a better chance to go well. Even less pleasant interactions should include the social conventions. If you have to, force yourself to say hello and goodbye to the colleagues you rather dislike. You may never develop a fondness for them, or they for you, but your work relationship will be enhanced by the social structure of detached friendliness that observation of the social conventions imparts.

Incongruence and Congruence

Incongruence is defined for assertion training as inconsistency between your verbal and nonverbal messages, while congruence in assertiveness is defined as consistency between your verbal and nonverbal messages. An excellent example of incongruence was seen in the early days of former President Jimmy Carter, who was heavily criticized by the media for sporting a wide smile while imparting news of grave consequence during his state of the union messages. Library incongruences could be:

- A librarian sitting on the edge of the chair, visibly shaking, eyes downcast, and saying in a barely audible voice: "I did a good job last year, and I want a raise."
- A librarian standing rigidly, with feet apart, fists clenched, chin jutting forward, and eyes flashing, saying "I'm really sorry I hurt your feelings."

Incongruence in your nonverbal message invalidates your verbal message, so congruent messages are highly recommended. Chapter 6 discusses in detail which nonverbal messages are perceived as assertive, which as nonassertive, and which as aggressive.

The Name Game

The name game is used to establish status relative to another person. The rules of the game are very simple: The person who has the highest status gets to be called by the most formal appellation. Theoretically,

- The *assertive* player calls others by the same kind of designation others use for her/him, e.g., first names used by both, formal titles used by both (with or without last names), or nicknames used by both.
- The *aggressive* player calls others by first names and nicknames, while requiring that they use her/his formal title.
- The *nonassertive* player calls others by their formal title and allows (sometimes even insists) that they use her/his first name or nickname.

The name game is tricky, however. Some people prefer to be called by names they are comfortable with, regardless of their perceived, real, or desired status. Others are uncomfortable calling people they perceive as authority figures by anything other than formal title and last name. In real-life situations, assertive people may fit all three patterns noted and separately classified above. The best rule to observe in the name game is the rule of your own cognitive assessment. If it is important to you in a given situation to be perceived as an equal by someone you believe is unlikely to accept your equality without equal kinds of designation, then you might choose to strive for name game status by responding in kind to whatever you are called. If, however, in another situation you are comfortable with an unequal designation (in either direction) and you believe the relationship would be significantly changed if you were to insist on name game rules, then you might rationally choose to accept the relationship as is.

In assertion training classes, librarians frequently ask how to move from one form of address to another without uneasiness, particularly when the move is from calling a supervisor/manager/director by formal title and last name to calling the same person by her/his first name. Even when librarians believe their supervisors will easily accept the change of address, or when they have actually accepted such a change, the librarians still find that they themselves remain uncomfortable with the change they believed was desirable or necessary. Practice is the only solution for this problem. A good way to practice is to do it in steps:

1. Use the boss's first name mentally until you are comfortable with it.
2. Call the boss by first name to others, when the boss is not with you, being careful not to revert to title with the same people, until you are comfortable with that.
3. Use the boss's first name in a group, not directly, but indirectly. Use statements like "As Del says..." or "I agree with Del on this." Keep it up until you are used to hearing yourself say this name aloud in that person's presence.
4. Finally, begin using the name directly. Again, practice with confirmatory statements, such as "I agree with you, Del" or "As you said yesterday, Del, ..."

Use the reactions you get at steps 2 and 3 (particularly the boss's reaction in step 3) to determine whether you wish to continue your practice. Your own discomfort in moving to the new behavior is insufficient reason to discontinue. Remember that your assertive use of the name game should be based on rational thought, not emotional reaction.

Power Give-Away

Power give-away is the catchy name given to our unthinking reactions when other people "push our buttons." The assertive philosophy can help us change unthinking reactions to considered responses, but for those who know us best, we may have incredibly strong habitual responses triggered by certain words or actions.

Typical power give-aways are:

- You make me sick.
- You make me so mad.

No one should have the power to *make* you feel an emotion. You, and only you, own and can control your emotions. Instead of using power give-away statements, you should replace them with ownership statements:

- I feel sick when you do that.
- I get angry when you do that.

This difference is more than simple semantics. In the give-away statements, you essentially say "I can't stop myself from feeling sick or angry when you act that way, and *every time* you do that, I will display my sickness or anger." If the other person is one who chooses to do you harm at any given moment in time, you have provided an excellent weapon for them. They need only act in the way you have defined as infallible for eliciting your emotions. In the ownership statements, you retain power over your emotions and can choose to display them or not. You essentially say "I don't like that action, and *I have chosen to show* that I am disgusted or angry by it. However, on another occasion, I may *choose not to show* anger or disgust."

Additionally, you are not responsible for the emotions of others, so if they use those typical statements with you, you have an obligation to disown them. Disowning statements are:

- I am not responsible for your feeling of sickness.
- I may have given you just cause to be angry, but you are responsible for choosing to show your anger.

It is recommended that you use I-statements to own your own emotions in place of power give-away statements and that you use disowning statements when others try to give you responsibility for their actions/emotions.

Reinforcement and Strong Assertions

Assertive librarians may occasionally feel a need to deliver a reasonably strong assertive statement to a person with whom they have had and want to continue to have a strong and positive relationship. If you believe your relationship may be somewhat hurt, even temporarily, by the force of your assertion or its content, you may wish to add some positive reinforcement concerning the relationship to your total assertive statement. Examples of this are:

- I don't like what you just said. I want you to know that, because I want to feel comfortable with you, even when we disagree professionally. I don't consider myself stupid, and I don't think you are stupid when you disagree with me, so I'd like to drop that word from our discussion before we continue. I respect and like you far too much to have this word hurt our relationship.
- I really appreciate your concern. You've always been a good friend, so I feel comfortable telling you that I have to make this decision alone.

The use of reinforcement within an assertive statement is highly recommended whenever you want to minimize potential injury to a relationship but have a strong assertion to make.

Repeat Back

This is a technique that has been known in the education profession for a very long time. Its use is to ascertain that the person you have been speaking to has understood your meaning. It requires a certain amount of tact to ask someone to tell you what they heard you say without implying that you think they might have been incapable of following you, so the assertive use of this technique frequently starts with an I-statement:

- I'm not sure that I'm being as clear as I had hoped to be about this. What have you heard me say so far?
- Have I been clear? What do you understand my position to be?
- I'm willing to be flexible about this if you have any suggestions. Please tell me what you have understood me to say before adding any suggestions, however.

This technique is recommended for those times that the specific meaning of what you are saying is very important, and you cannot be certain the other person has heard or understood you. It is also useful in disciplinary interviews, but special caution must be taken to ensure that negative implications are avoided.

Return the Question

This is a device that allows you to keep from answering inappropriate questions without outright refusal. Questions which you believe are too personal to be asked within the context of your professional relationship, and questions couched in good little victim traps are the usual focus of this technique, which is simply answering a question with a question. Some useful answer-questions are:

- Why do you ask?
- How would you have done it?
- Why do you think that would have been better?
- Do you know of other alternatives?
- Is your question relevant to this discussion?

Returning the question, like some of the other techniques reviewed, is a bit risky in some situations. In a job interview, a question that appears to border on infringement of your civil rights (for example, on your plans for marriage or a family) may be no more than an introduction to the subject of a university child care center, and a snappy "Why do you ask?" could be perceived as very negative. On the other hand, an interviewer who really does seem to be asking inappropriate questions may be indicative of the academic milieu or attitude, and you may feel a definite assertive response is necessary to indicate just where you stand, for you would not be happy in an institution that routinely violated your rights.

This technique is recommended only for the repertoire of skillful asserters who routinely analyze the situation so that they can rationally select the most appropriate technique/behavior to use. Others should use clipping until the intent of the questioner can be discerned.

Reversal

In a work environment, this is often a very useful technique. Reversal is a request for a direct refusal when you appear to be getting an indirect refusal, often known as "the run-around." The technique is eminently simple. First, you make your request for something, several times, in very clear terms. When you decide that acceptance is unlikely, but you are not getting a definite refusal, you ask for that refusal. The addition of a statement that you plan to delay your request and renew it at a later time may also be appropriate. For example:

Head of Technical Services: We have added five new people to the cataloging area since we added OCLC, and we are still short two desks. Terry and Pat have both been using the desk of whomever is off on the day they come in to work, and it's not a very satisfactory situation, to say the least. There are also four desks that desperately need repair or replacement—they're in terrible shape. This section of my budget request includes a very high increase for capital equipment because I'd like to purchase four new desks and repair two of the old desks. Of course, it includes two new desk chairs for Pat and Terry, too.

Director: The equipment budget is really tight this year.

Head of Technical Services: I'm not surprised. This economy has hurt everyone. But I really need this equipment.

Director: The controller is turning down practically all equipment requests.

Head of Technical Services: I know it will be tough to get it approved, but I would appreciate it if we could keep it in the budget request.

Director: I don't know how much we'll get of anything, this year.

Head of Technical Services: I could manage for this year with a loan of two desks from the old accounting offices, but I would definitely need the equipment next year. Shall I withdraw my request for this year and resubmit it next year?

One of the amazing things about reversal is that 10 to 20 percent of the time the request for a direct refusal is answered with acceptance of the original proposal. In most cases, however, the answer is no. Since the indirect answer was no, anyway, nothing real is lost. Studies also show that direct refusals are more easily remembered than indirect refusals and that, in unconscious attempts to be fair, most administrators balance out their yes and no responses. So reversal actually has an advantageous effect: a future request is more likely to be accepted if the administrator remembers giving a you a direct refusal at some earlier time (Shaw & Rutledge, 1976).

Scripting

Many assertion texts recommend the use of written scripts to make assertive statements. Although the scripts are written and can be placed in letters or memorandums, they are often delivered orally. They are useful in keeping the fledgling asserter on the main point and in control of her/his emotional responses. Like contracting, scripting specifies what the asserter wants and what the consequences will be of meeting the request or failing to meet the request.

One of the best texts covering a scripting technique is *Asserting Yourself; A Practical Guide for Positive Change* (Bower & Bower, 1976). This text describes DESCing, a formula way of writing assertive scripts. The four step process includes:

D = Describe	**Describe** the situation and/or behavior you want to have changed in exact and nonjudgmental terms.
E = Express	**Express** your feelings about the situation and/or behavior.
S = Specify	**Specify** what you want, when you want it, and how you want it.
C = Consequences	Promise the **consequences** that will result if the situation and/or behavior changes in the way you want, and the **consequences** that will result if the changes do not take place.

A recent graduate hired to assist the interlibrary loan librarian might use the following DESC script to get some needed instruction that had been promised but continually postponed during the first four months of work:

Describe	I have asked you several times to teach me how to use the state interlibrary loan coupons. You have agreed to do this, but you have not found the time to do it.
Express	I feel I am not learning an important part of this job. This is not only frustrating, it undermines my performance.
Specify	I want to arrange a specific time and date when you will teach me about this system.

Consequences   If I learn the system, I will know
when to use the coupons and when
to leave them out. I will know more
about my job and will be able to
perform better. If I don't have an opportunity to learn this system, I will
have to continue to interrupt you
with questions about including coupons in requests, and I will probably
make more errors.

Scripting can be stilted unless it is practiced, and Bower and
Bower advise writing the script and practicing it for several days
before trying it out. They recommend scripts for face-to-face confrontations, (you can try unobtrusively reading from your script by
keeping, for example, a brief script on the top of papers you're
holding); rehearse from a script before a confrontation, (but don't take
the script with you); for telephone responses (if urgently pressured
during a telephone conversation, you can use assertive disengagement
and write a script before calling back to resume the conversation); and
for written communication. Bower and Bower also note that briefer
scripts follow practice and some successful use with scripting.

Scripting is highly recommended for volatile and important work
situations and with volatile and aggressive people. An inability to work
successfully with colleagues in a given library may ultimately lead to
changing jobs, but a strong effort to maintain assertive relationships
can help in even the most drastic situations. Scripting is a highly
controlled way to practice assertion and is especially useful in highly
charged environments.

SUMMARY

The key elements in verbal assertion are I-statements, honesty,
and spontaneity or timing. The seven types of assertive statements
(simple assertion, empathetic assertion, soft assertion, angry assertion,
confrontation assertion, negative assertion, and assertive disengagement) can be used in a variety of ways and a variety of situations to
make requests of others, to refuse the requests of others, and to express
feelings. Simple assertions, soft assertions, and angry assertions are
especially effective and can be easily learned. An assertive person can

say no or set limits without damaging an interpersonal relationship and is comfortable deciding when, where, and to whom to say no.

The other half of saying things assertively is listening assertively. A special technique known as active listening can assist the communication process, just as certain disruptive habits can inhibit communication.

A variety of "tricks" and techniques have been structured by assertion trainers to help people practice assertive interactions. They have catchy names to increase their memorability, but they are essentially training aids that can be adapted or discarded once an assertive philosophy has been internalized.

Chapter 6
Nonverbal Assertion

Nonverbal behaviors, often referred to as body language, can include any reflexive or nonreflexive movement of a part or all of the body (Fast, 1970). For convenience, they are classified as two kinds: auditory and gestural. Auditory nonverbal signs include tone of voice, rate of speech, volume, inflection, and fluency in pronunciation. Gestural signs emanate from every part of the body, most commonly the face and hands, but also including posture, touch, and even perspiration (Argyle, 1972). The way your body moves tells others how you feel about yourself. A casual movement or fleeting expression can send much stronger signals than any words you utter (Robertson, 1978). Calabrese (1979) notes that 65 to 75 percent of the meaning from supervisory communications comes from the nonverbal components of the message.

Albert Mehrabian (1971) conducted a study that measured how much each part of the communication process was able to influence attitude change. He found that 7 percent of the attitude changes people made were brought about by the verbal content of the message they heard, 38 percent were brought about by nonverbal vocal characteristics such as rate of speech, tone of voice, and inflection, used by the message-giver, and 55 percent were accounted for by the facial expressions of the person giving the message. The dramatic significance of nonverbal communication has been shown in a variety of other studies that have demonstrated that nonverbal messages are one to four times more important than verbal content (Argyle, Alkema & Gilmour, 1971; Birdwhistell, 1970; Bugenthal, Kaswan & Love, 1970; Eakins & Eakins, 1978; Mehrabian & Ferris, 1967; Tepper & Haase, 1978). There are also studies showing that visual cues are more reliably and accurately interpreted than verbal messages (Berman, Shulman & Marwit, 1976; Levitt, 1964) and that, when nonverbal and verbal messages are inconsistent, judgments tend to be made on visual input rather than the verbal message (DePaulo,

Rosenthal, Eisenstadt, Rogers & Finkelstein, 1978; Posner, Nissen, & Klein, 1976).

The importance of nonverbal messages to the communication process makes nonverbal cues of major import in the practice of assertiveness because it relies heavily on effective communication. Therapists have found that nonassertive clients often lack the ability to display appropriate nonverbal, as well as verbal, behaviors (Serber, 1972). The ability to manipulate nonverbal cues can add much greater flexibility to the messages an assertive person can convey (Emery, 1975). As Flowers and Booraem note, the ability to use assertive nonverbal behaviors both reinforces the verbal assertive message and adds to the asserter's feeling of self-esteem:

> An assertive person doesn't merely say what they want, they say it in the way they want. The issue is for the asserter to be the "expressive package" that they wish to be. The non-verbal components of assertive behavior have two purposes. First, the other person is much more likely to perceive the client as assertive if the verbal and non-verbal components are consistent. Secondly, people do not feel the self-dignity that comes with assertive behavior until they are nonverbally as well as verbally assertive (1975, p. 31).

This chapter will consider many different nonverbal cues in order to determine which are most effective in assertive behavior. The nonverbal messages we will explore can be divided into five general areas: (1) facial expressions and the use of eye contact and eyebrows as communicators; (2) hand gestures and handshakes; (3) posture, distance, and touch; (4) the vocal variations of inflection, tone, volume, fluency, latency, and nonword verbalizations; and (5) appearance and physical room arrangements. The chapter summary will include a chart of assertive body language, annotated with phrases indicating what to do and what not to do in order to present an assertive nonverbal message. One word of caution, however, for librarians who find themselves in an emotional or confrontational situation with an obviously mentally ill patron. Here the librarian should present as much of a blank slate image as possible. Smiling, laughing, frowning, use of hand gestures, or other body movements can all be misinterpreted as provocative to a seriously disturbed patron.

YOUR EXPRESSIVE FACE

Facial expression, eye contact, and eyebrow movements are used extensively in human speech. Listeners provide a continuous commentary on their reactions to what is being said by "micromomentary" movements of the eyebrows and mouth (Haggard & Isaacs, 1966). Speakers accompany their words with facial expressions and movements that are used to modify or "frame" what is said, showing whether it is supposed to be serious, funny, important, shocking, etc. (Argyle, 1972).

Facial Expressions

People are much more likely to show pleasant facial expressions than hostile expressions simply because people are socialized to hide spontaneous negative expressions when they occur. However, even in facial expressions generally regarded as pleasant, such as smiles, there are signs that indicate the feelings behind the expression. Facial expressions are the composite of a wide variety of cues: smiles, frowns, wrinkled foreheads, bitten or pursed lips, chewing, wet lips, swallowing audibly, pallor, perspiration, tears, blushing, and "poker faces." Each has a specific meaning, and each affects the verbal message being delivered.

Smiles that do not involve the cheeks or nostrils indicate that you are shutting out the person who is talking with you. A slight smile that extends to the cheeks indicates you are listening and evaluating what is being said. An expansive smile that engages the nostrils and includes solid eye contact indicates you are enthusiastic about the other person or her/his message (Robertson, 1978). Research has shown that truth telling leads to increased smiling and greater facial expression of pleasure; however, there are additional studies that show deception is also closely related to increased smiling behaviors (Zuckerman, DeFrank, Hall, Larrance & Rosenthal, 1979). An unsmiling expression is read as haughty (Argyle 1972).

A poker face, or intentional effort to appear passive, is read as dishonest. It confounds observers by masking your feelings. If you rub your nose while conversing with others, they are likely to think you are nervous, disapproving, and perhaps dishonest as well. A wrinkled nose may be seen as a sign of amusement, but it may also be considered part of a worried expression (Broadwell, 1977). Worry is also indicated by tensed facial muscles, wrinkles at the corners of the eyes, a wrinkled forehead, and frowning. Pursed lips indicate disapproval, while bitten lips indicate nervousness and anxiety. Wetting the lips is read as a sexual invitation. Excessive swallowing, pallor, and facial perspiration indicate intense anxiety. Chewing indicates arrogance (Gazda, Childers & Walters, 1982).

Facial expressions that are of a calm and pleasant character, with appropriate, occasional smiles, and nods or headshakes that reflect the verbal message are perceived as assertive. Facial expressions that indicate anxiety or dishonesty are perceived as nonassertive, and those that indicate arrogance, hostility, or anger are perceived as aggressive.

Eye Contact

Eye contact has received more attention than any other kind of nonverbal communication because, of all the parts of the body, the eyes can transmit the most subtle nuances (Fast, 1970). The act of looking sends a signal to other people that a certain amount of interest is being taken in them. During conversations, people tend to look at each other intermittently for periods of one to ten seconds, with those times that they are mutually looking at one another usually lasting less than two seconds. The total time spent looking at the other person in a conversation can range from 25 percent to 75 percent of the total time of the conversation. People look roughly twice as much when they are listening as when they are speaking. People tend to look longer and oftener at other people whom they particularly like. When the distance between people is increased, their eye contact also increases (Argyle, 1972).

Staring is reserved for nonpersons because people are socialized that one does not stare at another person. We stare at animals, at people who have selected themselves for display (stage performers, for example), and at objects. Aggressors also stare at people who, in their eyes, have nonperson status, either temporarily or permanently. Nonperson status may be dictated by prejudice, social status, or age. Our socialized prohibition against ignoring people is as strong as the prohibition against staring, so we direct a brief glance toward others, even strangers, in order to acknowledge our awareness of their humanity. We look at people approaching us until we are roughly eight feet away and then divert our gaze (Fast, 1970).

Excessive blinking can indicate nervousness or guilt (Broadwell, 1977). Avoidance of eye contact or shifting gazes can be indications of dislike or embarrassment. A determined gaze radiates aggression as strongly as if it were an outright glare. Women tend to look more and give more eye contact than men. Pupil size increases when we look at someone we like, and we respond more positively to people when their pupils are enlarged as, for example, in somewhat darker rooms (Kleinke, 1975).

Looking down, looking at some object instead of at the person facing you, looking at the other person but looking away when looked at, covering the eyes with hands, and crying are perceived as nonassertive. Looking defiantly, glaring, staring, and squinting are perceived as aggressive. Looking steadily but calmly, looking away occasionally, looking at objects as they are discussed, and sparkling eyes are perceived as assertive (Gazda, Childers & Walters, 1982). Nonasserters report increased abilities to act assertively when they increase eye contact, and aggressors report that decreasing eye contact reduces their aggressive behavior (Flowers & Booraem, 1975).

In work situations, people who have higher authority tend to maintain greater eye contact. Good eye contact indicates better listening, and speakers feel more powerful when listeners give increased eye contact. An assertive subordinate wishing to impress an authority figure with evidence of self-confidence should maintain more eye contact than usual. This is especially useful in interviews, where it also helps keep you alert for indications of approval or recognition and indicates your close attention (Fast, 1970).

If you look away while you are speaking, you indicate that you are still conveying a message and do not wish to be interrupted. You may also indicate you are somewhat uncertain of what you are saying. A locking gaze at your colleague coupled with a pause in speech indicates interruption is acceptable. Looking at your listener indicates you are certain of what you are saying. Looking away while you are listening to someone else indicates some reservations about what you are hearing or a desire to hide what you are feeling. Looking at the speaker as you listen indicates agreement (Fast, 1970).

Eyebrows

Emotional messages include eyebrow movement for every emotion except happiness. Assertive messages can be tremendously enhanced when eyebrow movements are used congruently with the verbal message. Fully raised brows indicate disbelief or questioning. Half raised brows indicate surprise, interest, or mild questioning. Eyebrows at their normal level and position indicate no comment. Half lowered brows show puzzlement or confusion, and fully lowered brows indicate anger (Caputo, 1981). Nonasserters show excessive eyebrow movement, described as "animated" and constantly moving "up and down" (McFall, Winnett, Bordewick & Bornstein, 1982).

Studies of facial components in six emotions found that eyebrow movement was an integral part of the expressions used to convey these emotions:

Surprise. Raised curved eyebrows, long horizontal forehead wrinkles, wide open eyes, dropped open mouth and lips parted without tension.

Fear. Raised and drawn-together brows, short horizontal or vertical forehead wrinkles, open eyes with tension in lower lids, mouth corners drawn back, lips stretched, lips may or may not be open.

Anger. Brows pulled down, sometimes curved forehead wrinkles centered above the eyes, upper eyelids lowered, lower eyelids tensed and raised, squinting, lips pressed tightly together or open squared mouth.

Disgust. Brows drawn down but not together, wrinkles on bridge of nose, lower eyelids pushed up and raised but not tensed, deep creases from wrinkled nose, mouth open and lower lip forward or mouth closed with upper lip pushed up by raised lower lip.

Sadness. Brows drawn together with inner corners raised and outer corners lowered or level, or brows drawn in the middle and slightly raised at inner corners, eyes either glazed with drooping lids or upper lids tense, trembling lips.

Happiness. No distinctive brow-forehead appearance, eyes relaxed or neutral, outer corners of lips raised and drawn back (Kleinke, 1975, pp. 71–72).

YOUR EXPRESSIVE HANDS

We use our hands in many very expressive ways throughout our lives. In the work world, the way we gesture can assist or inhibit the verbal message we are trying to impart. It is very useful to study what hand gestures indicate to others in order to use our hands in effective communication. Another part of our professional behavior includes handshaking, a very special kind of touch. Other touching behaviors range from tapping someone's shoulder to get her/his attention to highly affectionate bear hugs. We need to be able to identify, however, not only which kinds of touching are appropriate for the library setting but also how to read when people are uncomfortable with these touching behaviors.

Hand Gestures

Although we may move legs, feet, or other parts of the body, the most expressive limb movements are those of the hands and arms, and particularly those of the hands. Hand gestures can be closely coordinated with speech, allowing speakers to illustrate their meanings and, in fact, are sometimes used to continue the message when words fail. Hands are especially useful to describe shapes (Argyle, 1972). We use our hands to make symbolic gestures like salutes or ritualistic signs, to demonstrate how to do something or how something happened, and to indicate size. We use them for signaling specific behaviors, as when we snap our fingers, hold a finger to our lips, point, beckon, shrug, or wave. We use them in the unconscious motions of rubbing, stroking, tapping, and fidgeting, as well as using them to play with various objects. Finally, we use them in various self-inflicting ways such as nail-biting, knuckle-cracking, and scratching (Gazda, Childers, & Walters, 1982).

Hand gestures are highly correlated with certain emotions, and a list of these can be seen in Table 5. Data for the following table came from studies reported by Ashby (1975), Broadwell (1977), Kleinke (1975), and McFall, Winnet, Bordewick, and Bornstein (1982).

Table 5
Emotions and Hand Gestures

Behavior/Emotion	Indicated by These Hand Gestures
Affection	Holding one or two fingers of one hand with your other hand while talking with another person.
Thoughtfulness	One hand held loosely over the other.
Determination	One hand in a fist, the other hand covering it.
Self-confidence	Steepling: bringing fingertips of both hands together to form a steeple.
Nonassertiveness	Jerky hand movements.
Shyness	Inactive hands.
Bewilderment	Hands held straight out, palms facing outward, fingers spread.
Shame	Hand to nose or hand to mouth movements.

Table 5
Emotions and Hand Gestures (continued)

Behavior/Emotion	Indicated by These Hand Gestures
Frustration	An open hand dangling between the legs (for men), or hands thrown into the air (for women).
Worship	Clasped hands.
Pleading	Open hands, palms up.
Passivity	Cupped hands.
Weakness, submissiveness	Hands hanging in drooping position.
Uncertainty	Shrugging.
Aggression	Clenched fists.
Suspicion	Two hands folded at the fingertips.
Immaturity	Hands pushing outward.
Restlessness	Hands rubbing arms of chair.
Hostility	Pounding objects.

Eisenberg (1979) writes that gestures are basically two types: purposeful and purposeless. Purposeful gestures contribute to the spoken message, while purposeless gestures detract from it. Purposeless gestures include:

1. Fooling with your keys.
2. Playing with the change in your pocket.
3. Fiddling with your hair.
4. Tearing paper into tiny pieces.
5. Continuously jiggling a part of your body.
6. Biting your nails or cuticles.
7. Cracking your knuckles.
8. Sucking air through your teeth.
9. Repeatedly adjusting your clothing.
10. Peeling off your nail polish.
11. Chain-smoking.
12. Putting pens, pencils, or paper clips in your mouth.
13. Frequently looking at your watch or the wall clock.
14. Cracking or popping your chewing gum.
15. Rubbing a part of your body.
16. Shuffling papers unnecessarily.

17. Straightening items on your desk unnecessarily.
18. Drumming your fingers.

Eisenberg believes that these gestures have little psychological meaning, that they are purposeless and should therefore be eliminated. They could easily be given intentional psychological meaning, however, if they are used while someone is trying to convey a message to you, and you want to either distract the person or imply disagreement, indifference, or hostility.

Handshakes

The custom of handshaking is ancient; it goes back far enough to have served as a sign that no weapon was held in that hand. In American culture, handshakes are used in greeting, saying goodbye, sealing agreements, and to express congratulations. Handshakes can be classified as strong, medium, or weak, but a more important classification is whether they are self- determined or other-determined. Self-determined handshakes are those that are influenced by the way you feel at that moment: confident or anxious, happy or depressed, healthy or sick. Other-determined handshakes are those that are influenced by the person with whom you are going to shake hands: an adult or a child, male or female, authority figure, or subordinate (Eisenberg, 1979).

Assertive handshakes are direct, firm, and convincing. They are not extreme in any sense, neither bone-crushing nor limp. They are brief, and accompanied by eye contact. They are offered to both sexes. People who shake hands are perceived as significantly more friendly, warm, sincere, and interested in their colleagues than people who do not shake hands (Kleinke, 1975).

Touch

Touching others, and being touched by them, is an important part of nonverbal behavior, but touching between adults, particularly in a work environment, can be risky. There are wide variations in the levels of comfort people have with touching behavior. Touching in the workplace must be nonsexual and comfortable. The two most important aspects regulating the use of touching are: (1) the level of trust between the two people involved and (2) the perception of the touch as sexual or nonsexual. The actual intent (sexual or not) is less important than the perceived intent in this latter regard. There are cultural restrictions governing which parts of the body may be touched by whom, but the perception of sexual intent in touching is not limited to these cultural restrictions (Gazda, Childers & Walters, 1982).

Touching may take many forms: tapping, hitting, stroking, pushing, patting, etc. Henley (1974) suggests that touching that is not reciprocal is an expression of interpersonal power. Higher status people (in libraries this could mean directors, managers, and librarians) in a work environment touch more than lower status people (which in libraries could mean secretaries, clerks, and student assistants) in the same environment. In American culture, Henley believes men have used touching behavior with women as a means of asserting male superiority, and she recommends either a significant decrease in touching behaviors of men toward women, or else an equally significant increase in touching behaviors of women toward men to bring opposite-sex touching to the same kind of reciprocal levels that same-sex touching occupies.

Assertive librarians may touch others to increase the effectiveness of a verbal message. When they do use touch as a nonverbal expression, they touch gently but firmly and for only a brief moment. They may include a maternal/paternal arm around a colleague's or staff member's shoulder on infrequent occasions. They do not use intimate touching behaviors, such as caressing or stroking, nor do they use rough touching such as grasping, pushing, poking, or slapping. Assertive librarians do *not* touch people who indicate discomfort when they are touched. Slight drawing-away movements and facial expressions that indicate touch discomfort must be noticed. Touch, like all other assertive behaviors, is a matter of personal choice and style and does not violate the right of others to choose whether they wish to be touched.

Certain touches have certain meanings in our culture. Table 6 lists some of them.

Table 6
The Meaning of Varied Touches

Description of Touch	Meaning
Tap on the shoulder	Trying to get attention.
Pat on the head	Belittling.
Pat on the back	Well-done.

Table 6
The Meaning of Varied Touches (continued)

Description of Touch	Meaning
Slap on the back	Camaraderie, boisterous greeting.
Slap or pat on buttocks	Sexual intent, ownership.
Brief touch on the wrist	Sympathy, empathy, understanding.
Poking finger into chest	Challenge, hostility.
Arm around shoulders	Affection.
Hugging	Caring, strong affection.
Taking hold of a hand	Caring.

YOUR EXPRESSIVE STANCE

Both posture and distance are messages conveyed by our bodies as a whole, rather than by individual parts of our bodies. Our posture conveys a message about the way we feel about ourselves, while distance conveys a message about the way we feel in relation to others.

Posture

Posture is definitely used as a means of communicating intrapersonal emotion. Mehrabian (1971) found that distinctive postures are correlated with the feelings of self-confidence, friendliness, hostility, superiority, and inferiority and that posture messages are particularly effective; we find them very easy to read. McFall, Winnett, Bordewick and Bornstein (1982) noted in their study of nonverbal components of assertiveness that overall body cues and arms conveyed far more information about level of assertiveness than eyes, mouth, forehead, and brows.

Nonassertive people sit and stand in positions described as "stooped," "shrugging," "droopy," and "hunched." They often exhibit "rotating," "rocking," and "squirming" activities, which interfere with the flow of verbal communication. They exhibit anxiety by maintaining tenseness in their hunched positions. If they are depressed, they show it by lowering their chins toward their chests even more and keeping their eyes downcast on their bodies. They may lean their heads far to the right or to the left when they speak, particularly if they feel what they have to say is childish or unimportant. Overall, they appear tired looking and slovenly even when well groomed. They may sit sideways or otherwise facing away from the person or people with them (Gazda, Childers, & Walters, 1982; McFall, Winnert, Bordewick & Bornstein, 1982; Robertson, 1978).

Assertive people sit and stand straight without appearing rigid. They keep their arms and legs in reasonably symmetrical positions. They have relaxed muscles and move with ease when they change positions. In attempts at persuasion they use slow, easy gestures originating from a comfortable position. To indicate interest, they lean slightly forward, toward the speaker. Overall, they appear eager to participate in conversations with others (Gazda, Childers & Walters, 1982; Flowers & Booraem, 1975; McFall, Winnert, Bordewick & Bornstein, 1982; Robertson, 1978).

When aggressive people are standing, they keep both arms and legs completely symmetrical, often with both arms at the sides and with clenched fists. They sit almost at attention when they are feeling hostile and relax into an exaggerated backward sprawl when they feel arrogant or over-confident. In this position, they may put their hands behind their heads, a signal that they are prepared to dominate. When they are ready to take charge, they signal by suddenly sitting up straight, facing others, and if necessary, moving to a central position. If the person with whom they are talking is perceived as influential, they are less likely to lean back but remain poised on the edge of the seat, seeking cooperation and approval. Their heads rarely leave the upright, vertical position, even when their bodies are slouched. When they are in groups, they may position their bodies (sitting or standing) in ways that effectively block others from joining the dyad or triad they have formed with one or two others (Argyle, 1972; Broadwell, 1977; Flowers & Booraem, 1979; Robertson, 1978).

There are also listening positions that convey messages. Assertive listeners lean back comfortably and may cross their legs. Uncrossed legs suggest slightly more openness than crossed legs. If they disagree, assertive people uncross their legs (if they were crossed) and lean forward slightly to respond and then resume their receptive position to listen again. Aggressive people may assume a similar listening posture, but if they disagree they exaggerate the sitting up movement, often sitting bolt upright to command attention. People who listen with their arms folded across their chests are indicating that they will not budge on their positions; they are immovable or implacable. In nonassertive people, crossed arms can indicate a desire for self-protection (Broad-well, 1977; Fast, 1970; Gazda, Childers & Walters, 1982).

Significantly, large postural changes indicate the person is ready to end the interaction. These changes include standing, moving to the extreme edge of a chair, or stepping away (Argyle, 1972; Broadwell, 1977; Fast, 1970).

Posture is not static but is in continuous motion, and it varies according to the individual's current emotional state. Argyle (1972) notes that this is particularly important, for when people control the reflection of anxiety in their facial expression, it may still be seen in their posture. If "leakage" of emotion is likely to occur anywhere, it is almost always expressed in posture.

Distance

Distance is part of the concept of personal space. Although there had been quite a bit of experimental investigation on distance and personal space before 1970, the results up to the early 1970s were somewhat meager. Researchers discovered that we stand closer to people we like than to people we dislike and that we stand closer to people who have their eyes closed than to people who have their eyes open, but the measurable differences in proximity were only two to three inches, and no significance was accorded to them since they were easily eclipsed by cross-cultural variations in personal space and distance. Studies undertaken as late as 1969 found no perceptions of personality differences in people sitting two, four, and eight feet away while talking with another person (Argyle, 1972). Yet the book *Personal Space,* which was also published in 1969 (Sommer), indicated definite correlations between our perception of a person's personality characteristics and the distance separating that person from ourselves or that person from others.

In American culture, distances of one and a half to three feet are considered appropriate social distances, and people are perceived as assertive within this space. When two people are seated, this distance may increase to six feet without a significant loss of perceived assertiveness. Assertive people lean back slowly, to increase interpersonal distance when they are facing an aggressive attack, even when the aggressor is not at close range. They then move forward again, slightly and slowly, to respond to the attack. Assertion trainers recommend regular practice of a slight move closer at the main point of an assertive statement, as long as the other person's personal space is not violated by such a move. Assertive people are characterized by taking initiative to move closer to people, by the graduality of their movements, and by the parallel movements they make in response to others—moving forward when the other person steps back, and moving back when the other person steps forward (Flowers & Booraem, 1975; Kleinke, 1975).

Distances of less than one and a half feet are perceived as aggressive, and fast movements carrying us toward another person are perceived as aggressive. These may even be characterized as "closing in" (Flowers & Booraem, 1975).

Distances greater than three feet when standing or greater than six feet when seated are perceived as nonassertive. People who stop just inside the doorway when invited to enter an office are also perceived as nonassertive (Flowers & Booraem, 1975; Gazda, Childers, & Walters, 1982).

We are more aroused by frontal approaches than by approaches from either side and respond sooner to perceived invasion of our personal space by people of the opposite sex than of our own sex. In arguments, we are more likely to agree with people who are farther away from us than with people who are very close. We use more discrete hand and facial gestures in conversation with people who are near us than with those farther away. Variations in personal space exist between ethnic subcultures in America as well as between American and other cultures, so that behaviors that are appropriate among some groups may be perceived quite differently by others even within our own limited environment (Kleinke, 1975).

YOUR EXPRESSIVE VOICE

The auditory components of speech are not words per se, and they are not truly nonverbal, since they are vocalized, yet they affect the messages we send as strongly as other nonverbal behaviors. Fast and Fast (1977) call this *meta*language:

> All of us speak two languages. There is the language we are familiar with, our spoken words. But behind these words, within them and around them, are numerous meanings that do not exist in the words themselves. This is a metalanguage, another form of communication whose meaning sometimes strengthens and sometimes weakens or even contradicts the words we speak. It accompanies the spoken words, and it includes resonance, pitch, stress, melody, and volume as well as dialect, accent, and the emotional overlay we give to words—sarcasm, tenderness, irony (p. 11).

In this section, we will look at how the tone of voice we use to say something and the inflections we place on certain words or on the beginning or end of a statement can affect how assertive others perceive us to be. We will also explore the effects of the rate of speech we use, the volume we project, the amount of time elapsing between a statement and our response, and the use of nonwords, as they affect others' perceptions of our assertiveness.

Tone of Voice and Inflection

Tone of voice can vary from a flat monotone that is devoid of feeling to a voice with strong, variable inflections which are perceived as bright, firm, confident, or vivacious. A flattened tone of voice is usually perceived as nonassertive. If the flattened tone appears to be the result of clenched teeth, however, it is perceived as aggressive. Rose and Tyron (1979), who conducted a study of how the degree of inflection influences the level of perceived assertiveness, revealed that accenting a greater percent of the syllables spoken significantly increases the amount of assertiveness perceived in the speaker. The experimental conditions included no syllables accented (monotone), 30 percent of the syllables accented, 60 percent accented, and 90 percent accented. The level of perceived assertiveness rose with each increase in inflection.

Listening to your own voice on a tape recorder can often give you an idea of how much affect you put into it. It is difficult and frustrating to try to accurately measure how many syllables you used without accent and how many were accented, but simply listening to your own voice as if it were another person speaking can give you a reasonably good idea whether this is a voice that would inspire confidence or one that would encourage mistrust. Adding inflections to your speech can also be a difficult task, but it is possible with practice. One good method for practicing is to read playscripts that include a wide variety of characters into a tape recorder, consciously trying to instill enough emotions into the different characters so that they are recognizable without trying to speak in an entirely different voice.

Rate of Speech and Latency

We all speak at varying rates of speed—fast, medium, and slow. In addition to the speed with which actual words are pronounced, the time in which we respond, called latency, can vary tremendously. Latency also includes pauses between words during a response, and these, too, show almost infinite variability.

Nonassertive speech is characterized as either very slow speech with frequent pauses of four seconds or more between words or the very rapid and breathy speech that has been correlated with high anxiety (Argyle, 1972; Serber, 1972). Even in reading, nonasserters have far more disfluencies,such as verbalizing "uhh," than assertive people (Norton-Ford & Hogan, 1980). Long latency is perceived as extremely passive. This is always true, even when it is exhibited infrequently. When you are taken by surprise and find yourself at a loss for words, other people perceive a delayed response as significantly less assertive than a quick filler response, such as "that surprises me," despite the fact that the filler says nothing relative to the immediate point (Flowers & Booraem, 1975).

An angry person is likely to speak more slowly than one who is afraid. Aggressive people speak more slowly when they are attempting domination over another person or the situation (Argyle, 1972). However, the latency of aggression is extremely short and frequently interruptive. Interruption, even polite interruption, is perceived as aggressive, and assertion trainers recommend hearing a person out even when the goal is to terminate a conversation, except in the specific situation where a person is running on extensively and limiting the use of the asserter's valuable time (Flowers & Booraem, 1975).

The study by Rose and Tyron (1979) showed that latencies of 16 or more seconds were invariably perceived as passive. Latencies from 5 to 15 seconds were perceived as reasonably assertive, while latencies of less than 5 seconds were perceived as very assertive. The closer the latencies came to 0, the more potential they had for being perceived as aggressive.

Volume

Nonassertive people use weak, hesitant voices; they may actually whisper or sound shaky and trembling. When they use low volume to project even a highly practiced strong assertive statement, the low volume negates the sense of the statement, and they do not accomplish their goal. They may complain that people just don't hear them or that they are not taken seriously whenever they do speak, and these complaints may be entirely justified. They can be eliminated, however, by practicing louder speech. Very loud speech is likewise characterized as aggressive, and people with booming voices may find themselves confused when others respond with avoidance or counterattack behaviors. They need to practice lower levels of volume (Flowers & Booraem, 1975; Norton-Ford & Hogan, 1980).

The Rose and Tyron (1979) study showed that speech at less than 68 decibels is perceived as nonassertive, speech louder than 84 decibels is perceived as aggressive, and speech within the 69-83 decibel range is perceived as assertive, with 76 decibels considered ideal.

Nonwords

Nonwords include head nodding, pauses in speech while maintaining eye contact, clearing the throat, coughing, "ahs," "ums," and "um-hmms." When any of these is used excessively, it is perceived as nonassertive behavior or as an indicator of anxiety, discomfort, or guilt. Aggressive people may use pronounced clearing of the throat as a means to attract attention or to indicate forthcoming disapproval (Broadwell, 1977). Assertive librarians can use occasional head nods as reinforcers to indicate listening. Studies clearly show that people increase the behavior they are engaged in if they are encouraged by a head nod from another person. Similarly, assertive librarians can use "um-hmm" as a reinforcer indicating understanding of the other person's message and pauses accompanied by eye contact to indicate a desire for input from another person. Clearing the throat and coughing are reserved for physiological need by the assertive person (Argyle, 1972; Cotler, 1975).

YOUR EXPRESSIVE LOOK

Many aspects of nonverbal behavior are under our voluntary control, and this is especially true in terms of the clothing we choose to wear and the way we arrange or use our work area or office furniture.

Appearance

There are books available for both women and men that recommend appropriate business attire, and they include some very useful suggestions. Such books, however, are advisory, not mandatory. Assertive librarians have sufficient self-confidence to consider these guidelines as contributions to their rational thought process and select their styles of dress based on personal likes and dislikes, an objective view of the environment in which their library work exists, and an analysis of the way successful people in their organization dress.

Clothing may be bold or unobtrusive, a current style, out of fashion, or "timeless." Whatever it looks like, its main purpose (after warmth and appropriate body covering) is to send messages about you to other people. People select some forms of dress to indicate status or occupation. Most bankers, for example, wear fairly conservative business suits rather than jeans to work. People also select clothing that conveys information about their personalities. For example, extraverts often wear bright colors, even if they must be limited to minor parts of a costume, such as a matched belt and shoes or a colorful tie. Whatever you choose to wear, the time, effort, and money you use in selecting clothing is an appropriate investment in nonverbal language because it sends a message about you (Argyle, 1972; Gazda, Childers & Walters, 1982).

The Office Environment

The way we move about an office setting also gives a message about us to our colleagues. Private offices and the immediate area around personal desks in larger work environments are a territorial extension of the personal space we all maintain as a buffer zone around our bodies. When someone enters our territory, and when we enter into someone else's territory, we begin sending messages about ourselves. Gazda, Childers and Walters (1982) tell us the following about our use of physical settings:

Nonassertive people sidle into other people's territory and either stand on the fringe waiting to be accepted or rejected or else hunch into a chair as unobtrusively as possible. They ask permission to talk with other people "if it's convenient." They prefer desks or other objects between them and the other person as a protective barrier even though they feel intimidated in this position. They turn their desks toward walls, and arrange shelving and other furniture to create "walls" surrounding them when they do not have private office space. However, when they do have private office space, they are reluctant to close their office doors for fear someone will think they are unapproachable.

Aggressive people stride boldly into others' territories and take a dominating position. They don't ask if the other person has time or inclination to talk with them but assume it is their right to interrupt. They may walk around a desk to stand beside and above the person they are meeting, or they may block the exit, close the door, or otherwise project a boxed-in feeling to the other person. They may move around the space a lot, as if claiming every piece of it, or they may simply ignore any territorial boundaries, moving in and out of the other person's territory at will. Their desks are placed in the center of their offices if possible, and visitors' chairs are placed directly in front of the desk. They face the door. They set up formal systems to guard their office door, often using secretaries or a visible approach area for this purpose.

Assertive people request time with other people by expressing their need, e.g., "I'd like to discuss something with you." They enter the other's territory confidently and take an open position that would seem too vulnerable to a nonasserter. This could be in the center of a room, next to someone on a sofa, or in chairs with nothing between them and the other person. Their offices reflect this openness with the use of tables as desks, comfortable chairs or small round tables for conferences, and the arrangement of their furniture, which typically has a chair to the side of the desk for visitors rather than in front of the desk. When someone enters their offices, they move from behind their desks and sit comfortably with their visitors.

SUMMARY

Nonverbal behaviors can be even more habitual than our verbal behaviors and changing them can thus be far more difficult than changing our verbal behaviors. Moreover, although we are all adept at reading the nonverbal messages we receive from others, we do this without much conscious thought, and we frequently don't recognize or even notice our own nonverbal messages unless someone else points them out to us. It is important, however, that our nonverbal messages be congruent with our verbal messages, so assertive librarians study their body language and adapt it to reinforce the assertive messages they wish to convey. The following table may help you to selectively adapt your own body language.

Table 7
Assertive Body Language

	What to Do	What not to Do
Facial Expression	Maintain calm, pleasant expression. Smile occasionally and appropriately. Use facial expressions that are congruent with the message you are sending/receiving.	Maintain poker face. Bite, wet, or purse lips. Frown and wrinkle forehead. Put hands over eyes, rub nose, or scratch ears. Swallow excessively or chew anything.
Eye Contact	Make direct eye contact. Look at materials (papers, etc.) together. Maintain eye contact at the height of your message.	Look away or down. Shift gaze excessively. Glare, stare, or squint. Discontinue eye contact at the height of your message. Blink excessively.
Eyebrows	Use them congruently with verbal message.	Use them incongruently with verbal message.
Gestures	Use hands naturally. Draw shapes, sizes in the air to demonstrate. Point out important items on written materials.	Hold hands rigidly. Play with anything, tap, drum, preen. Rub or stroke anything. Cover mouth when speaking.
Handshakes	Shake hands for hello, goodbye, sealing a bargain, congratulations. Use firm, brief grip. Maintain eye contact. Extend hand first. Offer to both sexes.	Refuse to shake hands. Use crushing grip. Pump the other's arm. Use limp hand. Break eye contact. Wait for other to extend hand first.

Table 7
Assertive Body Language (continued)

	What to Do	What not to Do
Touch	Touch to increase effect. Touch gently, firmly. Pat shoulder or back. Touch wrist for sympathy.	Touch in intimate ways (caressing, stroking). Grasp, squeeze, poke. Pat head or buttocks.
Posture	Maintain relaxed, comfortable posture. Cross legs if desired. Keep limbs reasonably symmetrical. Keep head on a level with the other person. Sit, unless specifically told not to sit.	Shift weight from foot to foot. Slouch, hunch, sprawl. Keep limbs rigidly symmetrical. Stand above, sit below the other person. Stand as if at attention. Pace, "freeze," clench fists.
Distance	Stand 1.5–3 feet from the person you are with. Sit 1.5–6 feet from the person you are with. Lean back slowly when attacked, then lean forward to respond. Lean back to listen.	Stand or sit closer than 1.5 feet to anyone. Stand farther than 3 feet or sit farther than 6 feet from anyone. Close in fast. Increase distance as you speak.
Nonverbal Aspects of Speech	Vary accents on syllables. Speak clearly without rushing. Use a variety of words. Respond within 1–15 seconds. Speak in easily heard voice.	Use monotone. Use flattened voice. Race through speech. Repeat the same words. Respond slower than 15 seconds. Whisper or shout. Interrupt. Speak through clenched teeth.
Nonwords	Use brief pauses with eye contact. Nod.	Say "ah" or "um" a lot. Clear throat or cough unnecessarily.

Table 7
Assertive Body Language (continued)

	What to Do	What not to Do
Appearance	Be neat and clean. Dress appropriately for the work environment.	Overdress. Underdress.
Physical Setting	Sit facing others. Respect territories of others.	Sit behind or in front of a desk when talking with others.

Chapter 7
Our Irrational Beliefs

Knowing what to say or do to be assertive is only the first step toward assertive living. People frequently learn appropriate assertive skills but fail to put them into practice by imagining disasters that will occur if they are assertive, by anticipating the guilt they will feel if they act assertively, or by convincing themselves they don't have the right to be assertive with certain people or in certain situations (Hulbert, 1982). The way we think, the way we feel, and the way we act are integrally related because the way we think influences the way we feel and the way we act (Caputo, 1981).

The founder of Rational-Emotive Therapy, Albert Ellis, developed an A-B-C model for understanding how our thoughts affect our feelings and behaviors. In this model, the irrational beliefs that are part of our habitual thought processes are determining factors in the creation of inappropriate feelings, which in turn lead to ineffective behaviors. The creation of appropriate feelings and the effective behaviors which then follow are dependent on an exchange of our irrational beliefs for rational ones.

THE A-B-C MODEL

In the Ellis model,

- A refers to an **activating event** or situation.
- B refers to the **thinking process** we go through, an "inner dialogue" about ourselves and the event or situation.
- C refers to the **feelings** and **behaviors** that we have and engage in when that event or situation occurs.

The activating event or situation, part A, occurs without any assistance or intervention on our part. Part B, our thinking process, may include some rational beliefs but is primarily characterized by irrational beliefs unless we consciously change our thinking habits. We seldom make such changes, however, because part B occurs so quickly that we believe our thinking is spontaneous and beyond our intervention; we seldom recognize its occurrence as a separate process at all. Nevertheless, part B represents a process that *can* be consciously controlled. With practice and objective analysis, we can put rational beliefs in place of our irrational beliefs. Part C is the result of what happens at part B. When our irrational beliefs prevail, we experience inappropriate feelings and behave in ineffective ways. When we form rational beliefs we experience appropriate feelings and behave in effective ways. In most situations, we assume A, whatever it is, always causes (and must always cause) whatever happens at C, which is usually a consequence that we find undesirable. We remain unaware that B, the thinking process, occurs at all, or that, if such a process did occur, we could affect it in any way to change the undesirable consequences of C.

Ellis (1976) summarizes his theory this way:

> The four general values that men and women most frequently hold seem to be these: (1) survival, or the sustaining of life once a person is born; (2) happiness, or survival with a decent degree of pleasure or satisfaction and a minimum of pain or dissatisfaction; (3) social acceptance, or survival in a group or community in which the person gets along reasonably well; and (4) intimate relations, or survival while relating lovingly to a few selected members of the larger social group in which the person resides...assuming it is legitimate for humans to pick the above-named values, it can be logically deduced that any thoughts, emotions, or actions through which they aid or promote these goals are rational, sensible, or healthy; while, by the same token, any behaviors through which they block or sabotage these goals are irrational, insane, and unhealthy....
>
> ...when an Activating Event or Activating Experience occurs in anyone's life, at point A, and he/she responds with a disordered Consequence (or emotion or behavior), at point C, A virtually never directly causes C. Rather, B, a cognitive mediating process, does. B is the individual's Belief System, or what he/she strongly concludes or interprets about A. Thus, if I get cheated by someone, at point A, and feel aggressively irritated and angry at the cheater, at point C, I really irritate and anger myself, at point B, by stoutly believing something about what happened at A.
>
> The A-B-C theory...not only indicates that an individual will normally feel both an appropriate emotion (irritation) and an inappropriate one (anger) when he is unjustly put upon, but also...operationally distinguishes between two different forms of Beliefs—a rational Belief (rB) and an irrational Belief (iB)—that creates these emotional consequences. For it hypothesizes that the irritation I experience at C when someone bilks me at A is caused

by my rational Belief, "I don't like being cheated. How unfortunate for me to be treated so unjustly! That was a rotten act the cheater performed." It also hypothesizes that the anger I experience at C is caused by my irrational Belief, "How awful for me to be cheated! I *shouldn't* have been! The person who cheated me is a rotten bastard!"

The first of these Beliefs is rational because it is a logical deduction from the basic values that I, the cheated individual, hold; namely the values (mentioned above) of my wanting to survive, to be reasonably happy, to get along in my social community, and to intimately relate to a few others. If I truly have been cheated, I probably will still survive and be able to engage in intimate relationships (though not as well as I might be able to do if I had not been cheated), but to some degree my happiness and my general relations with members of my community will definitely tend to suffer. Therefore, I can logically conclude that I *don't* like being cheated; that it *is* unfortunate (or disadvantageous, obnoxious, or inconvenient) for me to be treated so unjustly; and that it *was* a rotten act the cheater performed.

The second of my Beliefs is irrational because it does not stem from my basic values, has no empirical referent whatever, and is nothing but a magical set of assumptions or demands. Thus, it cannot be *awful* for me to be cheated, because *awful* does not mean exceptionally unfortunate, bad, inconvenient, or disadvantageous. When I say that something is *awful* (or *horrible* or *terrible!*) I mean that it is *more* than one hundred percent unfortunate—which, of course, nothing can be. When I say that I *shouldn't* have been cheated, I mean that there is an absolute, incontrovertible law of the universe that commands that anything that is highly unfortunate should not, must not, and ought not happen to me. But, obviously, there isn't, nor ever will be, such a law. When I say that the person who cheated me is a rotten bastard, I mean that he not only has performed rotten acts, but that *he* is rotten to the core; is a worthless *individual* who *cannot* ever do any good acts; and should be *completely damned* (and, naturally, preferably roasted for an eternity in hell) for having cheated me.

This is what normally, almost always, seems to happen when I feel anger, or any other inappropriate emotion, at point C, after something antithetical to my goals has occurred at point A. I not only sanely and empirically conclude that the Activating Experience is obnoxious and inconvenient and thereby feel appropriately displeased about it; but I also insanely and magically conclude that it is awful, horrible, terrible, and inconceivable; and that the person who perpetrated it is a complete 101 percent devil. I "awfulize" about the act and demonize its performer. I thereby *make myself* highly disturbed (Ellis, 1976, pp. 240, 247–249).

There are two central themes in Ellis's theory. The first theme is that we consciously or unconsciously *create* our feelings and have a choice between inappropriate feelings like murderous rage and appropriate feelings like rational displeasure (Ellis & Casriel, 1971). The second theme is that irrational ideas are the basic cause of emotional disturbance. When we believe the nonsense that we must always be loved and accepted or that mistakes are terrible, we will inevitably feel inhibited, hostile, guilty, anxious, ineffective, inert, uncontrolled, or unhappy. When we release ourselves from these nonsense beliefs, we find it exceptionally difficult to become intensely emotionally upset or to sustain an emotional disturbance for an extended period (Ellis, 1966). This theory has a tremendous implication for the practice of assertiveness. Research studies have shown that low assertive people are significantly different from high assertive people in their beliefs, expectancies, and self-instructions but not in their knowledge of appropriate assertive responses. Thus, changes in the cognitions (point B) associated with nonassertive behavior should lead directly to assertive behavior (Hammen, Jacobs, Mayol & Cochran, 1980). Similarly, Ellis states that the difference between assertive and aggressive behavior is based on our beliefs:

> When I am healthfully assertive, I am convinced that, "I want what I want and am determined to get it; but if I don't get it, that won't be the end of the world and I shall merely be frustrated." When I am unhealthfully combative or dominating, I am convinced that, "I *need* what I want and absolutely *must* have it; and it will be so horrible if I don't get it that I'll run roughshod over you, if necessary, to gain it" (Ellis, 1976, p. 249).

Ten Irrational Beliefs

What are our irrational beliefs? Ellis has identified 10 specific irrational ideas that are commonly learned (Lange & Jakubowski, 1976). Each of us accepts these in varying degrees, creating our own unique set of irrational ideas and corollaries. Our ability to use assertive skills hinges directly on our acceptance of these irrational thoughts. Ellis's 10 beliefs and their logical consequences in terms of assertive behavior are presented below.

Irrational Idea Number One: You must—yes, must—have sincere love and approval almost all the time from all the people you find significant (Ellis, 1962, p.61). This belief most commonly leads to nonassertive behaviors. For example, if you rationally assess that assertive behavior may lead to disapproval from someone whose opinion you care about, you may find yourself (1) being unable to express your opinions or needs, (2) avoiding participation in discussions, (3) accepting unreasonable demands on your time, and (4) tolerating the infringement of your personal rights. If you base your rational, assertive behavior choices on irrational fears of rejection or disapproval, your choices cannot be logical and realistic.

Irrational Idea Number Two: You must prove yourself thoroughly competent, adequate, and achieving, or you must at least have real competence or talent at something important (Ellis, 1962, p.63). This belief also leads to nonassertive behaviors. The critical ingredients in this belief are the absolute perfection of your expectation for yourself (I *must* do well) and the assumption that tragedy results when perfection is not attained (it will be *terrible* if I make a mistake). When we succumb to this irrational belief, we castigate ourselves for each human error with questions like "How could I be so stupid and careless as to do that?" and come to conclusions that "this always happens to me. I simply must be stupid. I should have known better than to try to do anything right." This form of thinking results in such nonassertive behaviors as (1) being too nervous to deliver a presentation at a professional conference; (2) worrying excessively, with a resulting increase in errors, over presenting the library budget; (3) prefacing nearly every task that requires the exhibition of some professional skill with profuse criticism of the external influences that make the accomplishment of your task less likely (and thereby leaving you free from blame for your inability to accomplish it); and (4) avoiding applying for a job with increased responsibility.

Irrational Idea Number Three: You have to view life as awful, terrible, horrible, tragic, and catastrophic when things do not go the way you would like them to go (Ellis, 1962, p.65). People who are strongly influenced by this irrational belief feel and act victimized. They complain, whine, and bemoan their awful life, often speaking bitterly against certain groups of people such as all women, all men, all bosses, or all secretaries. If they take any action to revise their lives, they do it in ways that produce negative consequences. They act highly emotional in their complaints, so that even when those complaints are justified, others are unwilling to listen or assist them.

For example, in a college library, an office assistant is treated unfairly by another library staff member. The office assistant immediately becomes highly agitated and launches a verbal attack which includes a tirade of bitterness against the staff member, the library, and the college itself. The staff member walks away, so the office assistant rushes into the library director's office to launch another emotional outburst. The director agrees to look into the matter, but two days pass with no action being taken. The office assistant then goes to the college personnel office and engages in another highly emotional outburst against this college which allows unfairness to run rampant. The personnel department directs the office assistant back to the library director without commenting on the situation.

In this true example, the office assistant did have a legitimate complaint, and the process of bringing it first to the attention of the other staff member, then to the library director, and then to the personnel department was appropriate. But the manner in which these steps were taken was so unreasonable in its excessive emotion and inordinate generalization from a single incident to a diatribe against the whole college that the office assistant was treated with avoidance at every step in the process, and the case was not resolved. If the office assistant had not "awfulized" the experience, it would probably have been resolved at step one or two.

Irrational Idea Number Four: People who harm you or commit misdeeds rate as generally bad, wicked, or villainous individuals and you should blame, damn, and punish them for their sins (Ellis, 1962, p.69). This irrational belief leads to aggressive behaviors. Overt behaviors include (1) constant criticism of others for incompetence, insensitivity, or ignorance; (2) continuous questioning of the motives of other people; (3) excessive vindictiveness against others who have actually been unfair or obnoxious; and (4) excessive self-punishment following failure or unintentional harm to someone else.

Irrational Idea Number Five: If something seems dangerous or fearsome, you must become terribly occupied with and upset about it (Ellis, 1962, p.72). There are many rational bases that lead us to reasonable concern and fear, but this irrational belief leads to unreasonable anxieties which in turn lead to preoccupation with the fear, inhibiting the clear thinking necessary to deal with the reality of a dangerous or fearsome situation. The anxiety caused by this exaggeration of a situation can be so severe it actually becomes debilitating, causing sleeplessness, nausea, and headache. The situations that trigger these unreasonably escalated fears might be rather innocuous until this irrational belief begins to build them up into major traumas. For example, worry over a certification examination could result in inability to concentrate on the examination when it is finally taken. Similarly, excessive concern over a job interview could stimulate physical illness, severe enough to force cancellation of the interview.

Irrational Idea Number Six: People and things should turn out better than they do and you have to view it as awful and horrible if you do not quickly find good solutions to life's hassles (Ellis, 1962, p.75). This belief leads to overreactions and feelings of inadequacy and guilt. People who succumb to this belief assume there is a magically perfect solution to everything, and that it can be found if only you try hard enough and are smart enough. But in reality, there are situations in which none of the possible alternatives available to us are truly desirable, and we must rationally assess which may be "the lesser of all the evils" rather than which will really meet all our needs. Looking for a perfect solution where none exists leads to anger and depression, which results in ineffectiveness. When librarians feel torn by too many responsibilities, they can become so highly disturbed by the demands on their time and their inability to create additional hours in a day or perfectly schedule the 24 hours that are routinely available that they are unable to accomplish anything at all.

Irrational Idea Number Seven: Emotional misery comes from external pressures and you have little ability to control your feelings or rid yourself of depression and hostility (Ellis, 1962, p.78). This belief almost invariably leads to avoidance and passive behaviors. Those who believe they have no control over their feelings may consider themselves to be "high strung" or "temperamental" or just people who are "naturally" pessimistic or depressed. This is not to say that such people continuously pout or complain about their own perceived inabilities, they simply feel that they cannot change either their feelings or their behaviors because they are completely controlled by some genetic factors of personality, whatever they perceive those to be. These people believe the same is true of others and, therefore, make no attempt to ask for behavior changes from other people. They do not recognize that they have any choice in the way they respond to things and ascribe blame for their feelings to an external cause or to someone else: "I just go to pieces when the work starts piling up that way, I can't help it," or "He *made* me so angry I couldn't talk." Similarly, they believe they can cause feelings in other people, so they hold back opinions for fear of *making* someone mad or say yes to things they don't want to do so that they will not hurt someone's feelings. They worry inordinately about the effect their opinion, feeling, or need will have on others and hold back, causing themselves increased tension and frustration.

Irrational Idea Number Eight: You will find it easier to avoid facing many of life's difficulties and self-responsibilities than to undertake more rewarding forms of self-discipline (Ellis, 1962, p.80). This belief commonly leads to nonassertive kinds of behavior, but it can also lead some people to aggressive behaviors. Nonassertive people frequently believe that avoidance of immediate discomfort is more important than long-term discounting of their personal rights. They easily see and feel immediate relief more easily than they can see or feel long-term effects that occur after purposeful and perhaps difficult behavior change. Nonassertive librarians subscribing to this irrational belief would be likely to (1) avoid participation in seminars with extensive group interaction, (2) prefer to deal with performance appraisals in writing rather than in person, or (3) tolerate inappropriate behavior in colleagues or subordinates rather than confronting them about their behavior.

Aggressive behaviors can result from this same irrational belief when people decide that learning to control their reactions to minor irritations would be intolerable because they must have the relief of immediate release of emotion: "I need to get this off my chest." Aggressive librarians who believe self-discipline is too hard a task would be likely to (1) blow up frequently over small annoyances in group meetings; (2) argue that it's unhealthy to bottle up anger, therefore it should always be displayed, immediately, and fully; and (3) yell or otherwise behave rudely to subordinates and yet expect continuous understanding that they are simply reacting to the pressures of their position and not intentionally hurting others.

Irrational Idea Number Nine: The past remains all-important and because something once strongly influenced your life, it has to keep determining your feelings and behavior today (Ellis, 1962, p.82). This belief not only leads to learned nonassertive behavior, it enhances the individual's feeling of helplessness. Librarians who believe this assume that change is impossible for them.

For example, a library director who has had a difficult childhood, including parental death, undesirable foster homes, and frequent relocations was told in elementary school that she is too impatient, too demanding of others. She learns to get along by decreasing her requests of other people and becoming increasingly self-sufficient. As a staff librarian she shows initiative, creativity, and high productivity. She rarely has to ask for additional time to complete a project and never has to ask a colleague for help. She is praised for her competence and self-sufficiency, just as she had been in childhood, and earns a promotion. Her promotion places her in a supervisory position with several subordinates. When she is criticized for not delegating responsibility and authority, as she overworks herself and underworks her staff, she feels "powerless" to change. She had decided, at an early age, that self-sufficiency was not only desirable, it was necessary. She believes she is incapable of patience (the irrational message she learned from elementary school), so she becomes incapable of waiting for others to perform tasks in the library. She therefore logically assumes all the important or immediate tasks herself. Although she is an adult, working in an environment that is totally different from her childhood milieu, her irrational belief that her past is inescapable and all-powerful leads her to give up the promotion she has earned and seek work where she can work alone with sole responsibility for a small collection.

Irrational Idea Number Ten: You can achieve happiness by inertia and inaction or by passively and uncommitedly "enjoying yourself" (Ellis, 1962, p.85). This is essentially a way of rationalizing a fear of activity. Unfortunately, it tends to increase passive behavior until the person who holds this belief becomes a bored and boring drone. Librarians who believe this find their work soon becomes a dull, routinized pattern in which contact with others is avoided. Their desks become the outer dimensions of their world. They are unable to talk about things unrelated to their work and are seldom stimulated even by anything new in the library. Their responses to changes in the library are first, "will it affect me?" and second, "how can I minimize that effect, so that little or none of my routine must change?"

THE A-B-C-D-E MODEL

In 1973, Ellis extended his A-B-C theory to include two more points, D and E. In this model,

- **A** refers to the **activating event** or stimulation.
- **B** refers to our **thinking process,** the inner dialogue we hold about ourselves, the other person, and the event or situation.
- **C** refers to the **feelings** and **behaviors** we base on point B.
- **D** refers to the **identification of the irrational beliefs** that are affecting points B and C.
- **E** refers to **the identification of rational ideas** that can be substituted for the irrational ideas.

At point D, there are two definitions that help in identifying irrational beliefs. It is *rational* to think that an event is unfortunate or inconvenient and to feel sad, frustrated, or irritated. It is *irrational* to catastrophize, convincing oneself that an event is awful or terrible and to feel destroyed by it. Absolute thinking is the hallmark of irrationality: "I *must* be accepted, *must* succeed, *must* be treated fairly. It will be absolutely awful if I am not." Once the irrational ideas can be verbalized, they can be disputed. Just as you ask yourself "So what, if..." in working out a fear of consequences, in fighting irrational beliefs you ask yourself similar realistic questions. For example:

- What would be so awful about asking that question ineffectively?
- How could that person's rejection destroy me?
- What if I don't get this raise?
- How would my boss' displeasure be terrible?

The answers to the questions posed at point D lead directly to point E, where rational ideas can be substituted for irrational ones. When the answers to the questions at point D are undesirable or negative, you can rationally think that *it would be better if things were different,* in place of thinking irrationally that things *ought to be* different. For example:

1. If I ask the question ineffectively, people may not understand me. But they can ask me questions, or I can take special care to notice if they seem to be following my thought and expand on my idea accordingly. Of course, I would rather ask the question effectively, but I know that sometimes I don't.
2. I don't want to be rejected by that person. But if I am, I can handle it. It will be inconvenient, it will probably hurt, I may feel lonely for a while, but I will find other friends.
3. If I don't get the raise I am requesting, I will not be able to do some of the costly things I was hoping to do. I can look for another job that pays more money, or I can look for ways to economize so that I can do some of those special things I want. Even so, I may not have enough money for the things I want. If that's the case, I'll just have to wait a little longer.
4. If my boss gets angry with me, I may have to endure some criticism or some undesirable tasks, but it won't be the end of the world. S/he can only affect my life at work and will only keep on affecting it here if I choose to stay in this job. I can tolerate whatever displeasure comes my way.

Ten Irrational Beliefs Revisited

The substitution of rational ideas for irrational ideas can be most effectively illustrated by briefly revisiting each of Ellis's 10 irrational beliefs once again. This time, however, the focus will be on rational statements that can be substituted for the irrational statements. A list of general rational beliefs, developed by Lange and Jakubowski (1976), which can be substituted for irrational ideas, has been adapted here for more applicability to the library environment. Rational substitutions which may be useful for assertive librarians follow each irrational statement.

Irrational Idea Number One: You must—yes, must—have sincere love and approval almost all the time from all the people you find significant.

1. It would be nice to be approved by my colleagues; I would like that very much. But I don't *need* that approval.
2. If I am not approved by a colleague whose good opinion I desire and respect, I can try to find out what it is that person doesn't like about *my behavior* (not about *me*) and then I can decide whether that behavior is something I want to change. If I believe strongly that my behavior is appropriate and I do not want to change it, I can handle having it disapproved of.
3. If I am not approved of, and I find this disapproval is not based on any inappropriate behavior on my part, and it appears this disapproval will inhibit a good relationship with that person, I can find other people whose company I can enjoy.
4. I am able to rationally decide for myself what I want to do and need not adapt myself to be what I think others want me to be.
5. If my boss disapproves of my work, and I rationally assess that I have a need to improve, I can ask for suggestions on how to improve. If I believe my work has been appraised unfairly, I can ask for a reappraisal and state my reasons for the request.

Irrational Idea Number Two: You must prove yourself thoroughly competent, adequate, and achieving, or you must at least have real competence or talent at something important.

1. I would like to be perfect or best at the professional tasks assigned to me, but I don't *need* to be.
2. I can be successful even when I do some things imperfectly.
3. In much of my work, there is no such thing as perfection. I am content when I have accomplished a task effectively, or when the person who has requested service is satisfied with the results I have obtained.
4. I may be happier when I am more successful and obtain tangible rewards of that success but level of success does not determine my worth as a librarian unless I let it.
5. I will be happier if I attempt to achieve at a realistic level rather than at a perfect level. Perfection is not possible, and there is no point in allowing myself to feel frustrated by

attempting the impossible. When I demand the impossibility of perfection from myself, I will always be pushing myself or worrying too much over mistakes. If I relax and accept a few mistakes, I will not only be happier, I will actually work better because I work better when I am relaxed.

6. I do have a desire to be a successful librarian, and if I am, I will likely be happier than if I am not very successful. If I am not very successful, I may be a little unhappy, but I need not be depressed or miserable.

Irrational Idea Number Three: You have to view life as awful, terrible, horrible, or catastrophic when things do not go the way you would like them to go.

1. This has really been a bad day so far. Well, I can't go back to this morning and start over, so I will just set the past few hours aside and begin making plans to make the rest of the day as pleasant and productive as I can.

2. I don't like the situation here at work. What can I do to change it? If there isn't anything I can do, I will accept it as somewhat frustrating and look for ways to accomplish my tasks in spite of the limitations I feel. If there seems to be something I can do to change the situation, I will try it.

3. My colleague treated me badly, and I am unhappy about it. I feel hurt, but I will get over it. It's not the end of the world. I will let the incident settle, and then I will talk it over calmly and rationally with her/him. It won't do either of us any good to tell everyone else all about it while I am feeling so upset.

Irrational Idea Number Four: People who harm you or commit misdeeds rate as generally bad, wicked, or villainous individuals and you should severely blame, damn, and punish them for their sins.

1. I am capable of directly telling the people I work with that their behavior has had unpleasant consequences for me; I don't have to berate them. I am assertive, not aggressive.

2. Even when I believe someone is very wrong, or has done something very wrong, and I am the boss, it is more appropriate for me to try to correct the misdeed and help that person avoid it in the future than to "punish" the person as if s/he is a bad child.

3. If I do have to apply disciplinary sanctions in my role as a supervisor, I can recognize that the person is capable of

correcting her/his wrong actions, and that everyone makes mistakes.

4. If I need to terminate someone "for cause" I can do it without violating her/his personal rights. I can specify the reasons for termination in behavioral terms, identifying wrongful *behaviors,* without labeling the *person* as a failure, or bad, or unprofessional.

5. When I try to punish someone I use a lot of my energy, and the punishment seldom results in correction. It would be better to use my energy in a more constructive way.

6. When a group that has been questioning certain acquisitions has a very specific focus, and I strongly disagree with their view, and they have questioned my competency and harmed my reputation, I have cause to feel very unhappy with the public attacks they have launched against me. Even though I think they are behaving badly, they have rights to their opinions. I can present my viewpoint rationally and clearly. Attacking them, calling them names, or accusing them of censorship is unnecessary and inappropriate.

Irrational Idea Number Five: If something seems dangerous or fearsome, you must become terribly occupied with and upset about it.

1. If I am not as good at presenting my ideas as I would like to be, I can handle it. The important thing is that I am heard, not that I am admired for my great oratorical skill.

2. An influential patron may go over my head to complain about library services about which we have different views. I cannot prevent this situation from happening by worrying about it, but I can try to anticipate problems resulting from the worst and prepare myself to meet them. Worry can be time-consuming and unproductive, so I will use it as a catalyst to spur me into constructive thinking and problem solving instead of worrying in a generalized and destructive way.

3. The probability is that the situation will be better than I think, not worse. Even if it is worse, I won't crumble. I will probably be uncomfortable, but I will survive.

4. I know that I decrease my personal resources when I worry excessively, so it is better for me to relax until I *must* face this problem. If necessary, I can think of diversions: absorbing tasks, reading, lunch with a special friend, a short walk outdoors, or other things that will help me keep my mind off the problem.

Irrational Idea Number Six: People and things should turn out better than they do and you have to view it as awful and horrible if you do not quickly find good solutions to life's hassles.

1. There are a lot of pressures on me right now. I have some things to do at home that take a lot of time. I am taking two tough classes toward a second master's, and I have exams in both classes this week. I have to work this weekend because of the illnesses of other people, and this morning the director added two special projects to my list of things to do. I cannot do everything this week that my family, teachers, and library director have asked for unless I do them poorly or ineffectively. I will assess my priorities and assertively communicate my limitations to the appropriate people so that I can accomplish some of these things successfully.

2. I feel depressed and angry when a lot is demanded of me and I feel helpless to refuse. I do not need to overreact in this way. I will say no to requests that I cannot fill, and if others are unhappy about my refusal, I will remember that saying yes may satisfy them but would give me cause to overreact and be firm in my refusal. I will just accept these realities and do the best I can.

3. It would be wonderful if things always went exactly the way I would like them to, but that is unrealistic. Sometimes things will go wrong for me. That is inconvenient but not awful. I can handle it.

Irrational Idea Number Seven: Emotional misery comes from external pressures and you have little ability to control your feelings or rid yourself of depression and hostility.

1. I *can* stand it when things go wrong. I always have an assertive choice to consider. I can choose to stand it if I want to, or I can choose to seek an alternative action for myself. I am not limited to an uncontrolled and uncontrollable emotional reaction when things go wrong.

2. I have quite a bit of control over how I react to certain situations. I am not willing to give that control over to someone else. No one can make me mad unless I choose to be angry.

3. Other people also have control of their reactions. I am not interested in manipulating anyone else's emotions, and I know that I do not have to take responsibility for their emotions,

even though I may agree that I have given them what they consider just cause to feel a certain way.

Irrational Idea Number Eight: You will find it easier to avoid facing many of life's difficulties and self-responsibilities than to undertake more rewarding forms of self-discipline.

1. It is difficult to discipline myself to control my emotions, but I can do it. It is worth it to try, because even though I feel a certain amount of relief when I avoid unpleasantness or let off steam by yelling, I feel dissatisfied with myself, and that is frustrating.

2. Each time I avoid facing an unpleasant situation or act aggressively when a minor irritation arises, I risk having the same situation happen again because I haven't taken any steps to try to resolve it.

3. Each time I practice self-discipline and take a positive action to face an unpleasant situation and resolve it, I strengthen my abilities to continue to act this way. In the long run, my relationships with other people will be enhanced.

Irrational Idea Number Nine: Your past remains all-important and because something once strongly influenced your life, it has to keep determining your feelings and behavior today.

1. My past experiences have some influence on my activities today, but I can change the way I behave, based on a realistic, cognitive assessment of myself. I am not stuck with behaviors that are no longer effective for me. When I have made mistakes in my job in the past, I learned from them. I can learn from past habits just as I have learned from past mistakes. I can review the habitual behavior I used, the consequences that resulted, and determine whether that behavior was effective for me or whether I should seek an alternative.

2. When I decide I need to change the way I act, people may not recognize that change right away, or they may not appear to believe it. I will remember that I can change if I want to, and not allow nonrecognition or skepticism from others to affect my attempts to change.

Irrational Idea Number Ten: You can achieve happiness by inertia and inaction or by passively and uncommitedly enjoying yourself.

1. I may be able to avoid some unhappiness by staying safely within a defined routine and a limited world, but I may lose many, many chances for greater happiness or pleasure by not meeting new people, listening to new ideas, or exposing myself to new situations.

SUMMARY

In his A-B-C theory, Ellis suggests that self-defeating and maladaptive behaviors and emotions stem from irrational beliefs. These irrational ideas are distorted, highly idealized, and perfectionistic, and they stimulate people to strive for impossible goals. These goals ensure failure since they are impossible to achieve and then encourage emotional overreactions to such "failures" (Alden & Safran, 1978). Ellis recommends cognitive restructuring—a means of changing the internal reference system of irrational beliefs—rather than changes in external forces to bring about appropriately assertive behaviors (Hung, Rosenthal & Kelley, 1980). This restructuring is accomplished by the substitution of rational ideas and beliefs for irrational ideas and beliefs, which then leads to more favorable emotional and behavioral outcomes (Schmidt, 1976).

Chapter 8
Coping

Every day librarians deal with conflicting demands from library users, colleagues, subordinates, supervisors, external authorities, and legislation of various types. Concerns for quality of library services, measurement of services, fluctuating patterns of user demands, and available financial support for collection development and its effect on services are continuous. Frustrations from chain of command delays, budget cuts, staff cuts, deadlines, and problem patrons can appear endless. Mandates of library boards, library committees, union contracts, affirmative action and equal employment opportunity rulings sometimes seem devilishly devised to destroy both short-term and long-term library goals. The result is job stress and, in severe situations, burnout.

Although much of their serious text on stress is of value, Morse and Furst (1982) are completely out of touch with the reality of library work when they state,

> The major stressor from being a librarian is the silence of libraries. Two other potential stressors are the necessity for evening and weekend work and the stiff competition for positions (p. 301).

Major stressors for librarians include professional role ambiguity, conflict, overload, anxiety, frustration, isolationism, rapidity of technological changes, legal proceedings, abusive library users, external controversy about the role of the library, internal controversy about the role of the library, the question of intellectual freedom and censorship, financial concerns, and a wide variety of management concerns (Albright, 1979; Anderson, 1974; Bailey, 1981; Biggs, 1981; Caputo, 1981; Cottam, 1970; Ferriero & Powers, 1982; Galvin, 1971; Groark, 1979; Hickey, 1972; Huber, 1981; Lowell, 1975; Prostano & Prostano, 1982; Steinmetz, 1981; Van Vliet, 1980). Librarians of the current decade are also victims of what has been described as an ancient Chinese curse: "living through interesting times."

Librarians are beset by all of the four types of stress recognized by Lyon (1980):

- Time stress: too much to do in too little time.
- Anticipatory stress: worry over problems that can be foreseen.
- Situational stress: worry over unforeseen events as they occur.
- Encounter stress: worry over interpersonal problems.

Like other people in other occupations, many librarians have learned to manage stresses by using defense mechanisms. Defense mechanisms work, but they are self-destructive over long periods of time, and thus the assertive philosophy recommends replacement of defense mechanisms with coping mechanisms, which are self-constructive rather than destructive.

This chapter will include a detailed review of defense mechanisms and coping mechanisms, with emphasis on adaptive ways to cope with stress. Ways to identify stresses will be reviewed, followed by recommendations of specific ways to cope with anger, feelings of guilt, and resentment over criticism. The chapter will conclude with descriptions of a variety of relaxation techniques.

DEFENSE MECHANISMS AND COPING MECHANISMS

The term "defense mechanism" was introduced by Freud in 1894 and was explicitly defined and expanded in 1936 by his daughter, Anna Freud (Wolman, 1973). Coping mechanisms are freely discussed in the current literature of psychology and assertiveness, but they are not as well-documented historically. Simple definitions of both terms reveal that they have the same function: they serve to reduce the level of anxiety that conflicts tend to produce. Both are successful in this primary goal, but there are two major differences between them. The first difference is in their effect on self-esteem: Defense mechanisms decrease self-esteem; coping mechanisms increase it. The second difference is their time frame. Defense mechanisms are long-term measures that effectively mask short-term anxieties as they build up long-term consequences within the individual. Coping mechanisms are temporary tension-releasing behaviors that do not mask the cause of anxiety but allow us time and space to step away from it so that we can return, refreshed, to face it anew. In 1965, Haan noted that "Coping is flexible, purposive, reality oriented, and differentiated whereas ego defenses are rigid, compelled, reality distorting, and undifferentiated" (Tanck & Robbins, 1979, p. 396).

This section will describe five commonly used defense mechanisms and the ways in which librarians use them. A review of seven commonly employed coping mechanisms will follow, with special emphasis on the most constructive coping mechanisms—talking things out and working things out. Assertive people try to replace defense mechanisms with coping mechanisms to reduce anxiety in ways that will increase self-confidence and self-esteem.

Defense Mechanisms

Defense mechanisms are essentially self-protective devices that we use to defend ourselves against psychological attack by others or by ourselves (McMahon & McMahon, 1982). Five commonly used defense mechanisms are avoidance, repression/suppression, projection, regression, and rationalization. These are habitual and tend to reoccur without conscious thought whenever our anxiety level is high. They are ritualistic, "cookbook" techniques that discourage spontaneity and free expression (Myers & Myers, 1982). We can easily feel the overt and immediate relief that follows the invocation of a defense mechanism, and this factor serves to make them highly resistant to change. In the short term, defense mechanisms work wonderfully well. They significantly reduce our anxieties—our primary short-term goal. Their deleterious long-term effects are less easy to discern, and we can remain unaware of their sabotage to our self-esteem and their disruption of our interpersonal relationships.

Avoidance is the defense mechanism that allows us to escape from or postpone unpleasantness. It minimizes the risk of rejection, embarrassment, or disapproval by counseling inaction or incomplete action. Avoidance always involves a sacrifice of some sort, which is irrationally weighed as less costly than the possible risks involved in taking action (Getter & Nowinski, 1981). (See Chapter 7 for a discussion of the irrational beliefs that often lead to avoidance and other defense mechanisms.) In the library environment, avoidance is translated into these kinds of inactions:

1. Not speaking up in meetings.
2. Spending a disproportionate amount of time on former kinds of assignments to avoid tackling new responsibilities.
3. Dealing only with problems we are confident we can solve rather than tackling critical issues.
4. Postponing a new activity until the deadline for participation has passed.
5. Interrupting or distracting a conversation that is headed toward a topic we consider dangerous.

The major disadvantages of avoidance behavior are inherent in the kinds of sacrifices made in order to preserve the feelings of safety and security which avoidance behavior seeks to preserve. For example, not speaking up in a meeting may mean that a change you want to consider never gets aired and thus has no chance of happening, or that you tacitly agree to an assignment that is undesirable or beyond your capabilities to complete, or that others get the satisfaction (and credit) of presenting your ideas.

Repression and suppression are defenses that protect us from motives or feelings we believe are inappropriate or undesirable. Repression is the unconscious burial of that feeling or desire, while suppression is the conscious burial of it. Both have the same effect: they keep these thoughts and feelings from our conscious awareness (Wolman, 1973). Examples of the kinds of feelings and intentions we are likely to bury through repression or suppression are:

1. Anger toward a library user.
2. Hostility toward a colleague.
3. Disgust or amusement over the topic a patron wants us to look up.
4. Resentment of justified criticism.
5. Happiness over another person's lack of success.
6. Desire for revenge.

Regular use of repression and suppression decreases our ability to deal with stress and conflict and increases the probability of physical illness (Weinberger, Schwartz & Davidson, 1979). When we repress or suppress the feelings that are generally considered socially unacceptable or that we believe do not fit our idealized conception of a professional librarian, we risk redirection of those feelings into inappropriate channels. Librarians who suppress anger toward a colleague may express it by turning it inward on themselves, becoming depressed. They may express it indirectly toward the colleague who had been the initial target by neglecting to relay some vital information, or they may express it outwardly toward innocent bystanders, either other members of the library staff, library users, or other people with whom the librarian interacts.

Projection is the defense mechanism that allows us to attribute the sins of our own worst faults, attitudes, and behaviors to other people. Although our consciences are always ready to tell us when we are not living up to our ego-ideals, it is difficult to live with the knowledge that we fall short of our own goals. Sometimes, instead of experiencing a conscious decrease in self-esteem that spurs us to some sort of behavior change, we counteract the felt decrease in self-esteem by discovering our own faults in other people (Levinson, 1968). Examples of projection are:

1. Being aggressive toward a colleague and justifying it by saying "I'm not the one who is hostile, s/he is hostile. Therefore I am perfectly right in being hostile and aggressive in return."
2. Feeling anxious or guilty over something and then attributing blame to the environment: "I'm not to blame for that. The circumstances demanded that I behave that way."
3. Being angry at a colleague and believing that s/he is angry at us to justify our negative feeling: "Of course I'm mad about that. If she hadn't gotten mad at me, I would have been able to keep my cool."
4. When being criticized or terminated for incompetence, projecting that assessment of professional inability onto those who have criticized or fired us: "The only reason they fired me is because *they're* incompetent. I was doing just fine before they came along."

McMahon and McMahon (1982) note that projection seems to be the weakest of the defense mechanisms in terms of its ability to reduce anxieties. It doesn't serve to make us less aware of the problem situation, and it doesn't reduce our stress over it. In fact, it may help focus the stress and thus enhance it.

Chalus (1978) notes that attributive projection occurs whenever we attribute to others the same personality trait or momentary feelings that we consciously possess and that this mechanism is most often employed for traits or feelings we see as undesirable. Projection can occur with positive traits as well, however, as when we feel particularly good about something and attribute any positive actions of other people to the same source: "This is such a beautiful day, I feel like singing. S/he must feel that way, too, to have given me that big smile."

Regression is a defense mechanism that allows us to reduce anxiety by returning to the satisfaction of lower level needs. Classic definitions include the idea that regression is a step backward in time to childhood, a return to less mature behaviors, caused by a wish to return to a time when life was easier and anxieties were significantly less (McMahon & McMahon, 1982). For a librarian, regression may take the form of spending time on low-level library routines in place of the higher level tasks that are anxiety provoking. Some lower level tasks that might be selected by librarians as a means of avoiding or postponing greater responsibilities include:

1. Reorganizing office furniture.
2. Sorting materials to be shelved.
3. Shelving materials.
4. Filing catalog cards.
5. Filing other materials.
6. Cleaning out files.

This is not meant to imply that doing these tasks is always a sign of regression, as we all know that there are times when the low-level routines of a library must take precedence or nothing will be available or accessible to library users and that librarians are sometimes the only staff available to perform them. But when these tasks are not immediately necessary and an anxiety-provoking higher level task is a priority, then time spent in these ways is indicative of regression.

Rationalization is perhaps the most frequently used defense mechanism. We have all found ourselves inventing excuses to justify our behavior or to explain away frustrations. Rationalization is an effort to distort reality in order to protect our self-esteem. Typical rationalizations include (1) the sour grapes type, which suggests that we wouldn't have gained any satisfaction out of succeeding because we don't want to admit we failed; (2) the type that makes us merely victims of circumstances beyond our control (Wolman, 1973); and (3) a don't rock the boat type, which allows us to explain nonaction in justifiable terms. These rationalization statements may look like this:

1. *Sour grapes:* I wouldn't have liked that assignment anyway, even if I had gotten it.
2. *Victim of circumstances:* I got that lousy performance review because I don't play tennis with the boss.
3. *Don't rock the boat:* I don't dare disagree with my boss; it's better to just leave things the way they are.

Rationalization allows us to avoid taking responsibility for the consequences of our behavior and also allows us to avoid the knowledge that not all desirable things are attainable.

Coping Mechanisms

All the defense mechanisms have some effectiveness for us, and many have become so ingrained that they are difficult to limit and impossible to eliminate. Their long-term effects are so deleterious, however, that limiting them is highly recommended. Unfortunately, when we limit the use of defense mechanisms, we experience an immediate increase in anxiety, so we need to find other effective means of reducing anxiety—means that will not serve to bring long-term undesirable consequences. The means that psychologists have found to replace defense mechanisms are short-term behaviors, called coping mechanisms, that can be used until tension decreases and can then be discontinued until they are needed again.

Successful coping with stressful situations, people, or tasks has four major components (Jacobson & McGrath, 1983):

1. Tolerating or relieving the felt distress.
2. Maintaining a sense of personal worth.
3. Maintaining rewarding interpersonal relationships.
4. Meeting the requirements of the situation or task.

Coping mechanisms can include almost any behavior that can be started and stopped at will, that can be (although may not always be) of limited duration, and that we find relaxing. Coping mechanisms are incredibly numerous but commonly fall into seven major categories. These are: (1) oral behaviors, (2) tranquilizers, (3) sleeping, (4) talking things out, (5) working things out, (6) pointless activity, and (7) retreating. Numbers four and five, talking things out and working things out, are of special importance because they are both highly effective and likely to increase self-esteem. The others can be effective, but they can also become maladaptive and have harmful effects for us. They are not likely to increase self-esteem, and if they become maladaptive, they may actually generate new stresses. They are also often inappropriate for use in a work environment.

Oral Behaviors. These include eating, drinking nonalcoholic beverages, smoking, and chewing gum or other materials. The most obvious risk in this coping mechanism is the effect it has on your health. Excessive eating or snacking can of course result in nutrition problems such as vitamin deficiencies and metabolic disorders or in obesity. Drinking coffee or other stimulants may decrease the situational tension but increase physiological tension. Smoking not only harms the smoker's health but may also affect others who work nearby. Chewing things at work is often perceived as inappropriate professional behavior. Oral behaviors are difficult to eliminate and are prone to overuse.

Tranquilizers. Those preparations commonly thought of as tranquilizers, such as medications, alcohol, and other substances that affect the senses are included, but tranquilizers can also be diversions such as television, reading, and listening to music, which allow you to selectively dull certain senses. The oral behaviors discussed above may also serve as tranquilizing agents. This coping mechanism is perhaps the one most likely to become maladaptive. Although medications may be prescribed as a method of reducing tension, their long-term use can become detrimental in that they may become habitual, they are prone to misuse and abuse, they may have physical side effects, and they do not encourage the individual to learn self-generated behavioral controls. The use of alcoholic beverages and unprescribed drugs is equally dangerous and carries the same risks. Moreover, most library environments do not allow excessive use of these types of tranquilizing agents.

Diversionary tranquilizers can be highly effective as adaptive coping mechanisms, but they, too, can be used in excess. Reading an enjoyable book during lunch may help you get back to your desk ready for anything, but it may also cause you to become too engrossed to ever come back from lunch at all. Diversions that take you out of the building for short periods are useful. If the library is located near a cultural center, lunch hours can be spent in museums, at concerts, at special exhibits, or at lectures. If you are in a more rural area, a nature walk might be a possibility.

Sleeping. As a coping mechanism, sleeping includes short naps, earlier bedtimes, and later rising from sleep. Excessive sleep can be an overt expression of the defense mechanism of avoidance. Planned periods of additional sleep can be refreshing and very useful as a coping mechanism. They are often difficult to work into a library work day, however. A place to nap and an ability to limit interruptions are necessary for the use of sleeping as a coping mechanism in the midst of the work day, while the flexibility to start work a little later sometimes is required to indulge in rising later than usual as a coping mechanism.

Talking Things Out. This is defined as discussing problems with a sympathetic listener, and it is a highly recommended and highly adaptive coping mechanism. You may choose a listener who is familiar with your environment and the people with whom you interact, or one who is not, but the listeners you choose should be people who can listen actively and objectively, providing an opportunity for you to verbally analyze the situation and decrease tension through the act of verbalization as well as providing you with valuable feedback.

In talking things out, you may choose to reappraise the situation, trying to reduce your anxiety by reinterpreting it in ways that are more adaptive for you. There are a number of effective ways to do this:

1. Reduce the importance of the situation by comparing and contrasting it with other possibilities. Phrases like ''At least

it's only..." and "It could have been..." are helpful in trying to do this.

2. Modify your expectations of both yourself and other people. When expectations are reduced from an idealistic level to a realistic level, tensions also decrease.

3. Convert what you see as a threat into a challenge. Instead of worrying that you'll never catch on to the new computer system, tell yourself that learning all about it is an opportunity to catch up to what the new generation of children are learning.

4. Convert unrealistic threats into nonthreats. Instead of worrying about losing your unique identity, tell yourself that creating another search analyst position will take a lot of the pressure off you and allow you to share the workload.

5. Look for the positive side in every situation. Instead of moaning over an unavoidable boring meeting, tell yourself that you will have an exceptionally good opportunity to observe body language messages.

6. Find something humorous in the situation. Remember how your New York background led you to the belief that choosing the right tie or shoes and suit for that rural southwest interview would make all the difference in the world, only to find when you arrived for it that the personnel manager, library director, and all the staff members routinely wore denim and western boots.

7. Look for ways others can help you. Approaching an anxious situation in the company of others is often much more comfortable than facing it alone. Perhaps a team approach is best for your particular situation.

Talking things out also serves as an opportunity to rehearse assertive strategies you think will help you resolve the situation when you return to it again. For this, you will probably need a listener who knows your environment well, knows the people you will be interacting with, and is discreet. You can practice using I-statements to state what you want or need, assess whether you want to include any expressions of feeling, design actual scripts, plan possible alternative strategies, try out humorous remarks or jokes, and seek new information about the situation.

Socialization is an important aspect of talking things out. A chance to get away from library users or from the co-workers with whom you have constant contact is very relaxing. Exchanging pleasantries with the people you normally see little of during your day helps build better relationships and gives you a place to voice frustrations that may hit too close to home with other people.

The special good in talking things out is the opportunity it gives you to air your concerns in a nonthreatening environment. Even if you feel you could not be truly open with a colleague about your mutual environment, you can find other people to listen to your concerns. Librarians in other libraries are an excellent resource. They are sympathetic to your professional concerns, can understand what you say without your having to define library terms, and may have had a similar experience in their own organization. In special libraries, managers in other departments can be good resources. They may not understand all the library terms you could wish, but they can relate to the same environmental concerns. Spouses, close friends, children, and relatives can all serve as listeners. Although talking with others is more effective and also more adaptive, since it is less likely to allow misperceptions to exist, in the infrequent times that you feel there is no one who could serve as a good listener for you, you may choose to talk things out with yourself, perhaps in writing a journal or diary or by holding a mental (or oral) conversation with yourself.

Working Things Out. Any physical activity that helps you release tension is included here. If you are a highly active person, this may be a relatively strenuous activity:

- Jogging or brisk walking.
- Tennis, raquetball, baseball, football, and other sports.
- Exercise routines, aerobics, or lifting weights.
- Shifting, sorting, or packing books.
- Dancing.

It can also be something that is less strenuous physically but which requires significant concentration:

- Playing card games or chess.
- Writing short stories.
- Playing a musical instrument or singing.
- Doing needlework or whittling toys.
- Working on jigsaw puzzles.

Regardless of the strenuousness of the activity, working things out is a way to do something that you enjoy and that uses some energy.

Many of the same activities that were noted earlier as regressive can be used as ways to work off energy—for example, engaging in low-level library routines like shelving. The difference is that, as *coping mechanisms,* these tasks are consciously performed for a period of time in order to work off some tension before resuming the anxiety-provoking task or situation. As *defense mechanisms,* they are performed as a means of avoiding and ignoring the anxiety-provoking task or situation in the hope that it will go away or be taken over by someone else.

Finally, the time spent in working things out may be used to think through the difficulty. This may be a conscious activity, as when running clears your head and you feel ready to reorganize your thoughts and explore new alternatives, or it may be an unconscious activity, as when you put the situation entirely out of your thoughts and discover, when you return to it an hour later, that a solution has miraculously appeared in the front of your mind.

Pointless Activities. These can also include many different actions that work off energy, but they are characterized by their nonproductive nature. Pointless activities are also usually extremely brief and may increase tension in the environment if they are performed in the presence of others. Examples of pointless overactivities are:

- Drumming your fingers on the desk.
- Pacing.
- Swinging a foot or leg.
- Twisting a piece of hair around your finger.

Retreat. Retreat can be either mental or physical. Mental retreats include fantasizing, indulging in daydreams, and selective inattention. These can be used in a variety of ways. If a particular person causes you to feel anxiety and thus inhibits your ability to behave assertively, a daydream of that person getting caught in a sudden cloudburst may amuse you, which then relaxes you, which then allows you to resume assertive behavior. Daydreams that are highly aggressive, however, such as imagining that person being run down by a car, are not likely to help you reduce tension. It is important to find a fantasy that allows you to reduce your current anxieties without building up others, such as guilt over fantasizing real harm to someone else.

Guided fantasy is a technique that therapists use to help people eliminate physiological symptoms of anxiety like sweating, blushing, and trembling. It works in a relatively simple way: If speaking in public usually results in your feeling shaky, you use a simple relaxation technique that allows you to rest comfortably in a place where you will be uninterrupted, and then imagine yourself in front of an audience of several hundred, speaking calmly and effectively, and feeling a great sense of satisfaction from your performance. After practicing repeatedly, when you must face an audience, you consciously recall the sense of satisfaction that you felt and the calm manner you used in your imagination to guide you through the actual experience (Montgomery & Heimberg, 1978).

Selective inattention is a way to retreat mentally without imagery. When a topic is causing anxiety, refocusing your gaze to a window or picture and allowing your mind to wander for a moment or two can help to reduce anxiety. Limiting the number of hours you will spend on a particular activity is another form of mental retreat that can lessen anxiety.

A physical retreat consists of actually leaving the environment in which the anxieties are being felt. Leaving your own office or the office of someone else, taking a brief walk, getting up for a drink of water (cup of coffee, etc.), or making a trip to the restroom are acceptable physical retreats in the library environment. Changing parts of your work schedule can also provide a physical retreat: instead of working at the reference desk both in the morning and afternoon on a day that has so far brought three troublesome patrons, two unscheduled school classes, and a stray dog to your attention, switch your afternoon assignment with the librarian who has had it with fighting the computer terminal all morning. Coffee break times and lunch or dinner hours, whether used to forage food and drink or used as a rest period, are very important. Whether your work break is scheduled to occur at an exact time every day, regardless of whether it is precisely timed to last an exact 10 or 15 minutes as prescribed by the rules of the organization, it is important that a concentration break occur every few hours. Attempts to continue concentration for more than a few hours are less effective than two bouts of concentration with a relaxation period separating them.

Like assertive disengagement, mental and physical retreats need not be lengthy to be effective. When more lengthy retreats are necessary, some possibilities are going home early, calling in sick for a day, or choosing to attend a meeting you had not planned to attend. Just as taking breaks and lunch or dinner hours is important, it is also important to take vacation time away from work. Long weekends or one-day mini-vacations in the midst of otherwise busy times are invaluable for refreshing your outlook. Busy librarians, librarians who work alone in special or small public libraries, and librarians who are working in unusually short staffed environments are often tempted not to take long vacations, as the work that piles up in their absence can make the vacation seem less than worthwhile upon their return. If this description fits you, remind yourself that there are myriad alternative solutions to every situation. For instance, if you are located near a library school, you may be able to find a graduate student who would enjoy spending a few volunteer hours in your library each week to check in journals and sort your mail into "immediate" and "to be reviewed later" piles while you are gone in return for some reality training, independent study supervision, or a future reference. In a special library, your administrator's secretary could be assigned to sort your mail until you return. Graduate librarians in the community who have chosen to be employed less than full time, or not at all, may be interested in a temporary assignment now and then to keep their skills fresh, and you may be able to convince your organization to pay them at the same rate other temporary employees are paid. Vacation time is important enough to be a priority for you, and it should not be a punishing experience to return to work following vacation. Be creative in your assertive requests to meet your vacation needs.

The Coping Continuum

Coping mechanisms, like assertive behavior, can be thought of in terms of a continuum. At one end of the coping continuum are maladaptive coping responses, while at the other end are adaptive coping mechanisms. Adaptive coping mechanisms are those that achieve the desired end of reducing your anxiety without decreasing your self-esteem. Highly adaptive coping mechanisms are those that not only keep you from reducing self-esteem but in fact are able to increase it. Adaptive coping also generates learning that can be generalized to later situations (Jacobson & McGrath, 1983).

Ferriero and Powers (1982) recommend the use of effective coping mechanisms to combat librarian burnout, the extreme physical and mental disability that continuous stress can produce in practitioners of the helping professions.

IDENTIFYING STRESS

One of the reasons we frequently rely on defense mechanisms to combat stress is because we don't recognize the fact that we are stressed until very late, usually after the defense mechanisms have already been triggered. The only way we can hope to replace defense mechanisms with adaptive coping mechanisms is to learn to recognize the signals of coming stress much earlier.

Physical stress occurs when you are engaged in unusual and excessive exertion, and it is easy to identify because this extra exertion is overt. Psychological stress, on the other hand, is concerned with foreseeing or imagining an emergency situation and is not always intellectually overt. You can, and frequently do, experience psychological stress subconsciously before you become consciously aware of feeling stressed. Psychological stress, however, has physiological effects on the human organism, and you can train yourself to become aware of these physiological changes as a means of identifying psychological stress in its early stages (Humphrey, 1982).

Intrapersonal Feedback

We will focus our attention on six particular kinds of inner or intrapersonal feedback: posture, muscle tension, sleep, the use of tranquilizers, emotional changes, and general physiological changes. Each person is unique, so it is unlikely that you will experience all of these signs of stress; you will have to note those that seem to pertain especially to you by recalling past stresses or observing yourself in stress situations in the near future. Once you have identified them as signs of your own stress, however, you can be on guard to watch for them well in advance of triggering a defense mechanism, which will allow you to employ a coping mechanism instead. References that were especially useful in compiling the following information were Apgar and Callahan (1982), Huber (1981), Humphrey (1982), and Jacobson and McGrath (1983). The information from these sources was supplemented and complemented by discussions held as part of the assertion training sessions offered to librarians by the Medical Library Association and Special Libraries Association since 1981.

Posture. Sudden postural changes often indicate the beginnings of stress. Signs to watch for include:

1. Inability to sit quietly in a chair for more than a few minutes.
2. Inability to lie quietly or to rest.
3. Hyperactivity expressed in moving restlessly about a room.
4. A sudden move to sit up straighter when in the presence of another person or a group.
5. Squirming in your seat while in the presence of another person or a group.

6. A sudden move to lean forward or backward, toward or away from the person (people) with whom you are conversing.

Working off your building energy may be the most adaptive coping mechanism for these signs of stress, but if you are currently engaged in discussion with others it can be difficult to disengage long enough to work things out. You may then choose to temporarily employ other coping mechanisms, including (1) the use of a tranquilizing agent, such as paying attention to background music, reading the papers handed out at a meeting, or even taking medication; (2) pointless activity such as swinging your foot under the table; (3) retreating physically, either in a minimal sense as in just leaning in the opposite direction or pushing your chair farther from the table, or in a greater sense, as in leaving your seat or leaving the room temporarily; or (4) retreating mentally by selective inattention, window gazing, or assertive disengagement.

Muscle Tension. Increasingly tense muscles are an excellent sign of stress, and they are usually easy to recognize. These are some of the many signs you might observe in yourself:

1. Increase in tension headaches.
2. Trembling, shakiness.
3. Nervous tics.
4. Stuttering and speech difficulties.
5. Clenched teeth or bruxism (unconscious grinding of the teeth).
6. Clenched fists.
7. Increased need to urinate.
8. Pain in the back of the neck and/or shoulders.
9. Pain in the lower back.
10. Tight feeling in the chest.
11. A feeling that your stomach is tied in a knot.
12. Weak knees—a feeling that you cannot stand up.

The best way to immediately deal with muscle tension signs of stress is to learn and employ a relaxation technique. Relaxation itself is not a coping technique useful to temporarily eliminate stress; it is a means of limiting the adverse effects of muscle tension and creating a state in which you can more easily employ a coping mechanism. Depending on your analysis of what has caused this particular stress, you may choose any of the seven coping mechanisms discussed earlier. Tranquilizers in this regard may include prescribed muscle relaxants.

It is important to note that these particular signs of stress may occur at times quite separate from the actual stressful situation. You may find yourself awakening with a sore jaw from grinding your teeth in your sleep, or you may find yourself too wound up to get to sleep although you "should be" tired from the physical activities of the day.

Sleep. Variations in sleeping habits are another excellent indicator of stress. These too, are reasonably easy to identify. Such variations include:

1. Insomnia, when you normally have no difficulty getting to sleep.
2. Falling asleep earlier than usual.
3. Taking catnaps when you normally sleep only at night.
4. Restless sleep when you normally sleep "like a log."
5. Unusually deep or prolonged sleep when you are normally a light sleeper.
6. Oversleeping in spite of normal routines or devices used to awaken you.
7. Waking early and being unable to go back to sleep.
8. Inability to calm your mind for sleep.
9. Disturbed sleep (nightmares, vivid dreams).
10. Reports from others that you "tossed and turned" although you had no recollection of restless sleep.

Like muscle tension, these signs may occur at times quite separate from the stressful situation, although they frequently occur immediately preceding some anticipated stress. Any of the seven coping mechanisms may be useful, depending on the source of stress that you identify. Prescribed medications to aid sleep may be one of the tranquilizing agents used if sleep disturbances are long-term. Working out activities may be particularly strenuous and scheduled late in the day in order to aid sleep. Talking out activities may be employed in a talking-to-yourself session in the middle of the night; it is certainly more productive to spend an hour talking something out with yourself (aloud if you like) than to spend four or five hours sleepless or in disturbed sleep. Retreating may include reading an enjoyable book in place of sleep; again, it is much more productive for you to relax with a book for several hours than to spend those same hours lying anxiously in a darkened room desperately trying to sleep.

The Use of Tranquilizers and Oral Behaviors. Although tranquilizers and oral behaviors of various sorts may be effectively used as coping mechanisms for other signs of stress, changes in the way you use tranquilizers or changes in your oral behaviors are themselves signs of stress. The key word is change, whether that change is an increase or decrease in your normal habits:

1. Increased use of prescribed sedatives.
2. Increased use, or beginning use, of nonprescription drugs and illegal drugs.
3. Increased use of alcoholic beverages.
4. Signs of alcohol or drug addiction.
5. Increased use of stimulants.
6. Increased smoking.
7. Increased appetite.
8. Decreased appetite.

These signs of stress have major adverse effects on human physiology and should be treated by health care professionals as necessary. These signs are also particularly harmful in that they are the ones you are least likely to recognize voluntarily. It is vitally important that you monitor your use of tranquilizing agents and oral behaviors in order to note those times that they cease to be adaptive coping mechanisms and become maladaptive for you. If others indicate any of these signs to you, love yourself enough to investigate the validity of their observations instead of denying them out of hand. If possible, get outside assistance to investigate such observations; don't rely on your own self-analysis. It is much better to be concerned about the possibility of addiction or malnutrition and to seek advice unnecessarily than to need assistance and avoid or ignore that need.

Emotion. Any changes in your usual emotional state or your likely emotional responses to incidents as they occur are signs of stress. These can take a wide variety of forms, and only you, the person who knows you best, can really discern whether the emotions you feel and display are usual for you or not. The signs to watch for include these:

1. General irritability.
2. Hyperexcitation.
3. Depression.
4. Impulsive behaviors generated by emotional instability.
5. Overpowering urges to cry.
6. Increased desires, felt as irresistible, for both mental and physical retreats.
7. Inability to concentrate.
8. Uncontrollable flights of fancy.
9. General disorientation in familiar surroundings.
10. Floating anxiety (a feeling of fear without being able to identify what you are afraid of).
11. Emotional tension and alertness, feeling "keyed up."

12. Loss of memory or inability to remember certain bits of information.
13. Inappropriate laughter.
14. Inappropriate rage.
15. Overreactions, both positive and negative.
16. Unexplained euphoria.

Although some of these signs may be overt enough to be observed by other people who know you reasonably well, they are all signs that should be self-observable. The difficulty will be investigating the cause of the stress because these signs may occur spontaneously at the time of stress, or they may occur immediately before or after a particularly stressful incident, but they may also occur at times when the stimulating stress is not present, imminent, or recent. Appropriate coping mechanisms depend on the identification of your particular stress, but the immediate coping mechanism of first choice is talking things out. This is not only a means of counteracting the unusual feelings you are experiencing, it is an excellent way to investigate their cause. Choice of listener is, as always, important, in that you will need to talk with someone who will respond in nonthreatening, nonjudgmental ways and who will allow you free rein to explore the depth of your feeling as well as its cause. In some cases, a professional therapist may be necessary. Do remember that you may be your own listener, if necessary.

Other Physiological Signs. There are some standard bodily reactions that nearly everyone experiences in times of stress, and these are:

1. A rapid heartbeat (often called "pounding of the heart").
2. Perspiration, particularly of the palms of the hands.
3. Elevated blood pressure.
4. Dilation of the pupils of the eyes.
5. Digestive difficulty.

In addition, there are a number of other physiological signs that some people experience:

6. Dryness of the throat or mouth.
7. Weakness.
8. Dizziness.
9. Higher pitched voice.
10. Loss of voice.
11. Blurred vision or other visual disturbances.

12. Disturbed hearing.
13. Diarrhea.
14. Nausea.
15. Vomiting.
16. Migraine or cluster headache.
17. Dysmenorrhea.
18. Impotence.
19. Loss of body heat, especially in fingers and toes.

We are not always aware of elevated blood pressure or pupillary dilation, but most of the other physiological signs of stress are things that we can discern immediately. Like muscle tension, sleep variation, and emotional changes, physiological signs may occur with stressful events or at a time quite remote from them. The five standard signs of stress are always expected during the stressful event itself, but biofeedback and relaxation techniques can be learned to help control them. The variable physiological signs are more likely to occur at any point in time as well as during the stressful event itself. The most effective coping mechanisms are retreat and talking things out. Retreat may be necessary to reduce or eliminate the physiological disturbance before talking things out can be initiated.

COPING WITH SPECIFIC EMOTIONS

Success as a librarian includes the ability to function effectively and intelligently in situations that are emotionally charged or that stimulate your own emotional responses. Humphrey (1982) defines emotions as inner forces that struggle to control your mind without being aware of or concerned with their effects on your welfare or the welfare of others. He notes six characteristics of emotion that affect our ability to routinely deal with them in a rational manner:

- There are variations in how long emotions last.
- There are variations in the intensity of emotions.
- Emotions are subject to rapid change.
- There are variations in the degree of frequency with which emotions appear.
- There are variations in our responses to emotions.
- The strength of an emotion is subject to change.

Anger, guilt, and resentment over criticism are often the most difficult emotions to handle in the library environment, where overt displays of such feelings may be detrimental to relationships, productivity, effectiveness, and status within the organizational hierarchy. A seven-step process to coping with emotion should be learned so that it can be employed when needed.

The first step in this process is to become *aware* of your emotion. The many signs of stress discussed in the previous section will help you to become aware that you are experiencing something different. Whether your emotion is anger, guilt, or resentment, it will precipitate some signs of stress that you can learn to observe.

The second step is to *identify* the specific emotion you are feeling. Analyze the signs that you observe to discern which specific emotion you are feeling. Although you will frequently know immediately that you are angry, you may mistake guilt for anger if your guilt has produced hostile behavior. Similarly, it is easy to mistake resentment for anger, since anger is a part of the resentful response.

Third, you must *own/accept* this emotion as yours. You have a right to feel any emotion, including those emotions that are considered "negative." You cannot effectively cope with your feelings if you do not admit that you have them and that you alone have chosen to feel that way. Remember, other people cannot "make you" feel anything, they can only give you cause to feel a certain way.

The fourth step is to *analyze* why you feel the way you do. Now is the time to look at the cause of your emotion and determine whether it is just or not. This analysis includes a look at past as well as current situations or experiences, for your feeling can be the result of cumulative incidents as well as a single incident. Be as objective as you can, so that you can determine whether you really have sufficient grounds to be angry or guilty or resentful.

The fifth step is to make a *plan*. If you have determined that your feeling is just, that you have sufficient grounds to justify feeling this way, you should begin making a plan to deal with your feeling in an assertive way. This could be confronting the person with whom you are angry, apologizing to the person you have injured, or actively disagreeing with the person who has criticized you unjustly. Your plan should not include aggressive behaviors at all and should not include nonassertive behaviors unless you feel the risks of potential consequences are too great to take action or that the incident was too trivial to be worth your assertive efforts. In those cases where you have determined that your feeling is not just, that you do not have sufficient grounds to feel the way you do, you should choose an appropriate coping mechanism to help you talk out or work off the feeling.

The sixth step is to *report* to yourself as you implement your plan. This is a vital step in the process. Keep a mental monologue going to monitor your progress as you take action. Tell yourself that you made your assertive statement just as you wanted to, that you feel better for having apologized, that you have made an effective presentation of why you disagree with that criticism, or that you are successfully ridding yourself of unjustified or inappropriate feelings. Reporting success is a way to reinforce your ability to handle emotion constructively, and success is defined as taking the action you planned, not on whether your assertive statement was accepted.

Finally, the seventh step is a culmination of the first six steps. In it, you *integrate your intellect with your emotion.* This is presented as a seventh step to indicate that the process is continuous, not finite. Your goal as an assertive librarian is to control your emotions and not allow your emotions to control you.

Coping with Anger

Humphrey and Stroebel (1982) note that anger occurs more frequently than any other emotion because there are so many conditions that can incite anger. Gazda, Childers, and Walters (1982) tell us that the emotion of anger has a very strong physiological component, which causes people to respond as if they are under physical attack. As the body signals "fight" or "flight" the mind is bewildered. Yet we retain the ability to choose one of four alternatives:

- Expressing the anger through rage.
- Denying the anger by stifling it.
- Expressing the anger through indignation and constructive action.
- Resolving the anger by removing its cause.

Rage is destructive and rarely acceptable as an option, particularly in a professional environment. Denial is also destructive, and, although it may be a tempting option in the library, anger can have seriously destructive long-term effects if it is allowed to cumulate until it is explosive. As children we are taught not to hit back, yell, or lose self-control, and this early training frequently results in adult denial of anger (Caputo, 1981). Studies show, however, that released anger runs a very brief course and does considerably less damage to ourselves and others than suppressed anger, which can be sustained immeasurably longer (Langdon, 1979; Miller, 1979; Novaco, 1975; Sanchez & Lewinsohn, 1980). Expression of anger through indignation and constructive action and resolution through removal of its cause are the courses followed most frequently and are the courses that are recommended. Gazda, Childers, and Walters (1982, pp. 225–229) recommend a two-step process for dealing with anger, which is presented below and which will repeat and thus reinforce some of the previous material in this chapter. Part I, "First Aid," is meant to buy time until physiological signs of anger can subside. Part II, "The Cure," is an attempt to deal with the roots of the anger, not just the overt sprouts that appear on the surface. The authors warn that many people omit Part II, but that this is a serious mistake, for if the roots of anger remain they will surely sprout again.

Part I, First Aid:

1. Remind yourself that even though you feel angry you are still in control of your behavior.
2. Turn your attention to something else, count to 10 or 200, focus on a nearby object, divert yourself from the cause of your anger.
3. Relax your breathing.
4. Retreat from the scene, even if only temporarily.
5. Maintain positive thoughts, fantasize.
6. Use music. Listen, play, or sing.
7. Channel your energy into physical activity.
8. Do something you enjoy.
9. Talk with a friend.
10. Talk with yourself, out loud, mentally, or in writing.
11. Relax.
12. Laugh.
13. Cry if you need to.
14. Measure the issue to see if it's worth your anger.

Part II, The Cure:

1. Learn to be aware of your anger and accept it as a legitimate emotional experience, even though you wish to remove it.
2. Undo any damage done to others, as far as possible.
3. Decide whether to eliminate the angry feelings or whether to take constructive action against the cause of the anger.
4. Find and analyze the sources of your anger. Talk with others about their observations of you, free associate words that the word "anger" brings to mind for you, or keep an "anger diary."

5. Look beyond the precipitating event. There is a high probability that emotional pressure has been building for a long time.
6. Make a firm commitment to yourself, and if necessary to
   others as well, that you will not be controlled by your anger,
   but will be in control.
7. Plan constructive actions: talk, confront, meet, forgive, seek
   outside help.
8. Rehearse your plan and carry it out.

Assertive Statements for Expressing Anger. Examples of assertive statements that are useful for librarians in expressing anger
include:

1. I am very angry that you....
2. I strongly disagree. I think....
3. I am very upset by this.
4. It bothers me when....
5. I think that's unfair.
6. I don't (didn't) like that.
7. I am so angry about this that I need a few minutes (an hour, a
   day) to think it over before I can respond.

Inappropriate Ways of Expressing Anger. There are four nonassertive and aggressive ways librarians occasionally choose to express
their anger, and all four should be avoided. The first is expressing
modified anger instead of declaring the extent of the actual feeling.
This is used by librarians who have been socialized to believe that
anger is always inappropriate. Instead of expressing anger they admit
to mild annoyance, irritation, or give a description of their physiological state:

1. No, I'm not angry about that. It's a bit irritating because now I
   have to reschedule my entire day, but I'm not really angry.
2. I just feel sick when I think of what happened.
3. It's just that I have this headache....

The second way of inappropriately expressing anger is to express
it indirectly. In this way, you attempt to instill guilt in the person who
has made you angry or to punish her/him in other ways. You may use
sarcasm, excessive compliance, or take passive-aggressive action to
punish the person, all the while avoiding a direct expression of anger:

1. Go ahead (sarcastically). I don't mind at all. I'm used to
   closing up alone while you leave early.

2. Do you want to leave early again? Well, you just go ahead, I'll be glad to close alone. I don't have as many evening obligations as you have, so it's no trouble at all. You go ahead and have a good time. Don't worry about a single thing. I'll be just fine.
3. Sure, I'll close alone. (Followed by doing no work whatsoever as soon as the other person leaves.)

The third way that librarians express anger inappropriately is to turn it inward, becoming depressed. This generates a feeling of hopelessness and helplessness, with despair governing the future as well as the present. This is extremely damaging to your self-esteem, as well as ineffective in eliminating the cause of your anger (Knowles, 1981). Depressed librarians might engage in the following kind of monologue, which indicates a cause of appropriate anger without identifying it as such and then uses that denial to move into self-defeating actions:

> I wish I could search as well as Superlibrarian. Ever since that computerized bibliography business started, I've been confused. If I could only go to one of the formal training sessions [indicator of underlying cause of anger], I might be able to do better. Still, I'm so slow I probably couldn't keep up with the rest of the class anyway [negative self-statement]. I'll never get the hang of it [negative self-assessment based on decreased self-esteem]. I'm sure it's useless to try [negative conclusion leading to self-defeating behavior]. Our library patrons deserve the best service we can give them [rationalization], so I might just as well give today's search requests to Superlibrarian and get it over with...[self-defeating behavior as avoiding the task cannot increase one's ability to perform it].

The fourth way of expressing anger inappropriately is with the use of violence. This can be verbal as well as physical violence and includes obnoxious, insulting, and abusive statements and action. These kinds of statements should be avoided:

1. You're stupid. (That's stupid.)
2. Why the hell did you do *that?*
3. Who do you think you are?
4. What do you *think* I think?!
5. When are you going to grow up?
6. You're full of baloney (or other things).

Similarly, these behaviors should obviously be avoided:

1. Pushing or shoving anyone.
2. Slapping or hitting anyone.

3. Grabbing anyone.
4. Spitting.
5. Slamming doors.
6. Kicking things (unless you're alone and sure that what you plan to kick won't hurt your foot).

Dealing with Anger Directed at You. In addition to controlling your own anger, you must find ways to deal with the anger of others when it is directed toward you. Most attacks of anger occur because of a precipitating event or a predisposition on the part of the other person to become angry. Sometimes the event and even another person's predisposed readiness to become angry are detectable, but often they are obscure and the attack of anger appears to be sudden and unreasonable (Gazda, Childers & Walters, 1982). Assertive communication is invaluable in facing the overt anger of others, and the following points need to be emphasized in planning your assertive response to anger:

1. Remember the other person has a right to her/his feelings, the right to express those feelings, and the right to make a mistake. You need not agree with the person's assessment of the situation to accept these rights.
2. Control your own response: stay calm, listen carefully, and assure the other person of your interest and concern.
3. Look for an immediate, if temporary, solution that can be implemented to give evidence of your concern, and that will allow the other person to assume control and calm down.
4. Allow the other person to communicate freely: don't interrupt, maintain a nonjudgmental and nonthreatening atmosphere even if you disagree, don't be trite or superficial in your verbal responses, and keep them minimal so that the other person can express her/his feeling of anger as necessary.
5. Admit culpability when you have been at fault.
6. Avoid aggressive verbal or nonverbal messages.

Coping with Guilt

Guilt is defined as "a feeling that one has transgressed a moral, social, or ethical principle, associated with a lowering of self-esteem and a need to make retribution for the transgression" (Wolman, 1973). Identifying when we feel guilty is relatively easy for most of us, because we either find ourselves apologizing or behaving defensively. The more difficult problem is discriminating appropriate guilt from inappropriate guilt (Caputo, 1981) because new assertive behaviors often generate feelings of guilt even though we may have acted in totally appropriate ways (Klass, 1981). As we have seen several times in earlier chapters, our socialization process often teaches us nonassertive behaviors.

Assertion to Prevent Inappropriate Guilt Feelings. As you begin to practice assertive responses, you may be plagued by feelings of guilt. A way to investigate the validity of these feelings is to carefully review the personal rights of each party in the interaction. If you find that you have not violated another person's rights in standing up for your own, the feelings of guilt are inappropriate and should be exorcised. If you discover that you *have* violated the rights of someone else when you attempted to stand up for your own rights, your guilt feelings are appropriate, and you must make some sort of attempt at retribution. In illustration, let's review the following situation, which takes place in a special library:

> A patron insists that the book for which you have sent a payment notice has been returned some time ago. In an angry voice, the patron says the library is too screwed up to have anything right, that there is *no* way s/he is going to pay for that book, and that if "you people" don't get your act together soon, s/he is going to start legal action for defamation of character because a list of patrons with outstanding overdue books has been posted at the library exit door. You respond by saying that you will investigate to see if an error has been made, that if one has, you will certainly correct it and apologize (in response to the patron's interruption demanding an apology when, not if, you discover you are wrong), and that the notice at the exit door is not an attack on anyone's character, simply an extra reminder to people who need to return materials to the library. The patron refuses to be mollified by your response and continues to be verbally abusive. You each speak several times, while you try to remember and use all the new assertive skills you have learned. Finally, in exasperation, you cut the conversation short, saying "I *said* I'll look into it. You don't have to be so nasty. If you don't like the way we do things in this library, go use another one." You then turn your back and walk away from the still expostulating patron. At the moment you feel totally justified, but five minutes later, you feel guilty and wonder whether you were assertive or aggressive. Should you apologize?

First, let's review your rights and the rights of the patron. You have the right:

- To be treated with respect.
- To be listened to.
- To make a mistake.

- To expect library materials to be returned.
- To request payment for unreturned library materials.
- To remind patrons of their obligations in legal ways.
- To discontinue fruitless discussions.
- To refuse to listen to verbal abuse.

The patron has the right:

- To be treated with respect.
- To be listened to.
- To make a mistake.
- To feel angry and to express that feeling.
- To question library notices.
- To question the legality of library policies.

Now, let's identify which of these rights have been violated. The patron has clearly violated your right to respect with the verbal abuse s/he has given. Interruptive behavior is indicative of a violation of your right to be listened to, and the patron's insistence that the library should not make any mistakes with her/his record indicates that the right to err has also been violated. Your final brusque statement and retreat has violated the patron's rights to be treated with respect and to be listened to, and your exasperation with the patron's behavior may indicate a violation of her/his rights to make mistakes and to feel and express anger.

This review shows that each of you violated the others' rights. What does that mean to you? The patron's violations came first, so were yours justified? Do they essentially cancel each other out, so no apology is necessary? If you were to apologize, what would you be apologizing for? Almost all of your half of the interaction was assertive, it was only that last exasperated statement that wasn't—so does the assertiveness you did use outweigh the one statement that was aggressive? Should the patron apologize to you?

You reviewed the incident because you felt guilty, and now you have found that you did violate the patron's rights. By definition, your feeling of guilt is appropriate and requires an attempt at redress. The fact that the patron also violated your rights means only that s/he also owes you some form of redress; it does not justify or cancel out your behavior. Any apology that is made should be made only for the actual violations—in other words, for your last statement and manner of retreat—not for the library's policies or actions and not for the decision to retreat, which was upholding your rights not to tolerate verbal abuse and to discontinue fruitless discussions. No matter how assertive you were up to the point of violation, you owe redress for the violation that did occur. Finally, the patron does indeed owe you redress, and you may choose to request an apology as you offer your own. Here is an appropriate assertive script for a follow-up telephone call to the patron:

> Hello, Ms./Mr. Patron. This is Ms./Mr. Librarian from the SooperDooper Library. I want to apologize for the way I spoke to you at the end of our conversation this morning. I felt we were not getting anywhere in our discussion and wanted to end it, but I am sorry I did not say so politely instead of simply walking away while you were speaking. I have investigated the matter of the book you brought to our attention, and...[first scenario]...so far it has not turned up in any of our searches. There are times when a book is returned and is missplaced, so we will continue to search for it, but our records do show that it has not been returned to date, so I would like you to look for it again as well. I am confident we will resolve the problem if we both take the time to search again. I know you are upset by this problem, and I am also upset by it. The conversation we had this morning was very unpleasant for me, too. I like to be on good terms with our library patrons. I will call you next week to let you know whether we have found the book.
>
> [or]...[second scenario] ...and it has been found. We *did* make a mistake in sending that notice to you, and I am sorry you were upset by it. I can understand why you were angry. I was angry too, when you talked to me the way you did. I like to be on good terms with our library patrons, however, so I hope that the next time you come in you will give me more of a chance to resolve the problem. I am confident we can talk together comfortably if you will state your complaints in a calmer way.

Let's assume now that, in the original situation, instead of saying what you did and walking away, you said: "I can see how angry you are about this. I am sure we can get to the bottom of it, but I will not discuss it with you until you stop shouting at me." Has this statement violated any rights? If you walk away when the patron continues to shout, have you violated any rights? If you said "I will not discuss it with you until you stop shouting at me. If you continue to shout, I will walk away," would you be violating any rights? Why would that be the best way to make your statement?

You have the right to set limits on the conditions under which you will continue the conversation, so stating that you will not discuss it unless the patron stops shouting is appropriate behavior about which you need not feel any guilt. Walking away when the patron continues to shout is not a violation of rights and would probably be interpreted as an unspoken consequence from the condition you stated. You might regret not stating the consequence, but there would be no need to apologize for forgetting to state it. Including the consequences, however, helps to make your statement more explicit, and the more specific your assertive statement is, the less likely you will be to fall into an impulsive violation of rights leading to appropriate guilt feelings.

When you feel guilt and discover that you have not violated any rights but feel guilty because you have been taught to feel guilty in similar circumstances (such as when you are doing something of which your parents would have disapproved), it is important to tell yourself that you have behaved appropriately in order to help extinguish the inappropriate feeling of guilt. Try telling yourself:

- This was not appropriate behavior for me as a child, but it is perfectly appropriate for me as an adult.
- I have not violated anyone else's rights by standing up for my own, and it is important to me to stand up for my own rights.
- I am very satisfied with my analysis of the way I behaved. I am really beginning to act assertively with ease.

When you do redress appropriate guilt feelings by apologizing, it is important that your apology be made in a timely fashion. If not, it will be perceived as insincere. It is also important to make your apology very specific. You have a right to make mistakes, so you do not need to apologize for being in error unless you sincerely regret having made a mistake. Most of the time, it is appropriate simply to apologize for the consequences of your error, not for the making of it, and it is often appropriate to offer redress without overt apology. Kelley (1979) notes that errors of judgment in interpreting records, facts, or figures can usually be redressed with recognition of the error followed by correction or revision, without apology. Errors in relationships with others, however, require apologies in addition to redress:

- I made a mistake and left your name off the mailing list for notices of library activities. I'll add your name and address right now.
- I can see my error was costly for you. I will correct the charge and give you a refund.
- You've shown me that my mistake has jeopardized our friendship. I am very sorry I said things that hurt you.
- I was wrong to assume you felt the same way I do about that and to include your name when I commented on it to the

director. I'm sorry you were called on the carpet because of my mistake.

Nonassertion to Avoid Guilt Feelings. As we saw in Chapter 3, there may be times that you would be more comfortable choosing not to be assertive because you would suffer feelings of guilt even though you had not violated another person's rights. For example, when you can see that the person who has just violated your rights is under unusual stress, you may choose to be understanding and nonassertive rather than feel uncomfortable asserting your rights. In order to reassure your self-esteem that you are rationally choosing nonassertive behavior, you may mentally tell yourself why you have decided to be understanding by thinking:

- I know s/he's had a rotten day, I'll just overlook that.
- Gee, s/he doesn't normally act that way, something must be really wrong today.
- I think that just came out wrong, and s/he didn't mean it the way it sounded, so I'll let it pass unless it happens again.

Sometimes you may feel it's necessary to also alert the other person that you are being understanding in order to prevent any misconception that you will always accept that behavior or that you don't recognize that your rights have been violated. At these times, you may choose to say something like this:

- I usually feel bad when someone yells at me like you did just now, but I know you've had an absolutely rotten day, so I won't let it bother me.
- Gee, you don't usually act like this. Is there something wrong? I'll be glad to help you in any way I can.
- I don't think you meant that the way it sounded, so I won't take it to heart unless you do it again.

You may also choose not to assert yourself with oversensitive people who will take your statement badly and begin overapologizing or engaging in excessive redress behaviors. Even though you have not violated any rights, you can end up feeling uncomfortably guilty for the obvious distress this sensitive person is suffering in response to your assertion. There are people whose self-esteem is so precarious that they cannot handle even a mild assertion from someone else. Their self-esteem is not your problem; it is theirs. But you may want to consider what kind of relationship you have and want to have with this type of person, whether the oversensitivity is consciously used in a manipulative manner, how frequently you interact with her/him, and who else might be affected by the overreaction you might stimulate as part of your rational decision about behaving assertively or not. Assertion is not harmful, but it is not used unthinkingly in situations where an overly sensitive person may perceive it as harm.

Coping with Emotional Reactions to Criticism

Criticism is often hard to accept. As Phelps and Austin (1975) state, when your self-esteem is low, it takes very little to put you into a panic when you hear critical remarks. A common reaction to criticism is to deny it and counterattack, engaging in a win-lose competition. Win-lose competitions, however, foster distance, unhappiness, and suspicion. Table 8 lists the diverse and very mixed feelings of the "winner" and "loser" in such competitions.

Table 8
Feelings in Win-Lose Encounters

Winner	Loser
Aggressive	Nonassertive
Offensive	Defensive
Triumphant	Hurt
Guilty	Angry
Fearful of retaliation	Desirous of retaliation
Powerful	Powerless
Judgmental	Judged

Neither the "winner" nor the "loser" finds closeness, understanding, personal growth, or satisfaction from a win-lose encounter. Yet criticism is a part of our professional lives, so we must find effective ways to cope with it while maintaining a solid sense of self-worth.

Smith (1975) outlines five necessary steps to coping with criticism:

1. Learn to distinguish between the truth in statements others tell you about yourself and the arbitrary judgments of right and wrong that are frequently implied in such statements. For example, if someone tells you "Your desk always has stuff

piled up on it," it is important to distinguish between the truth—that your desk is often piled high with materials to be processed, corrected, or filed—and the arbitrary implied judgment that there is something wrong in having a lot of things on your desk at the same time.

2. Learn to feel comfortable with criticism, so that you can respond to the factual content of the statement in agreement or disagreement, without reacting to the implied judgment in it. You do not need to defend yourself against another person's judgment that you are doing or have done something wrong; you need only to determine for yourself whether there is truth in the criticism, and if there is, whether you will choose to alter your behavior because you prefer to do something else rather than continue as you have been. When a colleague says your desk is piled high, respond with "Yes, I frequently have a lot of materials on my desk" or "Actually, I usually have much less piled on my desk than I do today."

3. Learn to deal with criticism by questioning the validity of the implied judgment. There is no reason for you to accept another person's value system if it differs from yours unless you choose to do so or choose to continue in a hierarchical relationship that authorizes the other person to create a value system for you, as when you accept the work conditions and judgments of a particular library and library director. If someone implies it is wrong to have your desk piled high with materials, you could choose to ask: "You seem to disapprove of my having materials piled on my desk. Do you see something wrong in that?"

4. Learn to distinguish the truth in statements others tell you about your actions and their arbitrary judgments that your actions are an error or mistake. Such statements are usually posed as a question of why: "Why did you give the patron *that* book?" Your response should be based on the confidence you have in that particular action and your total self-confidence as a competent librarian: "I think it is the best one to answer the question s/he asked" or "I wasn't sure exactly what s/he wanted, so I gave that one out as a starter. Do you have other suggestions?"

5. Learn to feel comfortable owning errors. The criticism you are given may be valid. You can admit to error when you are wrong without being defensive because you always have the right to make a mistake. Mistakes may be inefficient, nonpro-

ductive, or time-consuming, but they do not equal total
inefficiency, total nonproductivity, or a total waste of time.
They simply are actions that require some correction.

RELAXATION

Learning to relax is the key to counteracting anxiety, extreme
emotion, and stress (Morse & Furst, 1982). Many rigorous research
studies have shown that relaxation produces human physical effects
which are opposite to the effects of anxiety. Moreover, additional
studies show that when the effects of relaxation are counterposed to
the effects of anxiety-provoking stimuli, they significantly diminish the
anxiety responses that have been previously elicited (Wolpe, 1982).

Relaxation Techniques

Relaxation is clearly desirable in tense work situations, but how
do you *really* relax when you feel light-headed, you have the sweats,
your mouth feels like cotton, your hands are clutching the tabletop
like it's going to fly away any moment, and your knees have started to
wobble? There are a variety of ways to really relax, and some take very
little time. It's all a matter of training and practice. Deep breathing,
stretching, progressive relaxation, thought relaxation, autogenic training, Hatha Yoga, massage, meditation, biofeedback, and cued relaxation techniques are just a few of the many ways you can learn to
reverse the physiological arousal that emotions and stress produce.

Deep Breathing. Anxiety usually brings fast shallow breathing, so
breathing more deeply and slowly helps counteract tension. Even in
the middle of a stressful situation you can begin to relax by simply
paying attention to your respiratory pattern. You don't need to go
through a detailed exercise; if you simply will yourself to breathe in
and out slowly and deeply, you will find some quick relief. When you
have time, however, it is more effective to use an exercise in deep
breathing like this one from Donald (1980):

> ...Now focus your attention on your breathing...become aware
> of all the details of your breathing...feel the air moving in through
> your nose or mouth...feel it move down your throat and into your
> lungs...and notice how your chest and belly expand and contract
> gently as you breathe...be aware of whatever else you experience in
> your body as you breathe...now imagine that instead of you
> breathing air, that air is breathing you...imagine that the air is

gently moving into your lungs...and then slowly withdrawing...you don't have to do anything at all, because the air is doing your breathing for you...just experience this for a while...(p. 11).

Stretching. Extension and flexion of all the movable parts of your body can help to relax you. When muscles are used to stretch and flex, they follow that use with momentary relaxation. If you are experiencing very mild tension or are beginning to feel fatigued, this may be enough to counteract and reverse the physiological changes that are just beginning to appear (Piercy, 1976).

Progressive Relaxation. This technique was developed through the work of Edmund Jacobson and the psychologists who followed him in studying relaxation. Jacobson began his work in 1908 at Harvard University and by 1930 had developed the technique of Deep Muscle Relaxation, or DMR. There has been a vast accumulation of scientific studies measuring the reduction of tension through DMR, which has become more commonly known as progressive relaxation (Bernstein & Borkovec, 1973). Progressive relaxation can be taught in two different ways: (1) using a tension relaxation procedure and (2) using a procedure of relaxation without tension. It is a highly effective technique in either pattern, and a number of commercial audiotapes are available for home use. Progressive relaxation trainers generally make tapes of their specific routine available to those people who take personal training.

Pender (1983) describes progressive relaxation in a recent book on preventive health. She explains that both types of procedure should take place in a comfortable setting. Recliners, lawn chairs, or lounges of some sort are placed in a quiet (ideally, sound-proofed) room where lighting can be dimmed or softened to a low level. Tight clothing is loosened slightly, shoes and glasses are removed, and noisy watches are set aside. A completely prone position is discouraged because it is less restful than a reclining, slightly bent position. Both procedures include, and may begin, with a deep breathing exercise similar to the one presented earlier.

In the tension relaxation procedure, successive muscle groups are described by the trainer, and instructions are given to tense them, hold that tension briefly, and then relax them. In the nontension procedure, relaxation may be taught in one of three methods. The first method uses a slow, steady recall of previous relaxing experiences, as instructed by a trainer. The second method "counts down" through varied muscle groups or from head to toe, relaxing each part of the body in sequence. The third method is through the use of imagery focussed on pleasant scenes or sensations, such as the warmth of the sun, or a gentle breeze on a hot day.

Both procedures make extensive use of relaxation promoting phrases such as:

calm and quiet
heavy and warm
warmth is flowing
comfortable and relaxed
serene and still

Audiotapes are frequently used to induce relaxation. Such tapes can run from 15 to 45 minutes and usually include instructions for returning to alertness at the end of the tape.

Thought Relaxation. This is a five-minute exercise created by Fensterheim and reported by Baer (1976) which is used with people who are able to relax their bodies but find that they still have anxious thoughts racing through their minds. This tape consists of questions that can be answered "yes" or "no" (or "maybe"), spaced seven to ten seconds apart. A mental response or a muscle response are all that are necessary; the fact that you are answering a question is the key to relaxing the thought process, which cannot race to other things if it is busy investigating the answers to these questions. This technique is used to gain deliberate control of your thought process.

Can you let your eyelids feel heavier and heavier?
Can you let your right arm feel more relaxed than your left arm?
Can you imagine looking at an object in the far distance?
Can you imagine watching a beautiful sunset over a body of water?
Can you imagine what a painting of a sunset might look like if it were done by a modern abstract painter?
Can you remember the smell of fresh strawberries?
Can you remember as a child the good taste of ice cream on a summer day?
Can you imagine a country lake in the summertime?
Can you imagine a country lake in the winter?
Or in the fall when the leaves are burning?
Have you ever smelled fresh bread or cake baking?
Can you count the colors in a rainbow?
Can you imagine looking at a campfire on a pleasant summer night?
Can you let yourself feel the warmth radiating from that campfire?
Can you let your legs and thighs feel pleasantly heavier?
Can you imagine looking at a beautiful flower right in front of you?
Can you imagine smelling that flower?
Can you listen to the sound of your own breathing?
Can you imagine a pleasant scene or think of the word "calm"?
Can you allow your whole body to feel calm and relaxed?
Calm and relaxed?

Calm and relaxed? (pp. 123–124)

Autogenic Training. This is a brief technique that can be used easily in an office setting. It urges you to make mental contact with various parts of your body by phrasing certain descriptions. The aim of the exercise is to make specific somatic changes. If you are tense, for example, it may help you to relax if you could feel comfortably warm. You would lean back in your chair, close your eyes and mentally repeat "My arms are getting warm and heavy" until your arms feel both warmer and heavier. If that did the trick, you could open your eyes and go back to whatever you were working on. If not, you could continue the exercise by working toward warming up your legs or chest. This is rather like a combination of meditation and common sense which takes little training, not much practice, and only a little time (Apgar & Callahan, 1982).

Hatha Yoga. The ancient system of self-development called Hatha Yoga leads to physical and mental well-being. It is an excellent calming technique and is very effective in controlling moderate physical stress and moderate to extreme cognitive stress. It includes physical exercises, breathing techniques, nutrition, and concentration exercises. Many books are available on the subject, and classes are often available in adult learning centers, community centers, and local colleges. Formal instruction is recommended (Apgar & Callahan, 1982).

Massage. Massage is a direct, applied method of muscle relaxation. Easing of aching muscles is achieved through firm stroking and kneading of muscles and is made easier by the application of body oil. Massage can be self-applied, although this limits the muscles on which it can be used. Whole body massages are available commercially in private clubs, health spas, and some cosmetology establishments. Facial massages are even more readily available. Regular use of massage can improve posture and circulation as well as providing effective muscle relaxation (Apgar & Callahan, 1982).

Meditation. Many people have learned various techniques of meditation as an aid to relaxation. Whether they are practitioners of Hindu, Buddhist, Zen, or transcendental meditation, or use self-hypnosis, they can attain subjective feelings of relaxation and significant tension reduction in voluntary muscles. Experts in these techniques can achieve relaxation of involuntary muscles as well.

In 1975, Herbert Benson wrote a book called *The Relaxation Response* (New York: William Morrow) which did a great deal to popularize meditation. Benson studied human physiological responses to all types of meditation and summarized four basic elements necessary for simple relaxation through mediation:

1. A quiet environment with as few distractions as possible.
2. A mental device that consists of a single syllable sound or word which is repeated silently or in a low gentle tone in order to free the mind from logical or externally oriented thoughts by focusing solely on the single sound device.
3. A passive attitude in which distractions can be disregarded and no self-judgments (even as to success in meditating) are made.
4. A comfortable position to reduce musuclar efforts to a minimum, with support for the head and arms, shoes removed, feet slightly elevated, and clothing loose.

Biofeedback. In the process of biofeedback, you can be taught to control certain physiological reflexes when a monitoring device which can be either seen or heard (sometimes both) indicates a need to do so. This method of treatment is currently in widespread use for hypertension and tension headache and is being studied for use in other health problems, such as Raynaud's Disease and gastric acid secretion. Blinking is the reflex activity that ensures even distribution of moisture over the surface of the eye. Winking is the voluntary control of this reflex action, and it is learned in childhood by the process of biofeedback: by monitoring oneself visually in a mirror or getting audible feedback from an adult (Brown, 1977).

Biofeedback is not a self-taught technique, and everyone may not be a good candidate for it, but if you have special needs to control your physiological responses, this may be a method to investigate.

Cued Relaxation. Once you have achieved relaxation, you can condition yourself to correlate that state with specific cues. For example, you could train yourself to begin slower and deeper breathing whenever you lean back in your chair and cross your legs, by repeatedly leaning back and crossing your legs each time you start a deep breathing practice exercise. Then in meetings that are becoming stressful you can relax by merely leaning back and crossing your legs, which triggers slower breathing and starts the rest of the physiological reduction you need. If you are careful in your choice of nonverbal cues, you can also use them to reinforce the message you would like to give. Leaning back is read as being relaxed, so even if your relaxed state is somewhat slow to achieve, you will be perceived as relaxed while you work your way toward it.

A poem or work of art that has special meaning for you can also be used as a cue for relaxation. Keeping this object available in your office allows you to close the door for a moment of privacy and concentration and an opportunity to quickly achieve a more relaxed state. The following Japanese translation of the 23rd Psalm, by Toki Miyashani, has been used successfully by one librarian as a cue for relaxation:

> The Lord is my pace-setter, I shall not rush;
> He makes me stop and rest for quiet intervals.
> He provides me with images of stillness, which restore my serenity;
> He leads me in the ways of efficiency through calmness of mind, and His guidance is peace.
> Even though I have a great many things to accomplish each day, I will not fret, for His presence is here.
> His timelessness, His all importance, will keep me in balance.
> He prepares refreshment and renewal in the midst of my activity by annointing my mind with His oils of tranquility.
> My cup of joyous energy overflows.
> Surely harmony and effectiveness shall be the fruits of my years, for I shall walk in the pace of my Lord and dwell in His house forever.

SUMMARY

Everyone has to deal with unwanted or inappropriate emotions and stress. Most of us react to stress by triggering the defense mechanisms of avoidance, repression/suppression, projection, regression, and rationalization. These occur when we are inattentive to the signs of increasing stress or emotion. The many signs of rising stress include changes in posture, muscle tension, sleep, use of tranquilizers of various kinds, and emotional variances. Once we can identify a need for reducing tension, we can select a coping mechanism to replace the defense mechanisms formerly used. Defense mechanisms are destructive because they are long-term, rigid, involuntary, and do not allow personal growth to occur. Coping mechanisms are constructive because they are temporary, flexible, voluntary, and allow for personal growth. Coping mechanisms can become maladaptive, however, if they are used inappropriately. The most recommended coping mechanisms to deal with stress are talking things out and working things out. Coping with emotion is an intellectual process with specific steps of becoming aware, identifying, accepting, analyzing, planning, and reporting. Dealing with the feelings of anger, guilt, and resentment over criticism may be especially important for the library environment. A variety of procedures are available for assistance in achieving a relaxed state, and these are worth investigation and trial.

Chapter 9
The Assertive Library Supervisor

WANTED: ASSERTIVE LIBRARY SUPERVISOR who can work creatively with members of the library staff, stimulate career growth for all employees, and work respectfully and openly with both peers and patrons. This position requires someone who has high self- esteem, and who can build self-confidence in others. We are looking for a library manager who puts people first, someone who respects the human rights of library staff members. Requirements include understanding, firmness, kindness, objectivity, fairness, honesty, and a thorough knowledge of assertive skills and philosophy. Also required is familiarity with and ability to use I-statements, consistent nonverbal messages, and active listening. An innate sense of timing is also desirable. Salary and fringe benefits are negotiable; we are looking for applicants who are able to assess the value of their unique abilities and their worth to our organization.

It's highly unlikely that this ad will be seen in any library journal or newsletter or heard of through any job hotline. When library managers are sought, they are more likely to be asked to have budgeting experience, writing capabilities, grant experience, understanding of networks and cooperative efforts, and, as a catch-all for interpersonal skills, someone with X number of years of "administrative or supervisory experience." Most supervisory or management positions in libraries, however, are significantly more effective when the people who hold them are capable of assertive management.

Shaw and Rutledge (1976) are firm in their conviction that results-oriented institutions such as libraries can profit tremendously from the application of assertiveness at supervisory levels. They write:

> The image of the "assertive individual" is almost totally congruent with the image of the "effective manager." The effective manager is clear about goals and purposes. He or she is willing and able to confront conflict, to make tough decisions, to say "no" without guilt, embarrassment or shilly-shally.
> The effective manager is also capable of responding to and utilizing the resources of others. He or she is sufficiently confident

and self-possessed so that defensive and abrasive behavior which inhibits the enthusiasm, creativity and motivation of others is minimized. All of these attitudes and behaviors are part of the model of an assertive individual. So both the assertive individual and the effective manager value themselves, value fulfillment and achievement, and value others (p. 9).

WHAT IS A LIBRARY SUPERVISOR?

According to Barnhard (1980), a library supervisor is someone promoted from within or hired from the outside to train, guide, and oversee one or more other people. A supervisor may or may not be involved in the management tasks of planning, organizing, budgeting, or writing, but all supervisors have one major management responsibility: They must see that the people under them work to accomplish the goals of the organization. They also have one major personnel responsibility: They must see that the on-the-job needs of each individual under them are met. A position classification study from the University of Michigan library system (1979) defined library supervisors in much the same way by citing their responsibility for the work of the people whom they supervise but added that, if a library staff member is held directly accountable for even one other person's work, then s/he is that person's supervisor. According to this definition, any librarians who function in supervisory capacities, regardless of whether they hold a managerial title or are named on a formal organizational chart, are supervisors. In addition, librarians who have one part-time or volunteer assistant, or who have a few student assistants at minimal or no wages, are also library supervisors.

ASSERTION AND THE SUPERVISOR'S ROLE

As was seen in Chapter 3, library managers share all the general personal rights of other librarians and also have the right to evaluate staff members and the right to reassign tasks and responsibilities. With these rights are the concomitant responsibilities to be objective in evaluating others and to be thorough in exploring alternatives before effecting reassignments. Library supervisors, by the nature of their assigned roles, also have the right to evaluate and the right to make assignments. This chapter will take a detailed look at assertive behaviors that are appropriate in six specific areas of the supervisor's role: (1) staff conflict, (2) individual subordinate's problems, (3) motivation, (4) terminations, (5) praise and criticism, and (6) upward communication.

Staff Conflict

Staff satisfaction and ultimately the satisfaction of the library's users are significantly affected by the social climate that exists among the members of the staff, between staff members and their supervisor, and between groups of staff members, such as those defined by particular departments in the library. Conflict within any or all of these groups is inevitable (Calabrese, 1979). The presence or absence of conflict is no indication that a supervisor is good or bad because conflict itself cannot be characterized as all good or all bad. Our only concern with staff conflict will be how it can be resolved, and to explore this we need to identify the types of conflict that we might expect to encounter within a library.

The three types of conflict we will review are (1) interpersonal conflict, between two individuals; (2) intergroup conflict, between two groups of individuals; and (3) person-organization conflict, between an individual and the library. Whether a conflict between two individuals is called a "personality clash" or merely a fight, when two determined staff members oppose one another there are the makings of a serious interpersonal conflict. Causes of this kind of conflict may be:

- Use of power by one of the people.
- Poor or no communication.
- Rigid or one-way communication.
- Intense competition.
- Differences in style, values, philosophy, beliefs.
- Differences in status or credentials.
- Performance differences.
- Noncompliance with library policies and/or procedures.

Intergroup conflicts may arise from these kinds of causes:

- Differences in power between the two groups.
- Differences in status, size, or responsibilities of the two groups.
- Changes fostered on one group by the other.
- Little or no understanding of the functions of the other group.
- Differences in work orientation and each group's relationship to users.

- Differences in rewards and recognition accorded to the groups.
- Differences in workflow and scheduling between the groups.

Finally, conflicts between a single staff member and the library may stem from some of these causes:

- The individual's needs and the library's needs being incongruent.
- Too little individual autonomy.
- Too little individual recognition.
- Perceived inequities in salary and benefits with other libraries.

Previous sections of this book deal extensively with assertive ways to resolve conflict. The point to be made here is that, when a supervisor makes an attempt to resolve conflict, even if that attempt is made with appropriately assertive statements, in nonthreatening environments, with consistent body language, and with evident concern for the rights of all the individuals involved, there will be a short-term increase in hostility and tension aimed at the supervisor. This is usually very short-lived if the conflict has been resolved satisfactorily and long-term harmony reestablishes itself; but unless it is anticipated the assertive supervisor may be confounded by it.

Calabrese (1979) also points out that, in library work groups, social concerns take precedence over task concerns. This means that no one can work optimally in a conflict situation where hurt, humiliation, anger, or frustration pervade the social atmosphere, even if everyone is not actively involved in the conflict situation. This social concern is as important to the restoration of superior library service as is the resolution of overt conflict itself. The library supervisor must develop effective communication skills to develop a climate in which all staff members feel free to express themselves openly and to disagree without defensiveness. When this kind of communicative climate exists, the supervisor's ability to settle staff conflicts is tremendously enhanced.

In addition to developing assertive skills to assist in her/his own conflict resolution, the library supervisor will find that these skills also assist in the identification and investigation of conflict between others. Awareness of nonverbal messages will help the manager observe (1) who talks to whom; (2) who interrupts whom; and (3) who listens to whom, even when conversations cannot be heard. The assertive ability to seek the opinions of others and actively listen to them are primary components of any attempt to resolve conflicts between other people.

Subordinates' Problems

Just as assertive librarians can observe themselves for signs of stress, assertive supervisors can observe the library staff members under their supervision for the signs that often indicate that there is an underlying problem that is bothering them. It is more likely that underlying problems are personal than that they are work-related, but they have a significant effect on work productivity and intra-staff relations. Supervisors can watch for these signs of individual problems:

1. Changes in outlook, e.g., optimism to pessimism, or vice versa.
2. Increased irritability.
3. Appearance of signs of depression.
4. Sulkiness, uncommunicative behavior in formerly talkative, friendly people.
5. Increased formal communication, e.g., memorandums in place of informal chats.
6. Increased politeness in social transactions, especially exaggerated use of "please" and "thank you."
7. Increased absenteeism.
8. Decreased quality of work or slowing of rate of work.

When these signs occur, many supervisors have ambivalent feelings about approaching the employee. The employee may justifiably think it isn't anyone else's business if s/he has a personal problem, or s/he may open up with a problem the supervisor would much rather not know about. What should an assertive supervisor do? Let's review the rights of each person:

The supervisor has the right:

- To expect the employee to maintain her/his responsibilities despite personal problems or to indicate her/his inability to do so.
- To be concerned over a problem that interferes with work performance and to question the nature of it.
- To care about the individual and to express that feeling.
- To recommend appropriate reassignments or leaves of absence as necessary.

The staff member has the right:

- To keep personal problems to her/himself.
- To request work reassignments or leaves of absence as necessary.

- To continue to work with no change of assignment as long as s/he maintains a stable performance consistent with past work.
- To expect objectivity and confidentiality from her/his supervisor.

Given these rights, and the fact that an assertive supervisor remembers that each right carries with it a companion responsibility, the supervisor is ready to make the following kind of assertive statement after inconspicuously arranging for a private conference with the staff member:

Supervisor: Jamie, you were hired because of your excellent background in serials work and your previous experience at Former Library. I have been very pleased with your work in the two years you have been here and have tried to let you know how much I valued you as a member of the staff and how much I have enjoyed getting to know you better. In the past five weeks, your work has not been up to the high standard you usually maintain. You appear to be disturbed about something, and that worry seems to be affecting your work. Is there something happening in other areas of your life that is interfering with your concentration?

Jamie: Well.....yes.

Supervisor: I don't want to pry into your personal life. If you have something you want to share with a good listener, I want you to know I'm here. I also know about nearly every professional counseling service in town, because I had a special need for help last year and looked into what is available. I'll be glad to share that information with you if you want it. Right now, though, we need to come to an agreement about your work. I'm willing to consider temporarily assigning some of your tasks to other people, or making some deadline changes, but we still have that big renewal list coming in next month. What are your recommendations?

This kind of presentation allows Jamie to divulge the personal problem or keep it private, without applying pressure either way, yet makes the point that it *is* affecting performance and that therefore something needs to be done about it. The supervisor also provides a forum for mutual discussion and a joint decision on what to do but still leaves room for Jamie to say that the problem will not affect future work, and no changes are necessary if that's what s/he prefers. The supervisor has not only handled this difficulty in an assertive and caring way, it has been handled in a timely fashion with a major workload still a month away.

Staff members may occasionally respond to this kind of approach with a revelation they later regret. When that happens, you as supervisor must take special care to respect the staff member's right to confidentiality as you both return to the more customary social boundaries of the library work environment. You must also be sure you have written your assertive script in such a way that the employee does not feel compelled to reveal more than s/he wishes. There is a crucial difference between offering help and insinuating yourself into the role of "Supervisor/Confidante," particularly as a request for information coming from a supervisor may appear to be a demand for information rather than a matter of information given at the staff member's discretion.

Sometimes, upon investigation, the supervisor will discover that the staff member has a personal agenda. This is nothing more than a personal goal unrelated to the library work itself but which the library environment may promote. It is not the same as a "hidden agenda" (Barnhard, 1980). If this personal agenda is not contrary to the library's goals, the assertive supervisor may make an effort to assist the staff member toward her/his goal:

Supervisor: Mickey, you've been on the job for two weeks, now. How do you like working as a library assistant?

Mickey: Oh, I like the work fine, but I'm not meeting as many new people as I thought I would. See, I'm new to town, and I thought I'd meet some nice people if I worked here—people who would like reading as much as I do.

Supervisor: Well, I think I can help you with that. Every other week we have a special Young Adult Reading Club that meets in the garden room. Someone from the library staff has to preside over the members' sign-in book and note what books they've read for the meeting. If you would like to do that, I'll assign you to it and you'll be able to meet a lot of new people.

If the personal agenda does conflict with the library goals, however, the assertive supervisor has to set limits for the employee's pursuit of the desired goal:

Supervisor: Mickey, you've been on the job for two weeks, now. How do you like working as a library assistant?

Mickey: Oh, I like the work fine, but I'm not meeting as many new people as I thought I would. See, my brother is going to run for town council, and I thought I could campaign a little for him while I was here—people who read books are good prospects for voting.

Supervisor: I can't allow you to do that while you are working. The library has a policy against lobbying and campaigning of any kind. Your desire to help your brother is admirable, and you're quite right, studies do show that library users vote more often than nonusers. I'm sure some of our patrons will remember your face if you go door to door with your brother. There are no restrictions on how much campaigning you do *outside* of work.

Motivation

With all due respect to Frederick Herzberg and Douglas McGregor and the many management consultants who recommend myriad methods to motivate employees, the library world appears to be populated solely by people who are either self-motivated or immovable. The task of an assertive library manager is not to motivate but to create a climate that encourages self-motivation. This task has three components. The first is to remove obstacles to self-motivation; the second is to improve job content; and the third is to provide positive reinforcement.

Obstacles are defined as conditions that prevent job performance, such as inadequate time, instructions, tools, or resources; conflicting orders or multiple supervisors for individual staff members; and "red tape." There is a distinction to be made between dissatisfiers, which cloud the issue but don't really prevent job performance, and obstacles, which do. Dissatisfiers can be such things as salary, fringe benefits, parking facilities, and lounge facilities. Correcting dissatisfiers not only doesn't automatically increase self-motivation, it may actually inhibit it, as in the "but-what-have-you-done-for-me-lately syndrome." Obstacles that are controllable should be removed: Deadlines should be made reasonable, adequate instructions should be provided, and staff members should report to only one supervisor. Obstacles that cannot be removed should be recognized and allowances made to accept the best performance possible given the state of affairs, or available budget, or available staffing (Albright, 1979).

Improvement of job content can be difficult for some library work, particularly for those tasks that are relatively routine, tedious, and that require minimal thought. The concepts of job enlargement, job enrichment, and work rotation, all of which appear in the literature of management, are some ways to effect job improvement. The assertive supervisor's role in this regard would be to investigate possibilities, draft an assertive request for the changes to present to the appropriate authority, and finally, specify the changes to the affected staff members in a way that enhances their self-esteem.

Positive reinforcement is the final component of a climate for self-motivation. The assertive supervisor can use soft assertions, empathetic assertions, and simple assertions to provide positive statements to staff members recognizing their achievements.

Terminations

Firing a staff member is one of the most painful and difficult assertive confrontations a supervisor will ever assume. No matter how justified you are, no matter how much documentation you have completed, no matter how much administrative support you have, the face-to-face termination is painful for both parties. These key elements will help you prepare for it:

- Know in advance exactly what you plan to say and write yourself an assertive script.
- Stick to your script.
- Stick to your decision.
- Anticipate, and prepare answers for, any reaction you think the person might display.

Here are some sample reactions and reaction statements, paired with possible responses by the assertive supervisor:

Staff Member: You've got to be kidding!

Supervisor: I wouldn't kid about something as serious as this. I've given this situation a lot of thought.

Staff Member: But I've worked here longer than anyone else!

Supervisor: You have worked here a long time. This decision is based on your performance, which is not satisfactory.

Staff Member: No one else can (would) do what I do for you.

Supervisor: (Ignoring irrelevant comment): I have made an appointment for you with the personnel department; they will explain your termination benefits.

Staff Member: Give me a break, I'll improve....

Supervisor: You have had three opportunities to improve your performance in the past six months and have shown no improvement. My decision is firm.

Staff Member: Look, this is really a bad time for me, you just can't do this to me when everything else is going so lousy.

Supervisor: My decision is firm.

Staff Member: Look, I *know* I've made a couple big mistakes, but I know what I did wrong. You can't just throw me out in the trash.

Supervisor: My decision is firm.

Staff Member: [cries]

Supervisor: [hands staff member tissue box located on desk]

Staff Member: Well, You're being totally unfair. So this is what all those memos have been leading to all along? I'm not going to stand for this! I'm going straight to the personnel grievance committee!

Supervisor: You have the right to see them, if you choose.

Staff Member: And I'm going to the big boss! Right over your head, bozo!

Supervisor: If you want to discuss this any longer with me, you'll have to refrain from name-calling.

Staff Member: What's wrong? Didn't think I'd go to the big boss, huh? Surprised you!

Supervisor: I've discussed this at length with Dr. Big; we agreed that this decision is firm. However, if you wish to see Dr. Big, I will call right now to see if s/he is free to see you.

As soon as this assertive supervisor is alone, s/he will probably employ one of the relaxation techniques described in Chapter 8. Assertion is effective; it isn't always easy.

Praise and Criticism

Most libraries have some sort of systematized performance appraisal for staff. Whether or not a formal mechanism exists, the assertive library manager regularly reviews the work of staff members and applies praise and constructive criticism in ways that promote good interpersonal relationships. The guidelines to follow in this process are inherent in the assertive skills already described and illustrated:

1. Review the rights in the situation before you schedule a meeting, so that you can be sure you are not violating any of the staff member's rights, and so you are confident you know your own rights.
2. Be objective and honest.
3. Be specific in what you like and in what you don't like.
4. Discuss the performance , not the person.
5. Where you criticize, suggest ways to improve.
6. Actively listen to what the staff member has to say.
7. Use I-statements.
8. Use consistent nonverbal messages.
9. Give positive reinforcement where indicated.

At the end of conferences about their performance, your staff members should feel that they are worthwhile members of the staff.

They should not have any doubts that if you have given any criticism, the problem lies in their actions, not in them personally. They should feel they have had an opportunity to discuss their work mutually, not merely to listen to your views of it, and that they can reopen the discussion if they wish. They should feel confident that you are actively encouraging them in their personal growth.

Upward Communication

Although assertive people can free themselves from irrational beliefs about status differences, it generally remains much harder to give feedback in an upward direction than it is to provide it to subordinates, especially when the feedback is negative. Whether you are a middle manager reporting to a library director, a branch librarian reporting to the director of a library system, a public librarian reporting to a library board, a special librarian reporting to an administration within your organization, an academic librarian reporting to an academic administrator, or a school librarian reporting to a principal or school board, upward communication is inhibited by the unspoken undercurrents of the "boss-employee" relationship. There is a basic difference in real power between you and the person or people to whom you report, but assertive supervisors cannot afford to let this real difference distort their thinking when it comes to planning for changes in the library or planning for changes within the boss-employee relationship (MacNeilage & Adams, 1982).

How do you avoid the stalemate of a management that is reluctant to open itself to critical evaluation by a librarian and a librarian who is reluctant to open the Pandora's box of possible retaliation? The only way is through open communication. Library directors and supervisors are usually firmly agreed that, if management decisions are being made that will seriously affect the library in terms of its philosophy, goals, ability to provide service, or resources (both people and dollars), then librarians have a professional responsibility to speak and act in order to apprise management of the effects its actions will have on the library. But apprising management of a deleterious effect and successfully getting them to make a change to avoid that effect are two very different things. Management can decree changes for librarians; librarians are usually in the position of having to request changes of management.

One of the three basic assertive interactions is making requests. There is no single approach that can ensure upward communication will be heard, and there is no single approach for requesting change from authorities over the library, but assertive library managers and supervisors have a wide variety of skills to employ in this effort. This book and other books on assertive skills can help to introduce you to assertive living. The identification of your own goals, from those that are really not very important to those that are extremely significant, will give you many opportunities to practice making requests for change. With the reinforcement of success in achieving small and increasingly larger goals, you will be able to work your way toward the creation of your own requests for changes from your unique management structure, using similar kinds of statements, which match your own management style and which you can comfortably present. Here are some sample approaches that could work for assertive librarians:

> *Librarian 1* (special librarian in medium sized corporation, to vice president for research and development): I am very concerned about the effect the anticipated budget reductions are going to have on library service. I know that I am not alone in my concern and that you are aware these cuts cannot help but affect the library operation. I have put together some dollar figures for each separate library service that we offer, and I would like to discuss them with you. I recognize that in our current economic state, some reduction is inevitable. I plan to devote a significant amount of time during the next fiscal year to exploring ways that some of the library services can become partially self-supporting. In the meantime, I want to show you the conclusions I have drawn about next year's service. I am confident that we can make some reductions with minimal effect, but some of the targeted areas would suffer significant long-term effects and have relatively minimal savings for our organization. This document contains cost figures for our services, my conclusions about the effect of the current anticipated cuts, and my recommendations for reductions for the library budget. My total recommended reductions are 35 percent less than the total recommended by the finance committee. I would like to meet with you again next Friday to answer any questions you have about the material I'm leaving with you today.

> *Librarian 2* (director of a public library system with one main library and two branches, to president of the library board): I need your support. The budget reductions recommended by the library board include cutting three staff positions, and although it wasn't stated that way, I know the board expects that the three newest staff members will be let go. I have carefully reviewed our operation, and although I am not happy at the loss of staffpower the reduction represents, it's something I can live with. There are changes which can be made in workflow, in branch hours, and in our scheduling mechanism that will allow us to lose three positions and still maintain nearly all services at an adequate level. My problem is selecting the three people who will be affected. It's also not clear to

me whether these reductions are meant to be temporary and the library will retain three approved but unfunded positions, or whether they will be permanent eliminations. Either way, I have one special problem. We have a staff member who has been performing poorly for some time. I have been documenting this problem, which was brought to my attention by a supervisor about six months ago. The three of us met at that time to set goals for the staff member, who agreed to them but has not made any progress toward meeting them as yet. We have had two additional meetings to date. Under ordinary circumstances, we would continue to work with this staff member much longer before recommending anything as drastic as termination. However, my understanding of the situation is that it is not a new problem. This person had been shifted from supervisor to supervisor before the problem was brought up to me. I certainly hate to lose three excellent staff members simply because they are newer and keep this person who would likely face termination in the relatively near future anyway. I plan to recommend termination of this problem staff member as part of the budget reduction. How do you feel about that? Will you support my recommendation?

Librarian 3 (school librarian who has been asked to take on an emergency teaching assignment, to school principal): When I agreed to teach two classes for you during periods that the library is normally available for borrowing and reading guidance, I thought it would work out OK since we have volunteers available for the library during those times, and you only needed my help until the year ends. But I have found it is not working out as well as I thought it would. I would like to be released from my commitment to teach those two periods. The volunteer help I had anticipated has been intermittent at best, and the volunteers are not comfortable providing reading guidance even with the lists I prepared for them for each grade level. Students have either had no guidance at all or have been simply directed to the first book on the list without any attempt to see whether it meets their needs. Last week the head custodian was helping a student when the volunteer for that day failed to appear at all. I know it will be difficult for you to find a substitute for those two classes, but I feel that reading guidance is very important for our students. I am willing to teach for one more week to give you time to find a substitute.

Librarian 4 (academic staff librarian, to the Dean of Academic Services): It is never easy to be the "bearer of bad news" and I am very uncomfortable with the topic that prompted me to ask to see you. I will be very candid, and as specific as I can be, but I hope you will understand that I am feeling bad about this. In my opinion, our library director may be suffering from alcoholism. I am not qualfied to diagnose substance abuse problems, so I have discussed her/his unusual behavior (anonymously, of course) with a practitioner at the city health department, who gave me some educational materials to read. That discussion and the materials I read reinforced my opinion. I have been reluctant to discuss it with anyone here at the university because I did not want to jeopardize the director's reputation, so I have avoided discussions of unusual behavior with other members of the library staff, although several of them have stated a similar opinion to me. The director appears to be under the influence of alcohol more often than not, and I have not only seen liquor bottles in the desk drawers, I have been invited to join in for "a little nip" from the bottle. S/he fails to return from lunch approximately once a week and often does not come in to work until the afternoon on Mondays, even though our library staff meeting convenes every Monday morning at 11. I am concerned about her/his health and also about the effect this behavior will have on the library if it continues. I am not willing to be directly involved in a confrontation with the director over this. I trust you to be fair in investigating my belief, and to take appropriate action.

SUMMARY

This chapter is illustrative. It is meant to show how assertiveness skills can have a practical application to a variety of library situations. Assertive librarians, whether they function in supervisory or subordinate roles, can be effective in the enhancement of interpersonal relationships, conflict resolution, and proposing change. A thorough understanding of the rights of all parties in the situation and employment of the basic elements of assertive communication, I-statements, honesty, and timing are essential.

Chapter 10
Finale

Assertiveness means standing up for your rights without violating the rights of other people; being able to express all manner of emotions in an open, honest, and direct way; having the confidence to stand up for your rights without undue anxiety; and being free to choose or not choose to be assertive based on your assessment of the situation. Assertion texts are designed to teach ways to ask for what you want, refuse what you don't want, and express feelings to other people. Each of these interactions has a companion lesson that is equally important: assertion is being receptive to requests others make of you, accepting refusals from other people, and being receptive to the expression of the feelings of other people.

The assertive choice means that you can rationally choose to behave nonassertively, but it also means that no decision is inflexible, and any decision can be changed. The process of decision making includes investigation and experimentation, and assertive behavior is characterized by the flexibility of open-mindedness and continuous cognitive activity. The choice to alternate between assertive and nonassertive behaviors and among varied types of assertive behaviors is influenced by your self-esteem, rational assessment of risks, and perception of rights in the situation.

As children we learned that hiding feelings was a way to be accepted, and that other people (usually our parents) had a sense of responsibility for our feelings. As adults, in peer relationships, we find that no one else has responsibility for our feelings, and that we are not responsible for the feelings of anyone else. We can exchange the heavy and unnecessary mantle of responsibility for one of human concern. We feel human in hearing, telling, and sharing our feelings, and with practice, we lose the fear of vulnerability. We become warmer, develop a greater capacity to share and to love, and find a greater freedom to perform because we realize that when we make mistakes in performing, it means only that we have made a mistake, not that we are inadequate. Life becomes more fulfilling and rewarding.

In the library, assertive techniques help us build and maintain positive relationships with colleagues, library users, supervisors, and subordinates. Problem solving becomes easier when we apply assertive techniques. The communication process is enhanced by our ability to express ourselves assertively and to use and read nonverbal as well as verbal messages. Confrontations no longer have to end in deadlocks, fights, or withdrawal. Incompatible positions or goals can generally be managed in ways that meet some of the needs of all the participants. Assertive skills build confidence and a sense of self-worth that helps us grow and establish our library identity, be sensitive to colleagues and patrons, and present the library as a valued social organization. Assertion is not a panacea for all library woes, but it can and does give librarians an opportunity to be more effective in their own lives and in their profession.

PRACTICE AND FEEDBACK

Most assertion trainers agree that becoming an assertive person is not an easy task. It is a demanding, energy-consuming goal that requires a great deal of practice. This practice may take a number of different forms: (1) coaching, or being told what to do and say in a specific situation; (2) modeling, which consists of watching others model assertive situations; (3) role-playing in a classroom setting, including the acting out of artificial situations and real-life target situations of participants; (4) covert rehearsal, which involves thinking through situations assertively prepatory to taking assertive action; and finally (5) real-life practice with minor target situations. As in any other challenging endeavor, or any activity that requires some skill sophistication, the only way to excel is to practice, repeatedly, until your skill is developed to the point where it can be used with confidence and competence (Alberti & Emmons, 1982; Ames, 1977; Ashby, 1975; Caputo, 1981; Flowers & Booraem, 1975; Hauser, 1979; Hutchings, 1979; Jakubowski & Lange, 1978; Lange & Jakubowski, 1976; Shaw & Rutledge, 1976). Alberti and Emmons (1974) recommend a 13-step process for acquiring assertive skills. A major part of the process is feedback—information to guide and assist you as you learn about and practice assertion.

13-Step Model

The 13-step model suggested by Alberti and Emmons to assist you in building your own assertive skills includes the following:

- *Step 1:* Observe yourself to determine how effective you are in your interpersonal relationships.
- *Step 2:* Keep an assertiveness diary for a week, recording the situations in which you were assertive, those in which you blew it, and those that you avoided. Be honest and systematic.
- *Step 3:* Pick one situation and concentrate on it, how you handled it, how you felt at the time, and how you felt afterward. Review it as vividly as you can.
- *Step 4:* Analyze that same situation, in writing, in terms of body language, eye contact, gestures, voice, and the content of your message.
- *Step 5:* Watch someone else handle the same or similar situation, and if possible, talk it over, paying particular attention to the alternate approaches and the consequences you observed.
- *Step 6:* Imagine as many other alternatives as possible, and review them mentally for potential effectiveness.
- *Step 7:* Imagine your special situation again, this time inserting the best alternative you found and imagining how comfortable and succesful you are with this approach. Keep imagining the situation until you find the best mixture of an "assertive self" and "natural self" that you can.
- *Step 8:* Try your selected alternative out in a practice situation: role-play it with a friend.
- *Step 9:* Get objective, positive feedback. Positive feedback identifies the strengths in your behaviors and focuses on additional alternatives for the weaker areas rather than on the weaknesses themselves.
- *Step 10:* Repeat steps 7, 8, and 9 to firmly "shape" your behavior. You are striving to reach a point where you feel comfortable with your behavior so that you can take it into real life successfully.
- *Step 11:* Try your practiced behavior out in the real situation the next time it occurs (solicit its reoccurance if necessary).
- *Step 12:* Repeat steps 1–11 with as many situations as you wish in order to build up a repertoire of assertive responses.
- *Step 13:* Develop a system of positive reinforcements in your environment. For example, enjoy the good feelings you have

each time you use your assertive behavior and accept compliments from others.

Effective External Feedback

Feedback is not a one-way process but is a participative interaction with one or more other people (MacNeilage & Adams, 1982). Even when we realize that we can solicit feedback by requesting it, we don't always realize that we can direct it, guide it, and set limits on it, rather than simply absorbing it like a sponge. In an essay on feedback by David Johnson, feedback is defined as the provision of constructive information meant to help another person become aware of how her/his behavior affects you and how you perceive her/his actions (Johnson, 1982, p. 63). When you ask someone for feedback, it is important to remember that the purpose is one of constructive information, not destructive criticism, and to ask that the person give you helpful, nonthreatening feedback couched in positive terms. It is equally important to remember the purpose when *you* are giving feedback.

The characteristics of helpful, nonthreatening feedback include a focus on the behavior shown, not the person. The description "You raised your voice a lot" is far more acceptable than the attacking comment that "You sounded like a loudmouth." A focus on actual observations, rather than on inferences that could be drawn is also helpful: "Your comments to employee A were more specific than your comments to employee B" is better than inferring "You like B better than A, don't you?" First, your inference may be entirely erroneous, and second, it may be read as an attack and rejected as feedback. Similarly, it is important to focus on specific description rather than judgment: "I am disappointed that we are not meeting our circulation goals" is a specific description of both your feelings and the current state of affairs in terms of circulation goals and is much less likely to produce a defensive response than "You must not be working hard enough on the circulation goals." To be helpful in shaping assertive behavior, feedback should focus more on an exploration of all possible alternatives, not on supplying solutions or answers. Feedback is also more valuable to the recipient when it is presented in "more or less" terms rather than "better or worse" terms. A comment on a colleague's lack of assertiveness with a particular librarian could be described as being less assertive with that librarian than with others, which indicates the ability to be *more* assertive exists. A statement that "You are *better* at being assertive with others than you are with librarian X'' is more likely to indicate to the recipient that being *worse* at assertion with librarian X is a state of being that cannot be changed.

Feedback should be given at an appropriate time, not too far past the behavior that was observed, and at an appropriate place, where both giver and recipient can be comfortable and assured of as much privacy as each desires. It is also important to limit the amount of feedback that is given to the amount that can be absorbed. If you get more information than you can process, you have the responsibility to tell the giver that you have a lot to consider and must ask them to discontinue at this point.

Effective Internal Feedback

Covert rehearsal relies on internal feedback, the thought process you use to analyze your imagined behavior. It is vital that this feedback be as helpful and nonthreatening as any external feedback you might solicit. In addition to limiting yourself to descriptive and specific observations rather than inferences and judgments, you need to be able to distinguish between your objective view and your subjective view of the behaviors you want to employ. Your objective viewpoint is necessary to analyze your rights and the rights of the others in the situation, while your subjective viewpoint is necessary to analyze how you feel about your behaviors. In assertiveness, feelings are very important, and the integration of objectivity and subjectivity, not a separation of feelings from intellectual rationalizations, is what you must strive to achieve.

Internal feedback includes an awareness of your *intra*personal responses to situations. Chapter 8, which discusses coping with emotions, will provide much greater detail on the following intraper-sonal responses which should be used as internal feedback: muscle tension, posture, sleep behaviors, use of tranquilizers of varying kinds, and extremes of emotion.

SUMMARY

In the end, assertiveness means feeling good about ourselves, making our own decisions, and taking responsibility for our choices. It is not difficult to learn assertive skills, but it can be difficult to learn to implement them regularly. It takes practice, perseverence, and objectivity. As we go through steps of exploration, practice, and remediation, we need effective feedback. External feedback is an interactive process with at least one other person, while internal feedback is a part of our own thought processes. Both should be positive in effect, identifying strengths and exploring alternative behaviors for those areas identified as needing some strengthening.

In 1692, an unknown author wrote the following recommendation, which was found in Old Saint Paul's Church, Baltimore, Maryland:

> Go placidly amid the noise and haste, and remember what peace there may be in silence. As far as possible without surrender be on good terms with all persons. Speak your truth quietly and clearly; and listen to others, even the dull and ignorant; they too have their story. Avoid loud and aggressive persons, they are vexations to the spirit. If you compare yourself with others, you may become vain or bitter; for there will always be greater and lesser persons than yourself. Enjoy your achievements as well as your plans. Keep interested in your own career, however humble, it is a real possession in the changing fortunes of time. Exercise caution in your business affairs; for the world is full of trickery. But let this not blind you to what virtue there is; many persons strive for high ideals; and everywhere life is full of heroism. Be yourself. Especially, do not feign affection. Neither be cynical about love; for in the face of all aridity and disenchantment it is as perennial as the grass. Take kindly the counsel of the years, gracefully surrendering the things of youth. Nurture a strength of spirit to shield you in sudden misfortune. But do not distress yourself with imaginings. Many fears are born of fatigue and loneliness. Beyond a wholesome discipline, be gentle with yourself. You are a child of the universe, no less than the trees and the stars; you have a right to be here. And whether or not it is clear to you, no doubt the universe is unfolding as it should. Therefore be at peace with God, whatever you conceive Him to be, and whatever your labors and aspirations, in the noisy confusion of life keep peace with your soul. With all its sham, drudgery and broken dreams, it is still a beautiful world. Be careful. Strive to be happy.

This book has consistently emphasized that assertion is not aggression; it is the direct, honest, *appropriate* expression of opinions, beliefs, needs, or feelings. It is a way to survive in a difficult world as a healthier, happier, and more effective person. It is rational and based on objective, cognitive assessments of reality. You can be an assertive librarian: Your responsibility is to modify the skills and comments in this book to fit your own personal style in ways that will help you effectively stand up for your rights while protecting and maintaining the rights of others, allow you to build and maintain good interpersonal relationships, and encourage you to actively enhance interpersonal communications.

Appendix
Response Key
Librarian's Assertiveness
Inventory

Instructions: Compare your numbered response to the responses below, circling the response you made to each statement. Look for patterns: are most of your responses in a particular category? Do your nonassertive responses and aggressive responses occur randomly, or do they occur in similar type situations? There is no overall total score for this inventory; you should use it only as an indication of areas you might like to target for new behaviors, not as a measure of your overall assertiveness.

Response Key
1 = Never or almost never true of me, totally uncharacteristic.
2 = Rarely true of me, quite uncharacteristic.
3 = Sometimes true of me, depends on the circumstances.
4 = Usually true of me, quite characteristic.
5 = Always or almost always true of me, totally characteristic.

Inventory Statement	Aggressive Response	Assertive Response	Nonassertive Response
1. I am able to give constructive criticism to another librarian without jeopardizing our relationship.	1 - 2	4 - 5	3

Inventory Statement	Aggressive Response	Assertive Response	Nonassertive Response
2. I find it difficult to criticize or discipline a subordinate.	1	2 - 3	4 - 5
3. When I interview people, I put them at their ease.	1 - 2	4 - 5	3
4. People seem to take advantage of my good nature and willingness to help.	1	2 - 3	4 - 5
5. I serve on more committees than I would like to.	1	2 - 3	4 - 5
6. I tell people exactly what I think even when I suspect it will hurt their feelings.	4 - 5	3	1 - 2
7. If someone argues with me, I give in to avoid bad feelings.	1	2 - 3	4 - 5
8. I ask for the autonomy I believe I can handle.	5	3 - 4	1 - 2
9. I do not make exceptions to library rules.	4 - 5	3	1 - 2
10. I speak freely in staff meetings, voicing my opinion even when I know it is a minority view.	5	3 - 4	1 - 2

Inventory Statement	Aggressive Response	Assertive Response	Nonassertive Response
11. When I get a job evaluation I disagree with, I state my disagreement either orally or in writing.	5	3 - 4	1 - 2
12. I find it easy to give suggestions to my boss.	5	3 - 4	1 - 2
13. I don't bother to correct people who accept the librarian stereotype.	1	2 - 3	4 - 5
14. I have difficulty accepting criticism.	4 - 5	2 - 3	1
15. When someone teases me too far, I blow up.	4 - 5	1	2 - 3
16. When someone teases me too far, I cry.	2	1	3 - 5
17. I feel more comfortable with other librarians of my own sex than with librarians of the opposite sex.	3	1 - 2	4 - 5
18. When a co-worker asks me personal questions, I answer because I don't know how to get out of answering without offending him/her.	1	2	3 - 5

Inventory Statement	Aggressive Response	Assertive Response	Nonassertive Response
19. When a co-worker asks me personal questions, I never answer no matter how offended s/he is. I just ignore her/him.	4 - 5	3	1 - 2
20. I am a "risk-taker."	5	3 - 4	1 - 2
21. I can say "I don't know" easily.	1 - 2	3 - 4	5
22. Every time I disagree with someone, s/he gets mad at me.	4 - 5	3	1 - 2
23. When a colleague has really done a good job on something, I tell her/him.	1 - 2	4 - 5	3
24. I secretly tell annoying people off while I am driving home from work.	3	1 - 2	4 - 5
25. I brood over the things I say to people when I think I should have said them differently.	1	2	3 - 5
26. I am not afraid to take a controversial stand with the library board committee.	5	3 - 4	1 - 2
27. When I have a bad day at work, I usually wind up in an argument at home or out socially.	4 - 5	1 - 2	3

Inventory Statement	Aggressive Response	Assertive Response	Nonassertive Response
28. I won't ask a colleague to change work days with me, even though there have been times the schedule has wrecked my personal plans.	1 - 2	3	4 - 5
29. When a patron gets visibly upset about something, I remain calm.	2 - 3	4 - 5	1
30. When I think I am handling more than my share of the workload, I complain loudly.	4 - 5	3	1 - 2
31. When I am getting overcommitted, I say "no" to new requests for my time.	3	4 - 5	1 - 2
32. If I feel incapable of doing a task assigned to me, I won't admit it.	4 - 5	3	1 - 2
33. I find it difficult to relate to my boss as an equal.	1	2	3 - 5
34. Even when I agree with other people, I don't speak up in meetings.	1	2 - 3	4 - 5

Inventory Statement	Aggressive Response	Assertive Response	Nonassertive Response
35. I compliment myself when I've done something good, even where other people can hear me.	5	3 - 4	1 - 2
36. When someone has been unfair to me, I let her/him know I think s/he has been unfair.	5	3 - 4	1 - 2
37. If I am late to a meeting and the only seats left are in the front row, I stand in the back of the room.	1 - 2	3	4 - 5
38. I look forward to expressing my opinion at staff meetings.	5	3 - 4	1 - 2
39. I am often at a loss for words.	1	2	3 - 5
40. I don't know where to look or put my hands when I'm talking with someone.	1	2	3 - 5
41. I try not to hurt someone else's feelings.	1 - 2	3	4 - 5
42. When patrons are clearly disruptive, it is easy for me to calmly ask them to leave.	3	4 - 5	1 - 2
43. I try to swallow my anger when I'm at work.	1 - 2	3	4 - 5

Inventory Statement	Aggressive Response	Assertive Response	Nonassertive Response
44. I reciprocate when people try to "put me down."	4 - 5	1	2 - 3
45. I am willing to call other librarians for advice when I'm stumped.	1 - 2	4 - 5	3

Reference List

Aboud, F.E. (1976). The effect of stereotype generalization on information seeking. *Canadian Journal of Behavioral Science, 8* (2), 178–188.

Alberti, R.E. (1977). Comments on "Differentiating assertion and aggression: some behavioral guidelines." *Behavior Therapy, 8,* 353–354.

Alberti, R.E., & Emmons, M.L. (1974). *Your perfect right* (2nd ed.). San Luis Obispo, CA: Impact.

Alberti, R.E., & Emmons, M.L. (1975). *Stand up, speak out, talk back! The key to assertive behavior.* New York: Pocket Books.

Alberti, R.E., & Emmons, M.L. (1977). *Assertiveness; innovations, applications, issues.* San Luis Obispo, CA: Impact.

Alberti, R.E., & Emmons, M.L. (1982). *Your perfect right; a guide to assertive behavior* (4th ed.). San Luis Obispo, CA: Impact.

Albright, E.M. (1979). Handling employee problems. In R.E. Stevens (Ed.) *Supervision of employees in libraries.* Champaign, IL: University of Illinois.

Alden, L., & Safran, J. (1978). Irrational beliefs and assertive behavior. *Cognitive Therapy and Research, 2,* 357–364.

Ames, M.D. (1977). Non-assertion training has value, too. *Personnel Journal, 56,* 3 348–350; 366.

Anderson, A.J. (1974). *Problems in intellectual freedom and censorship.* New York: Bowker.

Apgar, K., & Callahan, B.N. (1982). *Stress management* (Workshop models for family life education series). New York: Family Service Association of America.

Argyle, M. (1972). Non-verbal communication in human social interaction. In R.A. Hinde (Ed.) *Non-verbal communication.* New York: Cambridge University Press.

Argyle, M., Alkema, F., & Gilmour, R. (1971). The communication of friendly and hostile attitudes by verbal and nonverbal signals. *European Journal of Social Psychology, 1,* 385–402.

Ashby, N. (1975). Stop putting up with put-downs. *Today's Health, 53*(7), 15–19.

Asheim, L. (1978). Librarians as professionals. *Library Trends, 27,* 225–257.

Bach, G.R., & Goldberg, H. (1974). *Creative aggression; the art of assertive living.* New York: Avon.

Baer, J. (1976). *How to be an assertive (not aggressive) woman in life, in love, and on the job. The total guide to self-assertiveness.* New York: Rawson Associates.

Bailey, M.J. (1981). *Supervisory and middle managers in libraries.* Metuchen, NJ: Scarecrow.

Barnhard, N. (1980). *CE 605-Human Factors in Library Administration* (4th revision). Chicago: Medical Library Association.

Becker, H.A. (1980). The assertive job-hunting survey. *Measurement and Evaluation in Guidance, 13*(1), 43–48.

Benson, H. (1975). *The Relaxation Response.* New York: William Morrow.

Berger, E.M. (1981). Self-acceptance scale. In R. Aero & E. Weiner (Eds.), *The mind test.* New York: William Morrow.

Berman, H.J., Shulman, A.D., & Marwit, S.J. (1976). Comparison of multidimemsional decoding of affect from audio, video, and audiovideo recordings. *Sociometry, 39,* 83–89.

Bernstein, D.A., & Borkovec, T.D. (1973). *Progressive relaxation training: a manual for the helping professions.* Champaign, IL: Research Press.

Biggs, M. (1981). Sources of tension and conflict between librarians and faculty. *Journal of Higher Education, 52*(2), 182–201.

Birdwhistell, R. (1970). *Kinetics in context.* Philadelphia: University of Pennsylvania Press.

Bloom, L.Z., & Coburn, K. (1975). *The new assertive woman.* New York: Delacorte.

Bower, S.A., & Bower, G.H. (1976). *Asserting yourself: a practical guide for positive change.* Reading, MA: Addison-Wesley.

Broadwell, M.M. (1977, July). Rediscover role playing. *Training Health Resources Development,* pp. 19,21.

Brockner, J. (1979). The effects of self-esteem, success-failure, and self-consciousness on task performance. *Journal of Personality and Social Psychology, 37,* 1732–1741.

Brockway, B.S. (1976). Assertive training for professional women. *Social Work, 21,* 498–505.

Brown, B.B. (1977). *Stress and the art of biofeedback.* New York: Harper & Row.

Bruch, M. (1981). A task analysis of assertive behavior revisited: replication and extension. *Behavior Therapy, 12,* 217–230.

Bugenthal, D.E., Kaswan, J.W., & Love, L.R. (1970). Perception of contradictory meanings conveyed by verbal and nonverbal channels. *Journal of Personality and Social Psychology, 16,* 647–655.

Butler, P. (1976). *Self-assertion for women: a guide to becoming androgynous.* San Francisco: Canfield Press.

Calabrese, R. (1979). Interaction skills and the modern supervisor. In R.E. Stevens (Ed.), *Supervision of employees in libraries.* Champaign, IL.

Caputo, J.S. (1981). *CE 669-Assertiveness and human relations skills.* Chicago, IL: Medical Library Association.

Cauthen, N.R., Robinson, I.E., & Krauss, H.H. (1971). Stereotypes: a review of the literature, 1926–1968. *Journal of Social Psychology, 84*(1), 103–125.

Chalus, G.H. (1978). The mechanisms underlying attributive projection. *Journal of Personality, 46,* 362–382.

Chenevert, M. (1978). Special techniques in assertiveness training for women in the health professions. St. Louis, MO: Mosby.

Clark, C.C. (1979). Assertiveness issues for nursing administrators and managers. *Journal of Nursing Administration, 9*(7), 20–24.

Clayton, H. (1970). Femininity and job satisfaction among male library students at one Midwestern university. *College and University Libraries, 31,* 388–398.

Cotler, S.B. (1975). Assertion training: a road leading where. *Counseling Psychologist, 5*(4), 20–29.

Cotler, S.B., & Guerra, J.J. (1976). *Assertion training: a humanistic-behavioral guide to self-dignity.* New York: Research Press.

Cottam, K.M. (1970). Student employees in academic libraries. *College and Research Libraries, 31* 246–248.

Cowell, P. (1980). Not all in the mind: the virile profession. *Library Review, 80,* 167–175.

Crowther, B., & More, D.M. (1972). Occupational stereotyping on initial impressions. *Journal of Vocational Behavior, 2*(1),87–94.

Dance, F.E.X., & Larson, C.E. (1982). Confirming and disconfirming responses. In Hill, S.E.K. (Ed.) *Improving interpersonal competence: a laboratory approach.* Dubuque, IA: Kendall/Hunt.

DePaulo, B.M., Rosenthal, R., Eisenstadt, R.A., Rogers, P.L., & Finkelstein, S. (1978). Decoding discrepant nonverbal cues. *Journal of Personality and Social Psychology, 36,* 313–323.

Dewey, M. (1876). The profession. *American Library Journal, 1,* 5–6.

Donald, K.M., et al (1980). *Before assertiveness: a group approach to building self-confidence. A manual for group leaders.* (ERIC Document Reproduction Service No. ED 186 814).

Duncan, P., & Hobson, G.N. (1977). Toward a definition of aggression. *Psychological Record, 27,* 545–555.

Eakins, B.W., & Eakins, R.G. (1978). *Sex differences in human communication.* Boston: Houghton-Mifflin.

Eisenberg, A.M. (1979). *Job talk; communicating effectively on the job.* New York: Macmillan.

Ellis, A. (1962). *Reason and emotion in psychotherapy.* New York: Lyle Stuart.

Ellis, A. (1966). The essence of rational therapy. In B.N. Ard, Jr. (Ed.), *Counseling and psychotherapy: classics on theories and issues.* Palo Alto, CA: Science and Behavior Books.

Ellis, A. (1973). *Humanistic psychotherapy: the rational-emotive approach.* New York: Julian Press.

Ellis, A. (1976). Healthy and unhealthy aggression. *Humanitas, 12,* 239–254.

Ellis, A., & Casriel, D. (1971). Debate: Albert Ellis vs. Daniel Casriel on anger. *Rational Living, 6*(2), 2–21.

Emery, R. (1975). *Staff communication in libraries.* London: Linnet Books and Clive Bingley.

Fast, J. (1970). *Body language.* New York: Pocket Books.

Fast, J., & Fast, B. (1977). *Talking between the lines; how we mean more than we say.* New York: Pocket Books.

Fensterheim, H. (1972). Behavior therapy: assertive training groups. In C.J. Sager & H.S. Kaplan (Eds.), *Progress in group and family therapy.* New York: Brunner/Mazel.

Fensterheim, H., & Baer, J. (1975). *Don't say yes when you want to say no: how assertiveness training can change your life.* New York: David McKay.

Ferriero, D.S., & Powers, K.A. (1982). Burnout at the reference desk. *RQ, 21,* 274–279.

Fiedler, D., & Beach, L.R. (1978). On the decision to be assertive. *Journal of Clinical and Consulting Psychology, 46,* 537–546.

Fischoff, S. (1977). The shortcomings of shallow assertiveness. *Human Behavior, 6*(1), 70.

Flowers, J.V., & Booraem, C.D. (1975). Assertion training: the training of trainers. *Counseling Psychologist, 5*(4), 29–36.

Galassi, J.P., Delo, J.S., Galassi, M.D., & Bastien, S. (1974). The College Self-Expression Scale: a measure of assertiveness. *Behavior Therapy, 5,* 165–171.

Galassi, M.D., & Galassi, J. (1977). *Assert yourself: how to be your own person.* New York: Human Sciences Press.

Galassi, M.D., & Galassi, J.P. (1978). Assertion: a critical review. *Psychotherapy: Theory, Research and Practice, 15*(1), 16–29.

Galvin, T.J. (1971). *Current problems in reference service.* New York: Bowker.

Gambrill, E.D., & Richey, C.A. (1975). An assertion inventory for use in assessment and research. *Behavior Therapy, 6,* 550–561.

Gay, M.L., Hollandsworth, J.B. Jr., & Galassi, J.P. (1979). An assertiveness inventory for adults. *Journal of Counseling Psychology, 47,* 16–24.

Gazda, G.M., Childers, W.C., & Walters, R.P. (1982). *Interpersonal communication: a handbook for health professionals.* Rockville, MD: Aspen.

Getter, H., & Nowinski, J.K. (1981). A free response test of interpersonal effectiveness. *Journal of Personality Assessment, 45*(3), 301–308.

Girdano, D., & Everly, G. (1979). *Controlling stress and tension.* Englewood Cliffs, NJ: Prentice-Hall.

Goldhaber, G.M. (1979). *Organizational communication* (2d ed.). Dubuque, IA: William C. Brown.

Gordon, T. (1970). *Parent effectiveness training.* New York: Peter H. Wyden.

Groark, J.J. (1979). Assertion: a technique for handling troublesome library patrons. *Catholic Library World, 51,* 172–175.

Groth, G.A. (1977). *Social conflict and negotiative problem solving. Trainer's manual.* Washington, D.C.: National Institute of Education (DHEW), Basic Skills Group. (ERIC Document Reproduction Service No. ED 150 120).

Haggard, E.A., & Isaacs, K.S. (1966). Micromomentary facial expressions as indicators of ego mechanisms in psychotherapy. In L.A. Gottschalk & A.H. Auerback (Eds.) *Methods of Research in Psychotherapy.* New York: Appleton Century.

Haldane, J.D., Alexander, D.A., & Walker, L.G. (1982). *Models for psychotherapy; a primer.* Aberdeen, Scotland: Aberdeen University Press.

Hall, C.S., & Lindzey, G. (1978). *Theories of personality* (3rd ed.). New York: Wiley.

Hamilton, D.L., & Gifford, R.K. (1976). Illusory correlation in interpersonal perception: a cognitive basis of stereotypic judgments. *Journal of Experimental Social Psychology, 12,* 392–407.

Hammen, C.L., Jacobs, M., Mayol, A., & Cochran, S.D. (1980). Dysfunctional cognitions and the effectiveness of skills and cognitive-behavioral assertion training. *Journal of Consulting and Clinical Psychology, 48,* 685–695.

Harper, F.D. (1981). *Dictionary of counseling techniques and terms.* Alexandria, VA: Douglass Publishers.

Harris, T. (1967). *I'm OK, You're OK.* New York: Harper & Row.

Hart, E.W. (1977). Levels of assertiveness. *Transactional Analysis Journal, 7,* 163– 165.

Hauser, M.J. (1979). Assertiveness techniques: origins and uses. *Journal of Psychiatric Nursing and Mental Health Services, 17*(12), 15–17.

Heffner, F. (1981). *A competency based course in job seeking and job survival skills.* Reading, MA: Berks County Employment and Training Office. (ERIC Document Reproduction Service No. ED 193 519).

Heimberg, R.G., Montgomery, D., Madsen, C.H., Jr., & Heimberg, J.S. (1977). Assertion training: a review of the literature. *Behavior Therapy, 8,* 953–971.

Heisler, G., & Shipley, R.H. (1977). The ABC model of assertive behavior. *Behavior Therapy, 8,* 509–512.

Henley, N.M. (1974). Power, sex, and non-verbal communication: the politics of touch. In P. Brown (Ed.) *Radical psychology.* New York: Harper & Row.

Herman, S.J. (1978). *Becoming assertive: a guide for nurses.* New York: Van Nostrand.

Hewes, D.D. (1975). On effective assertive behavior: a brief note. *Behavior Therapy, 6,* 269–271.

Hickey, D.J. (1972). *Problems in organizing library collections.* New York: Bowker.

Hoffman, R.A., Kirwin, P.M., & Rouzer, D.L. (1979). Facilitating generalization in assertiveness training. *Psychological Reports, 45*(1), 27–30.

Huber, V.L. (1981). Managing stress for productivity. *Supervisory Management, 26*(12), 2–21.

Hughes, P.L., & Mullins, L. (1981). *Acute psychiatric care: an occupational therapy guide to exercises in daily living skills.* Thorofare, NJ: C.B. Slack.

Hulbert, J.E. (1982). Interpersonal communication: replacing passive behavior with assertive behavior. *Business Education Forum, 36*(5), 25–26; 28–29.

Humphrey, J.H., & Stroebel, C.F. (1982). *A textbook of stress for college students.* Springfield, IL: C.C. Thomas.

Hung, J.H., Rosenthal, T.L., & Kelley, J.E. (1980). Social comparison standards spur immediate assertion: "So you think you're submissive?" *Cognitive Therapy and Research, 4,* 223–234.

Hutchings, H., & Colburn, L. (1979). An assertiveness training program for nurses. *Nursing Outlook, 27,* 394–397.

Jacobson, S.F., & McGrath, H.M. (Eds.). (1983). *Nurses under stress.* New York: Wiley.

Jacobson, W.D. (1972). *Power and interpersonal relations.* Belmont, CA: Wadsworth.

Jakubowski, P., & Lange, A.J. (1978). *The assertive option: your rights and responsibilities.* Champaign, IL: Research Press.

Jakubowski-Spector, P. (1973). Facilitating the growth of women through assertion training. *Counseling Psychologist, 4,* 75–86.

Johnson, D.W. (1982). Feedback. In S.E.K. Hill (Ed.) *Improving interpersonal competence: a laboratory approach.* Dubuque, IA: Kendall/Hunt.

Kelley, H.H. (1979). *Personal relations: their structures and processes.* Hillsdale, NJ: Lawrence Erlbaum Associates.

Kelley, J.D., & Winship, B.J. (1979). *I am worth it.* New York, NY: Nelson-Hall.

Kelly, J.A. (1982). *Social-skills training; a practical guide for interventions.* New York: Springer.

Klass, E.T. (1981). A cognitive analysis of guilt over assertion. *Cognitive Therapy and Research, 5,* 283–297.

Kleinke, C.L. (1975). *First impressions: the psychology of encountering others.* Englewood Cliffs, NJ: Prentice-Hall.

Knowles, R.D. (1981). Handling depression by identifying anger. *American Journal of Nursing, 81* 968.

Kroll, H.W., & Moren, D.K. (1977). Effect of appearance on requests for help in libraries. *Psychological Reports, 40,* 129–130.

Langdon, M. (1979). Assertiveness and Lewinsohn's theory of depression: an empirical test. *Behavior Therapist, 2*(2), 21–29.

Lange, A.J., & Jakubowski, P. (1976). *Responsible assertive behavior; cognitive/behavioral procedures for trainers.* Champaign, IL: Research Press.

Lange, A.J., Rimm, D.C., & Loxley, J. (1975). Cognitive-behavioral assertion training procedures. *Counseling Psychologist, 5*(4), 37–41.

Levinson, H. (1968). What an executive should know about his boss. *Think, 34*(2), 31–33.

Levitt, E.A. (1964). The relationship between abilities to express emotional meanings vocally and facially. In J.R. Davitz (Ed.) *The communication of emotional meaning.* New York: McGraw-Hill.

Levy, R. (1982). *The new language of psychiatry; learning and using DSM-III.* Boston: Little, Brown.

Liberman, R.P., King, L.W., DeRisi, W.J., & McCann, M. (1975). *Personal effectiveness; guiding people to assert themselves and improve their social skills.* Champaign, IL: Research Press.

Lowell, M.H. (1975). *Library Management Cases.* Metuchen, NJ: Scarecrow.

Lyon, B.L. (1980). *Stress management.* Indianapolis, IN: Health Potentials Unlimited.

MacNeilage, L.A., & Adams, K.A. (1982). *Assertiveness at work; how to increase your personal power on the job.* Englewood Cliffs, NJ: Prentice-Hall.

Mamarchev, H.L., & Jenson, M.P. (1977). *Assertiveness training.* Washington, D.C.: National Institute of Education (DHEW). (ERIC Document Reproduction Service No. ED 150 531)

McCauley, C., Stitt, C.L., & Segal, M. (1980). Stereotyping: from prejudice to prediction. *Psychological Bulletin 87,* 195–215.

McFall, M.E., Winnett, R.L., Bordewick, M.C., & Bornstein, P.H. (1982). Nonverbal components in the communication of assertiveness. *Behavior Modification 6,* 121– 140.

McMahon, F.B., & McMahon, J.W. (1982). *Psychology: the hybrid science* (4th ed.). Homewood, IL: Dorsey.

Mehrabian, A. (1971). *Silent message.* Belmont, CA: Wadsworth.

Mehrabian, A., & Ferris, S.R. (1967). Inference of attitudes from nonverbal communication in two channels. *Journal of Consulting Psychology, 31,* 248–252.

Milburn, T.W., & Billings, R.S. (1976). Decision-making perspectives from psychology: dealing with risk and uncertainty. *American Behavioral Scientist, 20*(1), 111–126.

Miller, C.H. (1979). Aggression in everyday life. *American Journal of Psychoanalysis, 39,* 99–112.

Montgomery, D., & Heimberg, R.G. (1978). Adjunctive techniques for assertiveness training: overcoming obstacles to change. *Professional Psychology, 9*(2), 220–227.

Morse, D.R., & Furst, M.L. (1982). *Women under stress.* New York: Van Nostrand Reinhold.

Myers, G.E., & Myers, M.T. (1982). Interpersonal skills: making it work. In S.E.K. Hill (Ed.) *Improving interpersonal competence: a laboratory approach.* Dubuque, IA: Kendall/Hunt.

Neiger, S., & Fullerton, E. (1979). The art of gentle assertive behavior. *Rational Living, 14*(1), 29–34.

Newcombe, N., & Arnkoff, D.B. (1979). Effects of speech style and sex of speaker on person perception. *Journal of Personality and Social Psychology, 37,* 1293–1303.

Nordby, V.J., & Hall, C.S. (1974). *A guide to psychologists and their concepts.* San Francisco: Freeman.

Norton-Ford, J.D., & Hogan, D.R. (1980). Role of nonverbal behaviors in social judgments of peers' assertiveness. *Psychological Reports, 46*(3, part 2), 1085–1086.

Novaco, R.W. (1975). *Anger control: the development and evaluation of an experimental treatment.* Lexington, MA: Lexington Books.

Numerof, R.E. (1980). Assertiveness training. *American Journal of Nursing, 80,* 1796–1799.

Nussbaumer, B. (1978, December). Assertiveness; the meek inherit the dirty work. *Occupational Health Nursing, 26,* 9–11.

O'Donnell, M., & Colby, L. (1979). Developing managers through assertiveness training. *Training, 16*(3), 36; 41.

Osborn, S.M., & Harris, G.G. (1975). *Assertive training for women.* Springfield, IL: Charles C. Thomas.

Pardue, S.F. (1980). Assertiveness for nurses. *Supervisor Nurse, 11*(2), 47–48; 50.

Paris, C., & Casey, B. (1976). *Project YOU: a manual of rational assertiveness training.* Vancouver, WA: Bridges Press.

Pender, N.J. (1983). *Health promotion in nursing practice.* Norwalk, CT: Appleton-Century-Crofts.

Perry, J.C., & Flannery, R.B. (1982). Passive-aggressive personality disorder: treatment implications of a clinical typology. *Journal of Nervous and Mental Disease, 1703,* 164–173.

Phelps, S., & Austin, N. (1975). *The assertive woman.* San Luis Obispo, CA: Impact.

Piercy, F.D., & Ohanesian, D.L. (1976). Assertion training in teacher education. *Humanist Educator, 15,* 41–47.

Position classification at Michigan: another look. (1979). *College and Research Libraries, 40,* 207.

Posner, M.F., Nissen, M.J., & Klein, R.M. (1976). Visual dominance: an information-processing account of its origins and significance. *Psychological Review, 4,* 398–406.

Prostano, E.T., & Prostano, J.S. (1982). *Case studies in library/media management* (Library Science Text Series). Littleton, CO: Libraries, Unlimited.

Pugh, J.B. (1979). Assertive interpersonal communication : what it is and how it can benefit nursing. *Military Medicine, 144,* 759–764.

Rathus, S.A. (1973). A 30-item schedule for assessing assertive behavior. *Behavior Therapy, 4,* 398–406.

Rathus, S.A. (1975). Principles and practices of assertive training: an eclectic overview. *Counseling Psychologist, 5*(4), 9–20.

Rimm, D.C., & Masters, J.C. (1974). *Behavior therapy: techniques and empirical findings.* New York: Academic Press.

Robertson, J. (1978). *How to win in a job interview.* Englewood Cliffs, NJ: Prentice-Hall.

Rose, Y.J., & Tyron, W.W. (1979). Judgments of assertive behavior as a function of speech loudness, latency, content, and gestures. *Behavior Modification, 3,* 112–123.

Salter, A. (1949). *Conditioned reflex therapy.* New York: Creative Age Press.

Sanchez, V., & Lewinsohn, P.M. (1980). Assertive behavior and depression. *Journal of Consulting and Clinical Psychology, 48,* 110–120.

Satir, V. (1972). *People-making.* Palo Alto, CA: Science and Behavior Books.

Schmidt, J.A. (1976). Cognitive restructuring: the art of talking to yourself. *Personnel and Guidance Journal, 55*(2), 71–74.

Serber, M. (1972). Teaching the nonverbal component of assertiveness. *Journal of Behavior Therapy and Experimental Psychiatry, 3*(3), 179–183.

Shaw, M.E. (1980). *Making it assertively.* Englewood Cliffs, NJ: Prentice-Hall.

Shaw, M.E., & Rutledge, P. (1976). Assertiveness training for managers. *Training and Development Journal, 30* (9), 8–14.

Shelton, J.L. (1977). Assertive training: consumer beware. *Personnel and Guidance Journal, 55,* 465–468.

Shuman, B.A. (1981). *The River Bend casebook: problems in public library service.* Phoenix, AZ: Oryx Press.

Smith, M.J. (1975). *When I say no, I feel guilty: how to cope—using the skills of systematic assertive therapy.* New York: Dial Press.

Smith, N.M., & Fitt, S.D. (1982). Active listening at the reference desk. *RQ, 21,* 247–249.

Smith, P.C., Kendall, L.M., & Hulin, C.L. (1969). *The measurement of satisfaction in work and retirement.* Chicago: Rand McNally.

Sommer, R. (1969). *Personal space.* Englewood Cliffs, NJ: Prentice-Hall.

Stead, B.A., & Scamell, R.W. (1981). A note on the contribution of assertiveness training to job satisfaction of professional librarians. *Library Quarterly, 51,* 380–389.

Steinmetz, C. (1981). Creating positive reactions toward reference services among young adults. *Top of the News, 38,* 57–59.

Sundel, S.S., & Sundel, M. (1980). Be assertive: a practical guide for human service workers. In *Sage Human Service Guides* (volume 11). Beverly Hills, CA: Sage.

Tanck, R.H., & Robbins, P.R. (1979). Assertiveness, locus of control and coping behaviors used to diminish tension. *Journal of Personality Assessment, 43,* 396–400.

Tepper, D.T., & Haase, R. (1978). Verbal and nonverbal communication of facilitative conditions. *Journal of Counseling Psychology, 25* 35–44.

VanVliet, V. (1980). The fault lies not in our stars—the children's librarian as manager. *Canadian Library Journal, 37,* 327–329.

Wasserman, P. (1976). *The new librarianship: a challenge for change.* New York: Bowker.

Weinberger, D.A., Schwartz, G.E., & Davidson, R.J. (1979). Low-anxious, high- anxious, and repressive coping styles: psychometric patterns and behavioral and physiological responses to stress. *Journal of Abnormal Psychology, 88,* 369–380.

Weiner, E.A. (1981). Self-image checklist, 1980. In R. Aero & E. Weiner (Eds.), *The mind test.* New York: William Morrow.

Wessler, R. (1975). Self-interest and assertion. *Rational Living, 10*(2), 2–6.

Williams, R.L., & Long, J.D. (1979). *Toward a self-managed lifestyle* (2nd ed.). Boston, MA: Houghton-Mifflin.

Wolman, B.B. (1973). *Dictionary of behavioral science.* New York: Van Nostrand Reinholt.

Wolpe, J. (1958). *Psychotherapy by reciprocal inhibition.* Stanford, CA: Stanford University Press.

Wolpe, J. (1973). *The practice of behavior therapy* (2nd ed.). New York: Pergamon.

Wolpe, J. (1982). *The practice of behavior therapy* (3rd ed.). New York: Pergamon.

Wolpe, J., & Lazarus, A.A. (1966). *Behavior therapy techniques: a guide to the treatment of neuroses.* New York: Pergamon.

Zimbardo, P.G., Pilkonis, P.A., & Norwood, R.M. (1975). The social disease called shyness. *Psychology Today, 8*(12), 69–70; 72.

Zuckerman, M., DeFrank, R.S., Hall, J.A., Larrance, D.T., & Rosenthal, R. (1979). Facial and vocal cues of deception and honesty. *Journal of Experimental Social Psychology, 15,* 378–396.

Index

Compiled by Linda Webster